THE SOVIET GERMANS: PAST AND PRESENT

The Soviet Germans
Past and Present

BY
INGEBORG FLEISCHHAUER
AND
BENJAMIN PINKUS

EDITED WITH AN INTRODUCTION BY
EDITH ROGOVIN FRANKEL

ST. MARTIN'S PRESS, NEW YORK
in association with the Marjorie Mayrock Center
for Soviet and East European Research
at the Hebrew University, Jerusalem

LC

© Marjorie Mayrock Center for Soviet and East European Research
at the Hebrew University, Jerusalem, 1986
All rights reserved. For information write:
St. Martin's Press, Inc., 175 Fifth Avenue, New York, NY 10010
Printed in England on paper with a guaranteed life of 140 years
First published in the United States of America in 1986

Library of Congress Cataloging-in-Publication Data

Frankel, Edith Rogovin.
   The Soviet Germans : past and present.

   Bibliography: p.
   Includes index.
   1. Germans--Soviet Union--History. 2. Soviet
Union--Ethnic relations. I. Title.
DK34.G3F73 1986   947'.00431   85-26188
ISBN 0-312-74833-7

ACKNOWLEDGMENTS

In December 1981 the Soviet and East European Research Centre of the Hebrew University held a conference in Jerusalem on the Ethnic Germans of the Soviet Union. The conference, which featured speakers from both Israel and abroad, enjoyed great success and the resulting interest encouraged the idea that there was need for a book which could introduce to the English-language reader the existing scholarship on the Soviet Germans (much of it in German or Russian), make use of materials not previously analysed, and provide a new synthesis. The present work embodies the historical and sociological contributions to the conference of two scholars, reshaped and considerably expanded.

As in all studies great and small, thanks are due to a number of people who, in one way or another, made the final publication possible. Those essays in this volume which were originally written in German or Hebrew were translated by Dr Dafna Alon of Jerusalem, who has provided the Soviet and East European Research Centre with excellent translations and editorial work for a number of years. Ella S. Frankel of London very kindly gave of her time translating some additional German material as well as reading over part of the manuscript. Appreciation should also be expressed to Ginette Avram, the librarian, and Shulamit Tsur, the secretary of the Centre. Christopher Hurst, the British publisher, has influenced the final form of the book with advice and editorial work.

The Leah Goldberg Fund for Russian Studies of the Hebrew University, to which the Centre is indebted for most generous help over the years, provided the funds for the translations. We would also like to express our appreciation to the following for the support which they gave in connection with this study: the Stiftung Volkswagenwerk, the Israeli Association of Slavic and East European Studies, the United States Cultural Centers in Jerusalem and Tel Aviv, and the Embassy of the German Federal Republic in Tel Aviv.

The editor, finally, acknowledges the characteristic generosity of her husband, Jonathan Frankel, in giving time, advice and encouragement, as well as reading over part of the manuscript.

Jerusalem   E.R.F.
September 1985

v

CONTENTS

vii

TABLES

PLATES

MAP

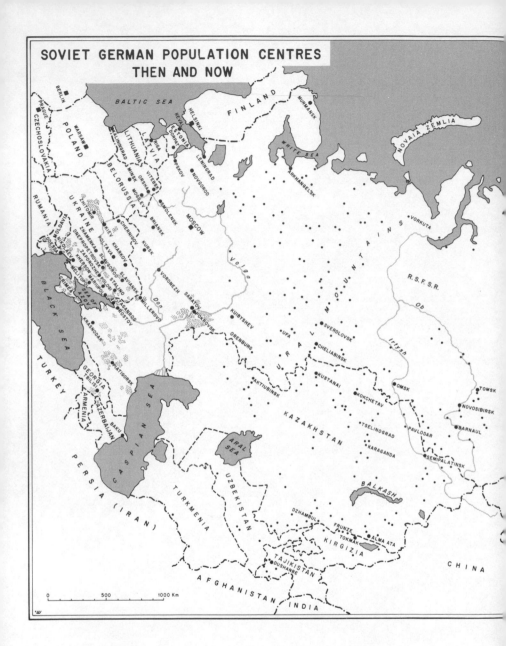

SOVIET GERMAN POPULATION CENTRES
THEN AND NOW

BERLIN

PRAGUE
CZECHOSLOVAKIA

BALTIC SEA

FINLAND

MURMANSK

NOVAIA ZEMLIA

POLAND

WARSAW

KALININGRAD
LITHUANIA
RIGA
REVAL
ESTONIA
DORPAT

HELSINKI

WHITE SEA

ARKHANGELSK

R.S.F.S.R.

VORKUTA

Ob

RUMANIA

BELORUSSIA
MINSK
ORSHA
MOGLEV

UKRAINE
ZHITOMIR
KIEV
CHERNIGOV

VISNU
KISHINEV
DNEPROPETROVSK
SLAVGOROD
KHERSON
MELITOPOL
SEA OF AZOV
CRIMEA

BLACK SEA

TURKEY

KRASNODAR

PIATIGORSK

GEORGIA
TBILISI
ARMENIA
AZERBAIJAN
BAKU

CASPIAN SEA

PERSIA (IRAN)

PSKOV
LENINGRAD
NOVGOROD

VITEBSK
SMOLENSK

BRIANSK
MOSCOW

KURSK

KHARKOV
POLTAVA
SLAVIANSK
ZAPOROZHE
STALINO
MARIUPOL
TAGANROG
ROSTOV

VORONEZH
SARATOV

Don
Volga

MILLEROVO

STALINGRAD

KUIBYSHEV

ORENBURG

UFA

SVERDLOVSK

CHELIABINSK

U R A L   M O U N T A I N S

Irtysh

KUSTANAI

OMSK

TOMSK

NOVOSIBIRSK

BARNAUL

AKTIUBINSK

KOKCHETAV

KAZAKHSTAN

TSELINOGRAD
PAVLODAR

KARAGANDA

SEMIPALATINSK

ARAL
SEA

UZBEKISTAN

TURKMENIA

BALKASH

DZHAMBUL
FRUNZE
TOKMAK
ALMA ATA

KIRGIZIA

TAJIKISTAN
DUSHANBE

CHINA

AFGHANISTAN
INDIA

0   500   1000 Km

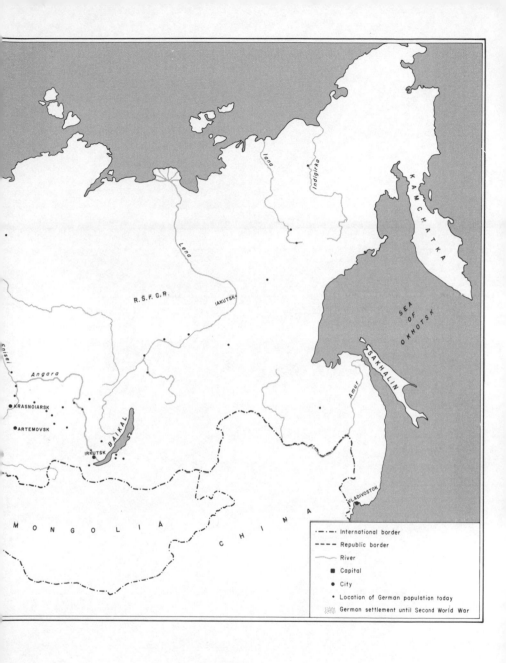

INTRODUCTION

Edith Rogovin Frankel

This is a study of official policy toward a national minority. The Soviet Union, as the successor-state, has retained much of the vastness and variety of population which characterised the tsarist empire. Among the many Soviet nationalities – there are some 130 today – the Germans, with just under 2 million members, are one of the larger groups, following those which are in possession of eponymous national republics. The principal focus of this work is the fate of the Germans under Soviet rule and the official policies towards them that have been implemented over the nearly seven decades since the revolution.

How to deal with minorities is, of course, not a uniquely Soviet problem. The modern world has witnessed upheavals and population flight, border changes and waves of migrant labour and *gastarbeiter* all on such a vast scale that most states – even those which had previously been homogeneous – have now to decide how to deal with multi-national (or multi-ethnic) societies. Whether, and how far, minority languages and national cultures are to be maintained is an issue which runs through this volume, but is likewise debated in many countries. For example, there are conflicting views in numerous locations in the United States, Canada and Great Britain on the value of teaching school subjects in a language other than that of the majority. What should be the objectives of national policy? Do the needs of the whole society in general necessarily run counter to those of the individual group? Are the interests of the whole and the part mutually exclusive?

The present study makes clear that the Soviet Germans do not represent one of the more successful examples of Soviet policy; they illustrate rather the most violent oscillations in that policy. During the period of Soviet rule the Germans have had to run the full gamut of governmental attitudes: they were granted their own territorial unit (indeed, several units of varying size and importance); they were deported and dispersed; and they were 'rehabilitated' but nonetheless remain an extra-territorial minority. This experience (together with that of the Crimean Tatars and the Meskhetians) provides the most extreme example of the vagaries to which minority groups have been subject in the Soviet Union.

National minorities became integral parts of the tsarist empire in a

1

variety of ways. Large nations such as the Georgians and the Kazakhs found themselves under Russian rule following conquest. Poles and Jews, Ukrainians and Belorussians were engulfed by the empire during the period of the Polish partitions. Some peoples voluntarily entered the empire for sundry reasons and were either absorbed or maintained their independent identity.

As for the German minority, who are they and what are their origins? The Soviet Germans or 'ethnic' Germans (*Volksdeutsche*) share a generally common history which should not be confused with that of the Baltic Germans. The Baltic German communities originated in the medieval colonisation led by the knights of the Livonian and Teutonic orders and by the burghers of Riga, Dorpat and Reval, and their region became part of the Russian empire with its expansion under Peter the Great in the early eighteenth century. They followed their own historical and sociological path within the empire and, following the Revolution of 1917, found themselves divided by the new state frontiers from the Germans under discussion here.

It is now more than two centuries since Catherine the Great issued her Manifesto inviting foreigners to come and settle in Russia. Coming from areas plagued by chronic instability and military conflict, the German colonists were attracted by the opportunities which Catherine's offer opened up. Thousands of German families entered Russia in the few years immediately following the promulgation of the Manifesto in July 1763; and they continued to come in a series of waves during the next century. Their backgrounds were disparate; they came from a wide range of German states – Baden, Württemberg, the Palatinate, West Prussia, Danzig – and even from German communities in Poland and Galicia; and they belonged to different Christian denominations. While most were Lutherans, there were also colonists belonging to the Catholic, Reformed and Mennonite Churches. It was usual for a single, homogeneous group to form a colony, although settlements were frequently contiguous, with the main street of the one village joining up with that of the next. In their social origin the settlers were rather more consistent:, largely they were from the lower strata of society and had earned their living in agriculture or skilled crafts. As we shall see, they met with varying degrees of success in their adopted country over the next century or more.

Most of Catherine's colonists were sent to the Volga region, and of these most settled south of Saratov on both banks of the river. It is estimated that some 25,000 came in this first wave of colonisation. Later groups settled in other areas: a large group in the lower Black Sea area and others in the Crimea, along the Dnieper, in Bessarabia, on the Dnestr, in the Caucasus, in Volhynia and Siberia.

Catherine's aim, as stated in the Manifesto, was to populate undeveloped regions of Russia and open them up to productive settlement. In order to encourage foreigners to settle in Russia, the government offered special conditions and privileges such as exemption from taxes for thirty years, material help in the construction of their homesteads, freedom of worship and permanent exemption from military service. It should be noted that the Germans came as free peasants to a country of serfs. It was hoped that their traditionally industrious character and productive farming methods would not only prove successful in Russian conditions but would serve as an example to the local farmers. In certain areas, where the native population was not Christian, the Germans were also to serve as a bulwark of European and Christian strength, performing the service of internal colonisation.

In a book published in Russia in 1905, which is sometimes didactic in its asides to the Russian-German reader, the Reverend Conrad Keller described some of the useful characteristics of the German colonist in South Russia in the early twentieth century:

The German colonist is courageous, valiant and able, and has a taste for order and discipline, which makes him an excellent and serviceable soldier, openly recognised as such by even the Russian officers. The general aspiration of the German colonists is directed more toward material than spiritual riches of life, for which reason even school affairs are still left far behind them. 'Money and land' is the cure-all cry among most German colonist.[1]

The degree of success among the German colonists and their descendents varied widely according to geographical area and, of course, native ability. Thus we find an acute land shortage among many of the Volga farmers (where, by the late nineteenth century there was a landshare of less than 4 acres per male)[2] and huge German landholdings in the Black Sea area where, for example, in the Odessa district nearly 60 per cent of the entire sowing area belonged to Germans.[3] In some regions the land hunger was eased by the considerable German emigration to the

1 Revd P. Conrad Keller, *The German Colonies in South Russia, 1804–1904*, vol. I, Battleford, Saskatchewan, 1968, p. 101. (This book was originally published in Odessa in 1905 in Russian.)
2 Fred C. Koch, *The Volga Germans in Russia and the Americas from 1763 to the Present*, Pennsylvania State University Press, 1977, p. 87.
3 Walter Kolarz, *Russia and her Colonies*, London, 1952, p. 71.

Western Hemisphere following the withdrawal of the military exemption in 1874,[4] but pressure for land continued.

Over time there was a dwindling of the privileged status of the German settlers, which had consisted of those rights set out in the Manifesto. Their tax exemption was not permanent, for example, and their immunity from the draft was repudiated under Alexander II. They continued to work the land which they had acquired, of course, some of them living the most modest of lives while others were great landowners, grain-growers and millers. And they continued to live largely in their own communities, marrying within the group and maintaining their separateness. A foreigner travelling through the Volga region in 1873 remarked that not only had the Germans had no effect on the Russian peasants, but they themselves had not been 'at all changed by their contact with Russians. . . The Germans look with dislike and contempt upon the Russians, a feeling which is returned by the latter with interest.'[5]

Twenty-five years later, Father Keller said much the same thing in his own way:

Distinctive intellectual characteristics of the colonists are: keen understanding, sagacity, good memory and rather slow but intensive power of comprehension. Among the colonists the ability to learn foreign languages is rare, for the Russian language is mostly incorrectly pronounced by them, to be sure, even if well learned in school. The German colonist is not much good at associating with foreigners, at which time his behaviour is mostly unnatural and awkward. The German colonist adapts himself easily among other peoples, but clings to his narrower homeland with devotion. . .[6]

In a variety of ways, the experience of the Germans under the tsars, both in its positive and negative aspects, was shared by other nationalities; the separateness of communities was by no means unique to this group. With the Germans it plainly emanated from tsarist policy as well as from the natural inclinations of the colonists themselves. Moreover, the hostility and envy often felt by the Russians toward the Germans

4 Adam Giesinger, *From Catherine to Khrushchev: The Story of Russia's Germans*, Battleford, Saskatchewan, 1974, p. 71.
5 Eugene Schuyler, *Turkistan*, I (London: Sampson Low, 1876), pp. 2–3, as cited in Isabelle Kreindler, *The Soviet Deported Nationalities: A Summary and an Update*, Soviet and East European Research Centre, Hebrew University of Jerusalem, Research Paper no. 59.
6 Keller, p. 101. Note that even in the twentieth century these people were still referred to as 'colonists'.

was consistent with their attitudes towards 'alien' groups generally.

This distrust manifested itself, in the German case, in the decision of the government of Nicholas II during the First World War to uproot and dispossess, first, those Germans living in the border areas and later those in the Volga region. But this policy was applied in the winter of 1914–15 to Jews in the same areas; and it had been employed by Alexander I in 1807 against Jews in the borderlands of the Pale during the Napoleonic wars and by Nicholas I against the Crimean Tatars during the Crimean war. (Ironically, in view of the impending catastrophe, the *Great Soviet Encyclopaedia* in 1939 criticised the policy of expulsion during the First World War: 'The overthrow of the monarchy prevented the implementation of this barbaric measure [expulsion of all Germans from the Volga area].'[7]

The compulsory study of the Russian language in German schools was a feature of official nationality policy under Alexander III. But, again, the same policy was applied in the schools of other nationalities, even those of the relatively privileged Finns. Furthermore, the tsarist policy of opening up lands to colonisation was not limited to the Germans alone. Other national groups (from Sweden and Switzerland, for example) entered Russia, albeit in smaller numbers, as settlers. And in New Russia, Jewish as well as German settlers arrived in large numbers from the period of Alexander I, who offered them various incentives to farm the land.

From the moment of their victory in October 1917, the Bolsheviks were faced with the awesome task of dealing with a prodigious array of national groups. Even with the territorial loss of Poland and the Baltic States (which included within their population *inter alia* the vast majority of Baltic Germans), the rest of the former Empire now under Soviet control still retained its multinational character. These groups ranged from those large enough to populate a good-sized country to tiny tribal remnants – besides, of course, the principal Slavic nationalities which dominated the European part of the state.

What was the basis of Bolshevik policy? It relied on a combination of long-term theory, short-term pragmatism and, to bridge the two, a flexible ideology. It seems clear that the Bolsheviks saw nationhood as a temporary, if tenacious, phenomenon, and held that the division of mankind into separate nations was a historical development which

7 *Bol'shaia sovetskaia entsiklopediia*, vol. 41, Moscow, 1939, p. 595.

would disappear in time. The Bolsheviks theorised that the nation had arisen during a particular stage of historical development, the period of rising capitalism. However, Lenin insisted at the same time that national aspirations – even if a temporary phenomenon – were often far too powerful a force to be ignored, let alone opposed. The dialectic duality and open-endedness of his approach can be seen in this characteristic statement from 1914: 'The proletariat . . . recognising equality of rights and an equal right to a national state . . . values most the alliance of the proletarians of all nations, and evaluates every national demand, every national separation *from the angle* of the class struggle of the workers.'[8]

And in trying to consolidate power in the turbulent years after the Revolution, the Bolsheviks developed policies designed to attract the ethnic minorities to their side or, at the very least, to neutralise them. But these were seen as interim measures for whatever period of time it would take for the basic differences between peoples to disappear or become insignificant. In this way Lenin saw the aim of socialism as 'not only to abolish the present division of mankind into small states . . . not only to bring the nations closer to each other, but also to merge them'.[9] The 'merging' has taken on different forms in Soviet theory over the past decades, moving uneasily between the ill-defined concepts of *sblizhenie* (drawing closer), *sliianie* (fusion) and *edinstvo* (unity). This variation in terminology points up the conflict the Soviet leaders have had to face in seeking to reconcile their own long-term theories with the reality of national problems. The dilemma has continued for nearly seventy years.

Thus Soviet policy towards the constituent nationalities has been characterised by two aspects: the promise – and provision – of rights and privileges intended to attract nations to remain within the Soviet framework during the early years of the régime and the acknow-ledgment in Soviet theoretical writing of the belief that nationality was a temporary phenomenon which would eventually disappear. Whether this is indeed a viable aim is a complicated question and in all probability the answer – despite Soviet theory – will vary radically from one nationality to another. These groups vary so widely that generalisations about one group cannot apply wholly to another.

It is not surprising that the ethnic Germans, as a fundamentally conservative, land-based, largely middle-class group, did not constitute

8 'On the Right of Nations to Self-Determination' in V.I. Lenin, *Selected Works*, vol. 4, London (Lawrence and Wishart), 1944, p. 265.
9 'The Socialist Revolution and the Right of Nations to Self-Determination' (March 1916) in V.I. Lenin, *Selected Works*, vol. 5, London, 1944, p. 270.

an ideal object for the socialist experiment. However, their very traits of down-to-earth farmer mentality coupled with a strong work ethic did prepare them to acquiesce in Soviet pressures to collectivise rapidly in the years after 1929 and to settle into a new sociological mould. Indeed, from the viewpoint of cultural administration, the first two decades after the Revolution – first the NEP, then the First Five-Year Plan – proved to be the zenith for the Soviet Germans. Up till the Second World War they had their own autonomous republic, a sub-section within the Russian Republic. This was located on the Volga in an area traditionally inhabited by German settlers since the time of Catherine, and was a natural choice for the establishment of a territorial base. However, as the German colonies had been quite far-flung, the autonomous republic served as a home base for only part of the German population. It was thus that Soviet Germans lived on both a territorial and extra-territorial basis. It is understandable that the very existence of the autonomous republic should have had important ramifications for all Soviet Germans wherever they lived and it assured them a far richer national life than was accessible to those groups who had no territorial unit at all.[10]

The chapters which make up this book deal with periods divided from each other by central events in Soviet history: the Bolshevik Revolution (October 1917), the German invasion of the Soviet Union (June 1941) and the victory over Nazi Germany (May 1945). However, if one were to determine the periodisation not from this bird's eye view but rather from the angle of the Soviet Germans themselves, the dates would have to be slightly different; certainly the October Revolution would constitute the starting-point, but the first period would then be perceived as coming to an abrupt end not in June but in August 1941. Until then, the Soviet German experience had not been out of the ordinary. As with so many other nationalities, its publications (books and newspapers) and schools had mushroomed in the decade following the Twelfth Party Congress of 1923, although, again true to a general pattern, the German section of the Communist Party was abolished in January 1930. And it was not picked out either for special treatment under the supremely tragic policy of collectivisation, with its toll of famine, and the accompanying assault on the Churches. Again, the reversion to a policy of

10 For an extremely interesting and detailed discussion of the German administrative units in the Soviet Union before the Second World War, see Meir Buchsweiler, *German Raiony and their Newspapers, 1927–1941*, Soviet and East European Research Centre, Hebrew University of Jerusalem, Research Paper no. 58.

preferential treatment for the Great Russian nationality after the mid-1930s adversely affected all the other nationalities as publications and other manifestations of their national culture were sharply reduced.

It does seem, however, that throughout this period the Germans maintained their national cohesiveness more successfully in various ways (lower rate of intermarriage, maintenance of mother tongue) than many other European national groups, such as the Poles and Jews. Largely a farming people, the Germans probably found it easier to maintain a degree of isolation. And this self-sufficiency may even have been made easier in some ways by the loss of the major portion of their intelligentsia through the emigration and physical separation of the Baltic German community with the border adjustments in the aftermath of the Revolution. Up to the present day the ethnic Germans have shown no significant inclination towards academic achievement or entry into intellectual fields which normally accelerate acculturation.

It was in the late summer of 1941 that the fate of the Soviet Germans suddenly deviated totally from the general pattern. It was then that the Soviet régime disbanded the autonomous republic and other territorial units of the Germans and systematically rounded up and deported them to various regions in Siberia and Central Asia, where they had to try to rebuild their lives in conditions of penal exile. The Germans, of course, were not the only victims of the wartime deportation policy. Seven other nations – the Crimean Tatars, Kalmyks, Balkars, Chechens, Ingush, Karachai and Meskhetians – were deported *en masse* by the Soviets during the war. But the Germans were the first to lose their autonomy and be deported. And they were also the largest among these nationalities. The subsequent fate of all the groups varied, as we shall see.

The deportation of the ethnic Germans was not limited to the autonomous republic; that is, although the deportations began in August 1941 and the legal abolition of the republic was decreed in September, it was not only the Volga Germans who were affected. Throughout the war years other Germans – even those living in Moscow and Leningrad – were collected and shipped out. Nor could the deportation be considered a specific form of punishment for collaboration with the Nazis: deportation largely occurred before the army of the Third Reich entered any of the Soviet German areas. It was a class action touching on all members of the group indiscriminately, even those who were members of the Communist Party.

The Soviet Germans were caught in a unique pincer-movement in this case. Not only did the Soviet administration act swiftly to deal with them, but the Nazis too had their own special plans for their fellow-nationals, many of whom they regarded as suspect either racially or politically. Even the chance to escape from the Soviet Union by trekking westward in 1944 with the retreating German army ultimately ended for most with their capture and internal deportation by the Soviet régime.

In the light of the treatment meted out to them during the Second World War and the accusations which have plagued them for decades since, it can legitimately be asked whether and to what extent the Germans remained loyal to the Soviet Union. In reality there were undoubtedly those among them who were not only disloyal to the régime but who actively worked against it; indeed it cannot be surprising, given the various grievances that must have been harboured against the Soviet state as a result of events of the 1920s and '30s, that there should have been a lack of enthusiasm among many in this group. However, there is nothing to indicate wholesale treachery on their part or even expressions or feelings of hostility which would distinguish them radically from other similar groups within the Soviet Union such as, say, the Ukrainians.

For the Soviet Germans the period ushered in by the deportations closed not in 1945 but, formally at least, a decade later with the amnesty decree of 1955. But this first stage of rehabilitation only provided relief from the special exile régime under which they had lived and restoration of their civil rights (for example, the ability to change their place of work). Not till 1964 was the onus of treachery and collaboration finally removed from the Soviet Germans by decree; yet of the eight deported nationalities only the Germans, the Crimean Tatars and the Meskhetians have not had their territories restored to them. The Germans remain in those areas to which they were exiled in the 1940s – the majority in Kazakhstan and Siberia. The districts belonging to the original Autonomous Volga Republic were transferred to neighbouring administrative units in September 1941 and are unlikely to be returned to form a German republic again. At a meeting with a delegation of former Volga Germans on June 7, 1965, A.I. Mikoyan admitted that for the Germans the re-establishment of the Volga republic 'would be the best solution of the problem', but he prefaced this with a significant statement: 'In the Virgin Lands it would now be impossible to carry on the economy without the Germans.'[11]

11 [R. Medvedev] *Politicheskii dnevnik, 1964–1970*, Amsterdam: Alexander Herzen

The ethnic Germans have, true to their original character, settled well in their new areas, industriously filling economic norms – Europeans in the midst of a non-European population. In his study of the Soviet system of camps and exile, Aleksandr Solzhenitsyn refers to the indefatigable ability of the Germans to root themselves successfully, quoting an old Russian saying: 'A German is like a willow tree – stick it in anywhere and it will take.' In the mines, he wrote, 'in Machine and Tractor Stations, in state farms, wherever it might be, the bosses could not find words enough to praise the Germans – they had never had better workers.'[12] According to Solzhenitsyn – and one can glean this too from official reports – the deported Germans fared relatively well by dint of their work ethic:

By the 1950s the Germans – in comparison with other exiles and even with the locals – had the stoutest, roomiest, and neatest houses, the biggest pigs, the best milch cows. Their daughters grew up to be much-sought-after brides, not only because their parents were well off, but – in the depraved world around the camps – because of their purity and strict morals.[13]

One cannot but marvel at this consistency of the national character which first induced Catherine the Great to invite them and which seems to have survived so many vicissitudes and catastrophes.

In many ways the Soviet Germans have fared relatively well in the past two decades; they are now once again allowed to publish a number of newspapers and books in their native language, they have been granted greater access to higher education; and they participate in successful farming communities – the *kolkhozy* and *sovkhozy* – in their new places of residence. Their position is in certain ways better than that of some other groups: unlike the Bulgarians, Crimean Tatars and Jews they have the opportunity for their children to be taught in their mother tongue. They have more periodical publications in their own language than do some other extra-territorial nationalities such as the Koreans, Jews, Greeks and Crimean Tatars. They have been relatively successful in maintaining their traditions, and a sizeable portion of the Germans are still Christian believers.

Foundation, 1972, p. 94. At this meeting one of the representatives, F.G. Shessler, complained: 'Now the accusation has been removed from us, but the punishment nevertheless remains' (p. 92).

12 A. Solzhenitsyn, *The Gulag Archipelago, 1918–1956*, vols V–VII, New York: Harper and Row, 1978, p. 400.

13 *Ibid.*, p. 401.

On the other hand, the number of children studying German has been declining and there is a drop too in those declaring German as their mother tongue. The circulation figures for German periodicals are low. The German intelligentsia is still only modestly represented in Soviet government institutions. Most important, in spite of the complete rehabilitation of the Soviet Germans in 1964 and the abolition of restrictions on their places of residence in 1972, the Germans have not been allowed to re–establish any national administrative unit.

The complexity of the situation will be more graphically understood in the detailed chapters which follow. What Soviet policy was, how it changed and in what ways the German population of the Soviet Union was affected; the national and cultural life of the people during the decades after the October Revolution; the vicissitudes which mark the Soviet German experience – all of these are put into perspective by Ingeborg Fleischhauer and Benjamin Pinkus in a narrative that tells one of the more fascinating stories of a national group in post-Revolution Russia.

A German peasant in Speyer/Odessa. (*Source*: Archive of Landsmannschaft der Deutschen aus Russland, Stuttgart.)

German peasants in the Black Sea area. (*Source*: as above.)

CHAPTER ONE

THE GERMANS' ROLE IN TSARIST RUSSIA: A REAPPRAISAL*

Ingeborg Fleischhauer

Along with many other national minorities of the former Russian empire, a German group numbering over 2 million fell to the share of the Bolsheviks when they established the Soviet state and entrenched their régime. In the Russian empire, this national group had been a powerful factor making a considerable contribution to its social and political stability while at the same time promoting steady, upward economic development.

There were three distinct historical and social sectors of German subjects of the tsars – the Baltic Germans, city and court circles, and colonists. Distinct though they were in their specific functioning and achievements, all three proved themselves pioneers of a dynamic economic and, in part, social outlook that bore the stamp of the West. In the epoch of modernisation, they served as one of the fulcra by means of which the spirit of reform and liberalisation was slowly but progressively implemented in Russian society and its institutions.

According to the first all-Russian population census of 1897,[1] there were 1,790,489 German-speaking Russian subjects of German origin (of the 1,813,717 persons who spoke German or cognate languages[2]). Of these Russian Germans, 1,312,188 (1,333,663) lived in the fifty *gubernie* of European Russia; 407,274 (407,780) in the ten *gubernie* of the kingdom of Poland; 56,729 (57,502) in the Caucasus; 5,424 (5,828) in Siberia; and 8,874 (8,947) in Central Asia. Of the 1.8 million Germans in Russia (in round figures), 1.3 million (76.62 per cent) belonged to the rural population and 401,960 (23 per cent) to the urban population. As

---

* The following is based on a comprehensive study of the role played by the Germans in Russia from the eighteenth century up to 1917, which the present writer has pursued over a number of years. The results will in due course be published in book form in German.

1 *Dépouillement des donnés sur la nationalité et classification des peuples de l'Empire russe d'après leur langue* (St Petersburg, 1899) and *Relevé générale pour tout l'Empire de Russie des résultats du dépouillement des donnés du premier recensement de la population en 1897* (St Petersburg, 1905).

2 For example, Swiss-Germans, Dutch or other ethnics who were for the most part culturally and socially assimilated to the Germans in Russia.

regards distribution by class and occupation, 1,033,282 (57.7 per cent) worked in agriculture and forestry and 375,953 (21 per cent) in industry; 112, 453 (6.3 per cent) were workers and servants; 97,796 (5.5 per cent) were engaged in trade, transport and communication; and 11,768 (0.6 per cent) were merchants. Some 50,000 Germans worked in academic professions; 35,000 were in the civil service and the armed forces. About 50,000 Germans belonged to the nobility and the distinguished group of 'Privileged Citizens' (pochetnyi grazhdanin). Of these, 24,854 (1.4 per cent of the overall Russian German population) were hereditary nobles and 17,134 (less than 1 per cent) knighted for personal merit or service to crown or country.[3]

In historical perspective, of these Germans, only the Baltic Germans (ostzeiskie nemtsy) were among the people subjugated under the Russian throne. All the others – the German urban population, those exercising the liberal professions and the colonists – had come to the Russian empire and become Russian subjects of their own free will. Yet the Baltic Germans of Livonia and Estonia had themselves concluded a Treaty of Submission with their conqueror, Peter the Great, which in the long run proved advantageous to them. The Peace of Nystadt (1721) had confirmed the privileges accorded to the Baltic Provinces under Polish rule (the Privilegium Sigismundi Augusti, 1561): freedom of religious practice and of the Protestant faith (later buttressed by the founding of the German Protestant University of Dorpat), German administration in town and country, and observance of German law. Courland, the third of the Baltic provinces, fell to Russia in the third partition of Poland in 1795. After 400 years of wars and struggling to survive, the Baltic provinces, which were joined into a general Baltic guberniia in 1801, entered a period of steady progress, while preserving their far-reaching privileges.[4]

---

3 J.Schleuning, Die Deutschen Siedlungsgebiete in Russland (Würzburg, 1955) p. 12.

4 Historical research by and on the Baltic Germans is rather voluminous. As an ethnic group which for centuries was overweeningly conscious of its social origins (the Livonian and Teutonic knights and Hanseatic burghers), religious faith (Protestantism) and national background (preponderantly North German), the Baltic Germans developed a historical tradition of their own that was quite unique in its East European context. Up until the second half of the nineteenth century, Baltic German historiography followed the historical lines of the development of the Ostsee-Provinces under Russian rule in the setting and against the background of general Russian history. From the mid-1860s on, a conflict of views broke out over the 'ostzeiskii vopros' (Baltic question) between Russian Pan-Slavists and overbearingly patriotic Baltic Germans, producing a marked nationalistic and later an autonomistic tone in

In the middle of the nineteenth century, some 100,000 Germans were living in the Baltic general *guberniia*, amounting to 7.52 per cent of the overall Baltic population.[5] The land-owning nobility constituted about 10 per cent of the Baltic German population. They were disproportionately strongly represented in the Russian state administration and at the court. The Baltic German urban population comprised a bourgeoisie of Hanseatic origin, active and fairly successful in trade and industry, a significant stratum of *literati* influenced culturally and politically by their former German fatherland, and a stratum of petty-bourgeois and artisans, which was broadened very considerably by a strong influx from the German lands, especially towards the end of the nineteenth century. In 1897 the Baltic Germans numbered 165,627 and this figure rose to 200,000 in the next two decades. Its percentage share of the overall Baltic population dropped in this period from 7.35 per cent to 6.2 per cent.[6]

The social and economic dominance of the Baltic German landowners

---

Baltic German writing (see E. Seraphim, *Grundriss der Baltischen Geschichte*, Reval, 1908). In the period between the two wars and the Nazi era, representatives of this nationalist wing among Baltic German emigrants to Germany accentuated the Baltic problem with a certain 'master-race' ideology and a national-political revanchism that marked them as 'experts' and mouthpieces of eastward expansion. The chauvinism of a small extremist minority of the Baltic Germans found its final expression in the appointment of Alfred Rosenberg as *Reichsminister für die besetzten Ostgebiete* (Reich Minister for the Occupied Eastern Territories). Even as eminent a Baltic German historian as R. Wittram allowed himself in this era to be seduced into a wilfully nationalistic view of Baltic German history (see R. Wittram, *Geschichte der baltischen Staaten*, Stuttgart, 1939.) It was no accident, however, that at the end of the 1940s, after a phase of personal and intellectual catharsis, Wittram became the central figure of a new Baltic German school of historiography (see R. Wittram, *Drei Generationen. Deutschland – Livland – Russland. 1830–1914* (Göttingen, 1949), and *Baltische Geschichte. Die Ostseelande Livland, Estland, Kurland 1180–1918*, Munich, 1954), which had been re-born in a fairly credible fashion from a purifying Protestantism and a new comprehension of Baltic-Russian relations (see, among many other works, G. von Rauch, *Geschichte der Baltischen Staaten*, Stuttgart, 1970; English edn. *The Baltic States: Years of Independence*, *1917–1940*, London, 1974). The younger generation is beginning to spread a profound historic comprehension of Baltic-Russian relations by means of critical historical analysis (see especially G. von Pistohlkors, ' "Russifizierung" und die Grundlage der baltischen Russophobie', *Zeitschrift für Ostforschung*, 1976, 25, pp. 618–31).

5 W.D.M. Stricker, *Deutsch-russische Wechselwirkungen oder die Deutschen in Russland und die Russen in Deutschland. Ein geschichtlicher Versuch* (Leipzig, 1849), pp. 230 ff.

6 *Die deutschen Ostseeprovinzen Russlands. Geschichtlich, kulturell und wirtschaftlich dargestellt von Kennern der Baltischen Provinzen* (Berlin, 1918), p. 137.

continued unchanged.[7] In 1900, Baltic German landed estates in Estonia comprised 1,145,128 hectares, or 59.8 per cent of the entire cultivable agricultural area of the *guberniia*, as against local peasant ownership amounting to 40.2 per cent. In Livonia in 1908, the Baltic German *latifundia* covered 60 per cent, and the local peasant land 39 per cent of the usable area. These ratios remained constant up to the First World War. In 1914 German landed property in the Baltic provinces made up a total of 4.4 million hectares, whereas local peasant land came to 2.7 million and Russian domain and Church land to 982,000 hectares.

The German Russian urban population and members of the liberal professions[8] numbered around 400,000 in 1897 and on the outbreak of war 500,000. They centred in metropolitan cities such as Lodz (67,248 Germans, 21.4 per cent of the city's population in 1897), Riga (65,332 – 23.1 per cent), St Petersburg (50,780 – 4 per cent), Moscow (17,717 – 1.7 per cent), Odessa (10,248 – 2.5 per cent) and Saratov (8,367 – 4.2 per cent). Smaller German urban 'colonies' were to be found in port and trading towns, among them Tiflis, Arkhangel'sk and Vladivostok.

The Russian German urban population could look back on a long history of settlement in Russia. There had been a sizeable German

7 S. Broederich-Kurmalen and others, *Deutsche Bauern in Russland* (Berlin, 1916), pp. 1–9.

8 Up to now no comprehensive research has been done on the Germans in the cities of Russia, but there has long been an interest in the subject – see Fr. Dukmeyer, *Die Deutschen in Russland* (Munich, 1916). Historians in Nazi Germany made contributions on this topic in the framework of the so-called *Deutschtums-Forschung* (research into *Deutschtum*), some of which were expanded and published after 1945. (It should be noted here that the word *Deutschtum* has no exact equivalent in English. Rather than use such clumsy words as 'Germandom' or 'Germanness', we will use the German word in this book.) See, e.g., E. Amburger, *Die van Brienen und ihre Sippe in Archangel* (Berlin, 1936), 'Aus dem Leben und Wirken von Hamburgern in Russland', in *Festschrift Percy Ernst Schramm zu seinem siebzigsten Geburtstag* (Wiesbaden, 1964), vol. 2, pp. 3–25, and 'Berliner und Märker in Russland', a filmed document of the Deutsches Auslandsinstitut (DAI) in *German Records* (GR), National Archives, Washington, DC, Microfilm Series T-512, Reel 294; A. Anzerova, 'Die ersten deutschen Handelsleute in Nordrussland', *Deutsche Post aus dem Osten*, 1941, 13, pp. 12–14; B. von Arseniew, 'Die Deutschen im Gouvernement Tula', *Deutsche Post aus dem Osten*, 1940, 12, 9, pp. 10–19; A. Mergenthaler, 'Vom Deutschtum in Moskau vor dem Weltkriege', *Deutsche Post aus dem Osten*, 1940, 12, 4, pp. 11–14; H. Sieveking, 'Die Hamburgische Firma Kunst und Albers in Wladivostok, 1864–1914' in *Vierteljahresschrift für Sozial- und Wirtschaftsgeschichte*, 1941, vol. 34, 3/4, pp. 268–99; G. Strauch, 'Deutsches Leben im einstigen Moskau', *Deutche Post aus dem Osten*, 1940, 12, 4, pp. 8–11.

population consisting of professional groups ever since the evolution of the Muscovite state.[9] The policy of Peter the Great, transforming Russia into a modern empire and therefore in need of skilled manpower, attracted German and other foreign elements *en masse*. They now increased by leaps and bounds in the growing cities as well as in the civil service and the armed forces throughout the empire. Under Catherine II this policy of bringing in well-trained foreigners assumed an elaborate legislative as well as technical-administrative form: the Manifestos of 1762 and 1763, which called for foreign immigrants and promised them exceptional privileges, promoted the influx of enterprising elements from the German territorial states. Renowned natural scientists and scholars, invited personally, as well as young and promising researchers came into the country along with manufacturers, entrepreneurs of all kinds, industrialists, merchants, artisans and peasants.[10] The hopes entertained by the Imperial Crown, and which inspired these Manifestos – hopes for Russia's economy and internal situation – were partly fulfilled. The granting of titles of nobility to particularly deserving Germans, as well as elevation to the status of 'privileged citizen' (*pochetnoe grazhdanstvo*) inaugurated under Nicholas I, became a frequent practice and a means of assimilating foreigners needed by the Russian polity for its economy, trade and culture. The Germans were a dominant group among these foreigners, together with members of other peoples affiliated with them in culture and language, such as the Dutch, British and Scandinavians.[11] In the mid-nineteenth century, when Russian German influence was at its height, the ennobled German urban population and the Baltic German nobility were especially well represented in the leading institutions of the Russian empire. They became the pillars of the Russian military establishment, diplomacy, higher administration and the court.[12] Even in the 1880s, when Russian German influence was

9 See E.F. Sommer, 'Die Anfänge der Moskauer Deutschen Sloboda' in *Deutsches Archiv für Landes- und Volksforschung*, 1941, 5, pp. 421–44.

10 See B. Ischchanian, *Die ausländischen Elemente in der russischen Volkswirtschaft*, Berlin, 1913; E. Amburger, *Die Anwerbung ausländischer Fachkräfte für die Wirtschaft Russlands vom 15. bis 19. Jahrhundert*, Wiesbaden, 1968; E. Jenny, *Die Deutschen im Wirtschaftsleben Russlands. Supplement: Die künftigen Beziehungen der deutschen Kolonisten in Russland zu ihrem Stammlande* (extract from the journal *Weltwirtschaft*, 1919), Berlin, 1920.

11 See E. Amburger, 'Mischehen im städtischen Deutschtum Altrusslands' in *Auslandsdeutsche Volksforschung*, 1937, vol. 1, pp. 266–73.

12 M. Raeff, 'Patterns of Russian Imperial Policy towards the Nationalities' in E. Allworth (ed.), *Soviet Nationality Problems*, New York-London, 1971, pp. 22–42; E.

checked in reaction to the establishment of the German empire and the rise of the pan-Slavic current in Russian society, the percentage of Russian Germans in the leading state positions was still fairly high, amounting to some 40 per cent of the army High Command, 62 per cent of the highest ranks in the Ministry of Posts and Commerce, 57 per cent in the Foreign Ministry and 46 per cent in the War Ministry. Generally, up to one-third of the high-ranking officers in the army and navy as well as civil servants or officials in the state institutions, including the ruling bodies of the Senate and Imperial Council, had German (or similar) names and in many cases were Protestants[13] – this at a time when the Germans comprised hardly more than 1 per cent of the population of the Russian empire.

By the end of the nineteenth century, the urban German population in which the Protestant element was predominant had developed its own institutions for welfare, health and social needs, as well as a network of German clubs of the various social groups, German press organs and schools.

In the same period, similar facilities of a fairly advanced nature were available to the German colonists in the different parts of Russia, who numbered 1,317,542 in 1897, far and away the largest German group in Russia. These colonists[14] had come to Russia on the strength of

Seraphim, *Führende Deutsche im Zarenreich*, Berlin, 1942; A. Noelle, 'Zur Wirksamkeit des baltischen Adels in Russland vor allem unter Alexander I und Nikolaus I' in *Der Wanderweg des Russlanddeutschen*, Stuttgart, 1939, pp. 138–46.

13 W. Laqueur, *Deutschland und Russland*, Berlin, 1965, p. 49.

14 Extensive research has been done on the German colonies in Russia, and it is relatively well covered in the relevant bibliographies. For the earlier and the more recent German research, see K. Stumpp, *Das Schrifttum über das Deutschtum in Russland*, Tübingen, 1980; and from the Soviet German side the older work by F. Schiller, *Literatur zur Geschichte und Volkskunde der deutschen Kolonien in der Sowjetunion, 1764–1926*, Pokrovsk, 1927. For research done under the Weimar Republic, H. Kniesche, 'Neues aus der Russlanddeutschen-Forschung' in *Vierteljahresschrift für Sozial- und Wirtschaftsgeschichte*, 1932, 25, pp. 261–5; and G. Leibbrandt, 'Forschungen zur Geschichte des deutschen Volkstums in Russland' in *Archiv für Kulturgeschichte*, 1931, no. 21, pp 81–94. For research done from the Nazi perspective, see M. Woltner, 'Die russland-deutsche Forschung, 1934–1937' in *Deutsches Archiv für Landes- und Volksforschung* 1938, vol. 2, pp. 471–95, and *'Die russland-deutsche Forschung* 1938–1941, ibid., and 1942, vol. 6, pp. 376–427; K. Stumpp, 'Sippenkundliche Werke und Beiträge über das Russlanddeutschtum' in *Der Wanderweg der Russlanddeutschen*, pp. 280–5. Recent American bibliographical research has produced: A. Giesinger, *Bibliography of the AHSGR Archives and Historical Library, Greeley, Colorado*, Lincoln, Nebraska (American Historical Society of Germans

Catherine II's two Manifestos and of the subsequent calls for immigrants. They gradually settled in different parts of Russia under the supervision of a special state administration for foreigners' colonies. They became a well-organized, privileged class, distinct from the Russian peasantry, with an internal self-government patterned on the institutions of their country of origin. In the mid-nineteenth century, after approximately a hundred years of development, there were some 300 German settlements or 'colonies' – the so-called 'mother-colonies':[15] 104 on the Volga, thirteen in the environs of St Petersburg and in the Russian heartland, and 181 in South Russia, Bessarabia and the Caucasus. In the period of their expansion, from the mid-nineteenth century to the outbreak of the First World War, their number increased to about 3,000 by means of land purchases and fresh settlement by the younger generation in the so-called daughter-colonies. Population growth, expanded land-ownership and capital accumulation in the German colonies appeared very considerable by comparison with the Russian peasantry, to the alarm of the Russian landed nobility, which was becoming steadily more and more impoverished.

In the first years of settlement, the German establishments on both banks of the Volga, which were among the earliest,[16] had been given some 489,000 hectares of Crown and domain land for utilisation in common.[17] In the mid-nineteenth century a similar quantity of land was

---

from Russia), 1976; J.W. Long, *Russian Language Sources relating to the Germans from Russia*, Fort Collins, Colorado, 1976; *The German Russians. A Bibliography of Russian Materials*, Santa Barbara, California/Oxford, England, 1979; M.M. Olson, *Bibliography of Materials in the Collection of the American Historical Society of Germans from Russia*, Greeley, Colorado, 1973; and *A Bibliography on the Germans from Russia. Material found in the New York Public Library*, Lincoln, Nebraska, 1976.

15 K. Stumpp, *The Emigration from Germany to Russia in the Years 1763 to 1862*, Lincoln, Nebraska, 1973, pp. 66–97.

16 G. Beratz, *Die deutschen Kolonien an der unteren Wolga in ihrer Entstehung. Gedenkblätter zur 150 jährigen Ankunft, 1764–1914*, Saratov, 1915; G.W.T. Bonwetsch, *Geschichte der deutschen Kolonien an der Wolga*, Stuttgart, 1919; K. Cramer, 'Zur Bevölkerungsstatistik des Wolgadeutschtums' in *Auslandsdeutsche Volksforschung*, 1937, 1, pp. 297–305.

17 The question whether the Crown lands allocated to the colonists were supposed to be their private property or community-owned became a matter for dispute. German nationalistic historians in the period of the First World War (R. Loew, *Deutsche Bauernstaaten auf russischer Steppe*, Charlottenburg, 1916) and German Russian historians in Nazi Germany (Th. Hummel, *Hundert Jahre Erbhofrecht der Deutschen Kolonisten in Russland*, Berlin, 1936) favoured the interpretation that the

allocated afresh to meet the renewed need for land. In 1861 there were some 200,000 German colonists living in the Volga colonies.[18] With the high population growth there also went a sharp rise in the amount of land owned; by the end of the nineteenth century, some 400,000 Volga colonists had at their disposal more than 1.3 million hectares in landed property. In 1914 the Volga settlers numbered 600,000, and their landed property had increased to 2.2 million hectares.

Other large-scale settlement activities initiated at the end of the eighteenth and beginning of the nineteenth centuries were carried out by, among others, approximately 60,000 German peasants and artisans in the three South Russian *gubernie* of Kherson, Ekaterinoslav and Tavrida, including the Crimea (1804–10),[19] as well as in the province of

original colonist laws enacted under Catherine II and the German law of inheritance introduced by the colonists had turned these lands into real German landed property. A stringent analysis of the juridical basis of the settlement process had however proved long before that the Russian legislation before 1871 left no room for this interpretation. Cf. A.A. Klaus, *Unsere Kolonien. Studien und Materialen zur Geschichte und Statistik der ausländischen Kolonisation in Russland*, Odessa, 1887 (Russian edition: A.A. Klaus, *Nashi kolonii. Opyt i materialy po istorii i statistiki inostrannoi kolonizatii v Rossii*. St Petersburg, 1869 and 1897), p. 191 ff.; J. Stach, *Ocherki iz istorii i sovremennoi zhizni iuzhnerusskikh kolonistov*, Moscow, 1916, p. 176 ff.; Fr. Matthaei, *Die deutschen Ansiedlungen in Russland. Ihre Geschichte und ihre volkswirtschaftliche Bedeutung für die Vergangenheit und Zukunft. Studien über das russische Kolonisationswesen und über die Herbeiziehung fremder Kulturkräfte nach Russland*, Gera, 1865, p. 253 ff.; as well as J. Keussler, *Zur Geschichte und Kritik des bäuerlichen Gemeindebesitzes in Russland*, St Petersburg, vol. 3, 1887, pp. 139–84.

18 A. Bohmann, *Strukturwandel der deutschen Bevölkerung im sowjetischen Staatsund Verwaltungsbereich*, Cologne, 1970, p. 23.

19 From the extensive literature on the South Russian (New Russian) colonies, see Stach, *Ocherki*; K. Stumpp, *Die deutschen Kolonien im Schwarzmeergebiet, dem früheren Neu- (Süd-) Russland. Einsiedlungs- und wirtschaftsgeographischer Versuch*, Stuttgart 1922; W. Ohneseit, 'Die deutschen Bauerkolonien in Südrussland von ihrer Gründerzeit bis zur Gegenwart' in *Preussische Jahrbücher*, 1926, 206, pp. 169–79; G. Leibbrandt, *Die deutschen Kolonien in Cherson und Bessarabien*, Stuttgart, 1926; J.A. Malinovsky, *Die Planerkolonien am Asowschen Meere*, Stuttgart, 1928; J. Stach, *Grunau und die Mariupoler Kolonien. Materialen zur Geschichte deutscher Siedlungen im Schwarzmeergebiet*, Berlin, 1942; H. Auerbach, *Die Besiedlung der Südukraine in den Jahren 1774–1787*, Wiesbaden, 1965; G. Hahn, *Die deutschen Bauernsiedlungen am Schwarzen Meer*, Stuttgart, 1965; C. Keller, *The German Colonies in South Russia, 1804 to 1904*, 2 vols, Saskatoon, 1968–73 (translation of the German lst edn, Odessa, 1905); and T.C. Wenzlaff, 'The Founding of the German Colonies in the Ukraine, Crimea, Bessarabia and Caucasia' in *American Historical Society of Germans from Russia, Work Papers*, Greeley, Colorado, 1971, pp. 43–52.

Bessarabia (1814–20).[20] Up to the First World War, the number of these 'Black Sea Germans', whose population had already risen, by virtue of population growth and new waves of immigration, to 136,000 by 1858, grew more than tenfold: in 1914 there were as many as 660,000 German settlers in South Russia. The land they owned reached almost legendary proportions: in 1910 the 154,000 German colonists living in the Kherson *guberniia* alone owned about one million hectares of real estate and the 112,000 settlers in the Ekaterinoslav *guberniia* more than 900,000 hectares, which represented about one-seventh of the cultivable area in these *gubernie*. In Tavrida during this period, 97,000 German colonists farmed one-sixth, and in Bessarabia 73,000 settlers owned about 600,000 hectares, as much as one-fifth, of the usable area of these *gubernie*. In all four South Russian provinces the German colonists had been allocated 671,000 hectares of Crown land for their first settlement; in 1914 they accounted for more than 4,209,280 hectares of well cultivated land.

German peasants and artisans settled in the Caucasus (mainly in Transcaucasia)[21] in 1814–42. In 1869 about 4,000 colonists there possessed some 26,000 hectares of land; in 1908 there were 49,000 Germans living in the Caucasus and in 1914 about 100,000.

German settlement in Volhynia[22] was marked by particularly swift growth from the 1870s on, coinciding incidentally with the strengthening of the new German *Reich*. Immigration movements of not very great size from neighbouring Poland in the years 1816, 1831 and 1861 had brought some 6,000 people there. By 1881, however, their number had already grown to over 100,000 and by 1911 to 200,000. Their landed property, according to German data, comprised about 300,000 hectares and according to Russian data as much as 700,000 hectares by the outbreak of the First World War.

Along with the Volga colonies and those in the Russian heartland, the German colonies in St Petersburg belonged to the oldest German settlements in Russia. They had a population of some 4,000 in 1865 and some 10,000 on the eve of the First World War. Together with the heartland German colonies in the Novgorod, Chernigov and Voronezh

20 See A. Kräenbring, *Bibliographie über das Bessarabiendeutschtum*, Hanover, 1970.
21 Fr. Schrenk. *Geschichte der deutschen Kolonien in Transkaukasien. Zum Gedächtnis des fünfzigjährigen Bestehens derselben*, Tiflis, 1869.
22 See A. Karasek-Langer and A. Kleidienst, 'Das Schrifttum über die Deutschen in Wolhynien und Polesien', *Deutsche Wissenschaftliche Zeitschrift für Polen*, 1931, 22, pp. 123–36, and A. Karasek, 'Das geschichtliche Werden des wolhynischen Deutschtums', *Deutsche Monatshefte für Polen*, 1937/8, 4, pp. 23–30.

gubernie, they possessed about 450,000 hectares of land in 1914.

In the Russian-Polish *gubernie* with their large German peasant concentrations, some 2 million hectares, according to Russian estimates, or
1 million hectares, according to German estimates, were in German
hands by 1914.

Finally, in the course of large-scale Siberian colonisation, carried out
as part of the agrarian reform of the Russian government between 1904
and 1914, there was a flow of numerous German colonists to Siberia and
Central Asia.[23] While in 1897 there were only 8,874 Germans living in
Central Asia and 5,424 Germans in Siberia, at the outbreak of the First
World War there were 44,838 German settlers with 371,000 hectares of
land registered in Siberia and 50,160 settlers with 332,100 hectares of
real estate in Central Asia.[24]

Besides some 4 million hectares of German-owned land in the Baltic
provinces, in 1914 landed property in the possession of German peasants
in other provinces of the Russian empire amounted to about 10 million
hectares. Most of this German-held land occupied an extraordinarily
wide belt stretching from the western to the southern borderlands of the
empire. The greatest part was held by private individuals, small independent farmers, as well as owners of medium-sized and large estates.
Besides this, property was held in common by some colonists' communities. But only a few of the Volga colonies went over at a relatively early
stage to the *mir* system[25] and, like the Russian peasant communes, they
were affected by land-hunger and desolation in the middle of the nineteenth century and by pauperisation and proletarisation by the end of it.

In the period of expansion, beginning in the 1860s, the growth of the
colonies went along with a rapid rise in productivity and increasing
occupational and social differentiation. At the same time, they converted
themselves in increasing measure from exclusively agricultural and artisan production to manufacturing and industry. The tools and machines,
the ploughs and vehicles with which the German colonists in South
Russia provided the Russian peasants played as great a role in opening up

23 See H. Anger, *Das Deutschtum in Sibirien. Reise durch die deutschen Dörfer
    Westsibiriens*, Berlin, 1930, and J. Stach, *Das Deutschtum in Sibirien, Mittelasien und dem
    Fernen Osten*, Stuttgart, 1938.
24 Bohmann, *Strukturwandel*, p. 124.
25 See the essay by J.E., written in accord with the Soviet-German line, on the ques-
    tion: 'Wann in unseren Wolgakolonien der russische Gemeindebesitz mit seinem
    Seelen-system eingeführt worden ist?' in *Unsere Wirtschaft*, no. 12, 30, June 1924, 3,
    p. 345 ff.

and intensifying the agrarian economy there as did the windmills and later the steam-driven mills of the German cereal production in the Volga region for the cereal trade in the empire.

The taxes paid by the colonies, which already came to over 1 million rubles annually in the middle of the nineteenth century, likewise indicated the contribution of the German settlements to Russia's national economy.[26] The extension of the railway network and freight-steamer traffic raised the colonists' production and trade balance very notably up to the end of the century.[27] By the turn of the century, numerous settlement complexes had developed into capital enterprises of the first order. It can be ascertained from the insurance of the buildings of the 126 German colonies located in the Ekaterinoslav *guberniia* at the beginning of the 1890s that the real estate owned by them was valued at 14,617,670 rubles.[28] The immovable property in the then 513 German colonies in South Russia were valued at about 50 million rubles. To this must be added the urban property owned by individual colonists towards the end of the nineteenth century. In 1893 estimates of the value of all German-owned buildings in South Russia, plus the land, came to 360 million rubles. The total assets of the South Russian German colonists were valued at 410 million rubles in 1893. Besides all this, private capital deposited in the German *volost'* banks testified to the wealth of many colonists. The sum-total of private accounts in the German *volost'* bank in Khortitsa alone in 1888 reached the handsome figure of 1.3 million rubles.[29]

Seen in a historical perspective, the special juridical-social status of the foreign colonies, anchored in the so-called Colonial Code[30] and valid throughout the first century of settlement, provided the framework for this economic upsurge. The momentum was by no means lost, however, in the course of the great reforms enacted under Alexander II, although they either annulled the provisions of the Colonial Code or modified them step by step, and made the German colonists – while preserving

---

26 Matthaei, *Ansiedlungen*, p. 203.
27 G. von Schultze-Gävernitz, *Volkswirtschaftliche Studien aus Russland*, Leipzig, 1899, p. 312.
28 A.A. Velitsyn (pseud.), *Nemtsy v Rosii. Ocherki istoricheskogo razvitiia i nastoiashchego polozheniia nemetskikh kolonii na iuge i vostoke Rossii*, St Petersburg, 1893, p. 143.
29 *Ibid.*
30 'Svod uchrezhdenii i ustavov o koloniiakh inostrantsev v Rossiiskoi imperii' in *Svod Zakonov Rossiiskoi Imperii*, vol. XII, part II, bk. 4, edn of 1857 g.

their substantial privileges – part of the Russian peasantry.[31] In exchange, their inclusion in the new institutions of the reform era opened up a field of political-social activity for them in the overall Russian sphere. With the inauguration of the zemstvo (1864), they were also given access to the new local self-governing administration. The administrative reform of 1866 annulled the separate administration of the colonies and substituted the general state administration. The Military Reform of 1874 extended general compulsory military service to the colonists as well.[32] All told, the outcome was that towards the end of the nineteenth century and the beginning of the twentieth, the former colonists were about to relinquish their ethnic-cultural and social-class isolation and become an active, dynamic component in general Russian economic and social life.

In 'pre-constitutional' Russia, numerous ties had already formed between the three segments of the German national group. On the one hand, the Russian Crown had chosen to appoint Baltic Germans and urban Germans to administer the colonies; on the other hand, ties developed between the three sectors of the population through eminent personalities in the economy, in science and in culture as well as through common educational institutions as, for example, the University of Dorpat.

In 'constitutional' Russia, that is from 1905 till 1917, tendencies arose for closer contact between the three parts of the German national group.[33] The October Manifesto of Nicholas II proclaimed in 1905 was followed by the spontaneous formation of German clubs and unions in all the centres of German life. Representatives of the urban intelligentsia in Odessa united with the spokesmen of the South Russian colonies, their journalists, zemstvo activists, teachers, clergymen and publishers, in the Südrussischer Deutscher Bildungsverein (South Russian German Cultural Union); in St Petersburg a Deutscher Bildungs- und Hilfsverein (German Cultural and Aid Union) came into being around

---

31 'Pravila ob ustroistve poselian-sobstvennikov (byvshikh kolonistov), vodvorennykh na kazennykh zemliakh v guberniiakh: S.-Peterburgskoi, Novgorodskoi, Samarskoi, Saratovskoi, Voronezhskoi, Chernigovskoi, Poltavskoi, Ekaterinoslavskoi, Khersonskoi, Tavricheskoi i Bessarabskoi' in Polozhenie o Sel'skom Sostoianii, Osob, Prilozh. k Tomu IX, Svoda Zakonov 1876 g.

32 Ustav o voinskoi povinnosti, Moscow, 1874. For the Mennonites a substitute service was introduced, the so-called 'Forest Commandos' (lesnye komandy).

33 See E.F. Sommer, Die Einigungsbestrebungen der Deutschen im Vorkriegs-Russland (1905-1914), Leipzig, 1940.

the publisher of the newspaper *St. Petersburger Zeitung*, the Baltic German Karl von Kügelgen. In Moscow, Baltic German and urban circles of the liberal professions formed the Moscow Deutscher Verein. In Saratov, Adolf Lane, the new editor of the *Saratower Deutsche Zeitung*, founded the Saratower Deutscher Verein. German unions were also created in Piatigorsk in the Caucasus, in Aleksandrovsk-on-the-Dnieper, in Novorossiisk and in Vladivostok.

Particular significance was attached to the German unions in the main German population centres in Poland and first and foremost in the Baltic *gubernie* on account of their numerical and economic weight. Here some minor parts of the Baltic German nobility that were gravitating progressively toward the German *Reich* exercised decisive influence: Eduard Freiherr von Stackelberg held the chairmanship of the Deutscher Verein in Estonia; Karl Wilhelm Baron von Manteuffel-Katzdangen led the Deutscher Verein in Courland; and a member of the von Sievers family headed the Deutscher Verein in Livonia. Like the Polish German *Vereine*, the Baltic German ones, registered as educational institutions, pursued national aims far more strongly than the Russian German *Vereine* did. It was also at their instigation that the first endeavours were made to bring about an organisational unification of all the German national groups in Russia.

The peasant unrest raging in 1905 and 1906 in the Baltic provinces brought to light and exacerbated the political divisions existing within the Baltic German population. The conservative, landowning forces loyal to empire and Crown and strongly represented in the Senate and Imperial Council, together with the moderate conservative and liberal forces within the nobility and upper middle class, which inclined towards the 'Union of the 17 October' and represented it in the Imperial Duma, stood for the solution of the Baltic problem in the setting of overall Russian reforms. A marginal nationalist wing of Baltic Germans, consisting of fervent Protestant *literati* and lower noblemen, which held the leadership of the Baltic German unions, strove to unify all the sections of the German national group and to create a German nationalist movement in Russia. It was also ready to cooperate for this purpose with the Pan-Germanic League of the German Empire as well as with its local groups (*Ortsgruppen*) formed by *Reich* Germans residing in Russia.

These nationalistic attempts to merge all the German national forces within one movement led by some Baltic Germans met, however, with defeat. Even the project for a congress of all the German unions in Russia that would lay down a binding overall statute was wrecked by the lack of support given by both the liberal urban population and the colonists. Likewise, their proposals to create common trade associations, banks and insurance companies open to the Baltic nobility, shaken by the agrarian unrest, and to the financially strong colonists got no hearing from the latter. And finally their plan to 're-settle' impoverished Russian-German colonists in the Baltic provinces (Estonia, Livonia and Courland) in order to strengthen the German element there, met with opposition from those colonists concerned except for a number of uprooted families from Volhynia and the Volga region. As for a system of national German schools and studies under Baltic German leadership, which was intended to create and nurture a national élite, it met by and large with indifference and hardly had time to produce results.

The vast majority of the colonists, who were politically conservative, and the moderate conservative-to-liberal German urban population were not to be won over to the national idea as mediated by some Baltic German elements. Loyal to the Russian Crown, they based their hopes on the spirit of the Imperial Manifesto of October 30, 1905.[34] The colonists' demands for cultural autonomy in the colonised regions, wide scope for local self-government and administrative de-centralisation along with the maintenance of political centralism and moderate agrarian reforms, brought them in the first instance into the October Union (Octobrists) or the Constitutional Democratic Party (Kadets). The spokesmen for the colonists had become active and experienced *zemstvo* representatives by the mid-1890s, and they now proved themselves effective party leaders and parliamentarians. The high proportion of Germans participating in the voting and the effectiveness of their candidates secured them relatively large representation in the Russian parliament. In the first and second Dumas (1906–7) most of the German deputies strengthened the ranks of the Kadets and the moderate centre. Some German delegates belonged to the Kadet left wing or even took a stand close to the Socialist Revolutionaries. In the third and fourth Dumas, the representation of the German delegates shifted largely to the October Union. These German Octobrists, among them Alexander von Meyendorff, who was for some time vice-president of the Duma, displayed a marked degree of political-ideological independence. In the

34 These questions and the following ones, which can only be summarily indicated here, are the subject of the research by the present writer already referred to at the beginning of this chapter. Information on political parties and their programmes is to be found in P. Scheibert (ed.), *Die Russischen Politischen Parteien von 1905 bis 1917*, Darmstadt, 1972.

third Duma (1907–12) they stood solidly behind the projects for agrarian reform as submitted for parliamentary approval by the Prime Minister, Stolypin. To be sure, in the course of the Russian nationalist hardening in the third and fourth Dumas, the German Octobrists lapsed into something like isolation. The debates over land held by Germans in the borderlands, an issue inflated by the Russian nationalist right wing into the question of Russia's being 'under the German yoke', now forced them on to the defensive.

The outbreak of the First World War rendered the situation of the Germans in Russia extraordinarily difficult. Their hitherto proverbial loyalty was called in question by the now strengthening nationalistically Russian mood. Economic boycotts, directed indeed mainly against the German empire, produced among them uncertainty and a sense of helplessness. German settlers and property-owners together with the Jews were forcibly evacuated from the combat areas and the hinterland, reaching deep into Poland, Volhynia and the Baltic provinces. The approximately 250,000 German colonists serving in the Russian army were withdrawn from the western front after the serious Russian defeats in the spring of 1915; people with German names and language seem to have been removed in some cases from strategically sensitive positions. High-ranking officers of German origin still made up some 15 per cent of the Russian General Staff during the war, but they could come under suspicion for military treason, as the fate of General Rennenkampff testified. War-economy measures taken against subjects of enemy nations, a matter in which Russia followed her allies only with hesitation, also affected numerous Germans within her borders. The so-called 'liquidation laws'[35] regarding the property of enemy aliens in strategically endangered zones led to the forced sale of some 500,000 hectares of German landholdings.[36] German-held concerns and trusts, trade and industrial undertakings were subject to compulsory alienation if they were not working for the war industry; the owners' accounts were blocked.[37]

35 K.E. Lindeman, *Prekrashchenie zemlevlaneniia i zemlepol'zovaniia poselian sobstvennikov. Ukazy 2 fevralia i 13 dekabria 1915 goda i 10, 15 iiulia i 19 avgusta 1916 goda i ikh vliianie na ekonomicheskoe sostoianie iuzhnoi Rossii*, Moscow, 1917.

36 D. Rempel, 'The Expropriation of the German Colonists in South Russia during the Great War', *Journal of Modern History*, 1932, 4, 1, pp. 49–67.

37 B.E. Nolde, *Russia in the Economic War*, New Haven, 1928, as well as, from the German viewpoint, A. von Vogel (ed.), *Der Wirtschaftskrieg, herausgegeben vom Königlichen Institut für Seeverkehr und Weltwirtschaft der Universität Kiel*, part II: *Russland*, Jena, 1918.

The February 1917 Revolution brought to a standstill the operation of these measures, implementation of which had in fact only just begun. The Moscow German Octobrist group around Professor E. Lindemann petitioned the Provisional Government, and the special wartime measures directed against Germans and other hostile aliens were discontinued and the laws suspended. The Germans of Russia had had their faith in the tsar's rule shattered and they welcomed the February Revolution and the Provisional Government with enthusiasm. The German-language press, which had been banned since the outbreak of the war, soon burgeoned again. German unions and leagues resumed activity afresh. When the Provisional Government issued its Decree of March 21, 1917, proclaiming the equality of rights of all nationalities and religions in Russia, intensive activity started up in all the centres of German settlement. After the experiences of the war and in the flush of the general springtime of the nationalities, the idea of creating a large organisational network comprising all the German groups in Russia, which had found so slight an echo before the war, was adopted by the leading strata of the German population whose main interest consisted of some form of cultural autonomy. But even now this idea of unification was subservient to the general constitutional and democratic restructuring of the whole of Russia, of which the overwhelming majority of Russian Germans felt themselves a loyal component.

At assemblies and congresses in Moscow, Odessa and Saratov, plans were worked out for the foundation of an all-Russian union of Russian citizens of German nationality and Mennonites (Allrussischer Verband der russischen Bürger deutscher Nationalität und Mennoniten). The initiators and heads of this organising activity were the former Duma delegates and party spokesmen of German origin. They now tried to work out some common platform concerning their economic and political demands based on a democratic, constitutional consensus with some local deviations to left or right, national or liberal orientations. In all procedural questions they voted for unconditional support of the Provisional Government. The organisational network of the *Verband*, which consisted of central committees in the urban centres of German settlement and of regional and local committees in the rural regions, was soon extended to German 'colonies' in towns and countryside throughout the entire empire, reaching from Bessarabia to Omsk and from Transcaucasia to Petrograd. The All-Russian Central Committee of the *Verband*, with its head office in Petrograd, was already in existence when all further organisational activity began to be paralysed by general chaos in the economy and communications.

At the moment of Lenin's take-over, the German movement was at an advanced stage of its organisational formation. The *zemstvo* elections had strengthened German activity in the local bodies. The central, regional and local committees of the union had begun political and educational work as well as preparations for the elections to the Constituent Assembly. The network of German schools and press organs was expanding well. Moreover, against the background of the deep cataclysm in the last months of the Provisional Government, a political consensus was in the making within the numerous different historic, social and religious sectors of the German nationality.

This activity of the German groups did not come to a standstill at the exact moment of the Bolshevik seizure of power in October 1917. Except for the German inhabitants of Petrograd and Moscow, most of the local German communities came to experience all the short-lived hopes and long-lasting agonies of the Civil War. In those years the great majority of German peasants and property-owners fought on the side of the White armies. Here they joined their efforts for social and economic self-preservation with those of officers and generals of German and Baltic German origin striving to defend and re-establish the *ancien régime*. In the Civil War the Volga and Black Sea colonies suffered exceptionally heavy losses of life and property. The agrarian terror of the left Socialist Revolutionaries hit them just as hard as the plundering, sacking and murders of the Makhno gangs* and the requisitioning practices of the Red Army units. Some colonies vanished entirely while others survived, half demolished and depopulated.

The loss of the western provinces of the Russian empire with the independence of Poland and the Baltic states, as well as the implementation of the provisions of the Treaty of Brest-Litovsk which manifested little concern for its fate, left the German population of Russia diminished and desolate. The Baltic Germans living in Russia proper now had the right to opt for one of the new states, and the majority of them sooner or later left the Russian Federation. With the Baltic provinces the Russian Germans lost not only some important centres of their Protestant schools and educational institutions, but a whole cultural

---

*Anarchist armed detachments active in the Ukraine during the Civil War, and organised by N.I. Makhno (1889–1934).

landscape that had been engraved on their historical consciousness. Finally, the Bessarabian Germans – some 80,000 German peasants with landed property of 345,177 hectares – became for a short while citizens of the Democratic Moldavian Republic and from 1918 were Rumanian citizens.

While the German national group had been the foe of the nationalistic and right wings in late imperial Russia, it now became one of the main adversaries of the revolutionary leftist government of the People's Commissars in the course of its stabilisation. With the fall of the Kaiser's *Reich* and the failure and defeat of the White armies and regional governments, the Russian German population was faced with the threat of the annihilation of its centuries-old, guaranteed, privileged status. Flight, emigration and opting for other states were the responses of the mobile sections of the Germans to this threat to their existence. Those who remained – among them the overwhelming majority of the peasants – became the object and plaything of an internal and nationalities policy pursued by the new holders of power on the thorny path of construction of the socialist Soviet régime.

CHAPTER TWO

FROM THE OCTOBER REVOLUTION TO THE SECOND WORLD WAR

Benjamin Pinkus

There have been two principal foci in research on Soviet national groups. One deals from the outside with the administration's attitude towards the national minority in question in order to ascertain its legal-political status. The other is internal, which is to say that it deals with the way of life of the national minority, partly or entirely unrelated to administrative policy (the external environment). Hence these methods are often one-sided, tend to distort complex Soviet realities, and fail to get to the roots of the problem.

The history of a national minority is not one-dimensional; it evolves on more than one plane or it can be envisaged as made up of concentric circles, wheels within wheels, connected with each other and fitting into each other, influencing each other dynamically. Research on national minorities has to develop a system of organic connections covering both external and internal aspects in all their complex and changing relationships. The first and outermost circle of research here looks into the legal-political status of the Soviet Germans, the degree of autonomy accorded them and the degree of their participation in the public, political life of the country. The second circle inwards deals with demographic and socio-economic processes. The third, innermost, circle embraces the minority's national life in the full sense, religious and cultural. Finally, an attempt should be made to evaluate the degree of identification of the Soviet Germans with their German nationality, the strength of their sense of national identity. The scope of this work does not allow us to dwell at any length on some important aspects of the ties between the Soviet Germans and their fatherland (the two Germanies of today) and their sister-diasporas in the United States, Canada and elsewhere, ties which certainly influenced their national consciousness.

As the first chapter made clear, the Germans in Russia underwent particular hardships during the First World War. They suffered from discrimination, restrictions, organised rioting directed against them, and deportations. They welcomed the Revolution of February 1917 with frank enthusiasm in view of the changes it brought with it in their legal-political status, and they took part in the feverish and wide-ranging

31

political activity in the ensuing months in a way unknown to the Germans in Russia until then. As against this, the great majority of the German population took a completely different attitude to the October Revolution. The German voting patterns in the elections to the Constituent Assembly in November 1917 show that the German national parties received 121,614 votes, while all the socialist parties (mainly the SRs and the Mensheviks) got only 42,156 votes.[1] Furthermore, many Germans fought in the war against the Bolsheviks, whether in the ranks of one or another of the White armies or in the defence battalions created in the German colonies during the Civil War.[2] The special social structure of the German population – a broad stratum of well-off peasants, independent, closed communities, strong attachment to traditional religious values and, allied to all this, their inbred national-political conservatism – was not exactly propitious to the processes of accelerated and forced sovietisation.

The legal-political status

The national question, as is well known, held a central place in the debate that was carried on in the Bolshevik Party both before and after the October Revolution. When the Bolsheviks took power, they were forced to come to terms with the reality of the existence of a multinational state on the one hand and, on the other, their aspiration for a state that was centralized and monolithic. Lenin remained faithful to his mentors, Marx and Engels, and was long opposed to any federative solution. After the October Revolution, however, his basic approach to every political problem was that it must be dealt with concretely and that solutions must be weighed up in the context of the given concrete historical situation. Approaching the nationalities problem in this way, he came to the conclusion that for Russia the best solution would be the

---

1 O.H. Radkey, *The Election to the Russian Constituent Assembly of 1917*, Cambridge, Mass., 1950, p. 17.
2 Soviet historiographers tried to create a myth about large-scale, active German participation in the Bolshevik forces fighting in support of the new Soviet régime. This line taken in the 1920s is still followed today in the German press in the Soviet Union. What is interesting is that German dissidents also talk enthusiastically of 'battalions of Volga Germans fighting on the front in the Civil War'. See *Unsere Wirtschaft*, 1923, pp. 608–10; *Neues Leben*, Feb. 21, 1963; June 1, 1976, and July 13, 1976; *Repatria*, A.S. no. 1176, p. 24.

federative one. Lenin was also one of the fiercest and most consistent opponents of the Austrian Social-Democratic idea, espoused by the Bund, of national-cultural autonomy. The central leadership of the Bolshevik Party therefore adopted the territorial solution as the only possible one. Nevertheless, by an irony of history this solution, as it was handled in practice in the 1920s in the Soviet Union, became a copy on general lines, if not always a successful one, of the tenets of the Bund that had been wiped out.

It did not prove possible to combine the two contradictory doctrines – national-cultural autonomy built on the extra-territorial principle and the Leninist-Stalinist doctrine of regional autonomy built on the territorial principle. The attempt to bring about a combination of the two led to inconsistency, jostling for position and endless complications.

The solution of the national question in general and that of the extra-territorial nationalities in particular was stated in numerous official documents such as the constitutions and proclamations of independence of the various Soviet republics; in laws, decrees and regulations of different kinds and in the decisions and resolutions of the Communist Party.[3] These documents laid down in clear terms the right of free development of the national minorities and ethnic groups living in Russian territory. Equal rights were formally proclaimed for all citizens regardless of their racial and national origin; national institutions were to be established, the mother tongue must be used in administration, education and culture, and representatives of the national minorities must be given their place in all the general, Soviet elected institutions.

From 1918 until 1941, the Germans in the Soviet Union were in fact divided into two separate categories as regards their legal-political status: those living in the Volga region, who were granted a national federative unit of their own, a solution on the territorial principle, which was the most solid basis in the shifting Soviet reality; and those living dispersed in different republics (mainly Russia and the Ukraine), with a solution based on the extra-territorial principle. Obviously, the differences between the two categories were not just formal ones; they had substantial significance in whatever was concerned with the long-term possibility of establishing national, educational and cultural institutions. The Soviet administration does not appear to have intended to

3 See *Istoriia sovetskoi konstitutsii, Sbornik dokumentov, 1917-1957*, Moscow, 1957, pp. 20, 111, 250–3; *Desiatyi s"ezd RKP (b)*, Moscow, 1963, p.606; *KPSS v rezoliutsiiakh*, part 1, 7th edn, Moscow, 1954, pp. 709–18; V. Durdanevskii, *Ravnopravie iazykov v sovetskom stroe*, Moscow, 1929, pp. 47, 147–59, 162–3 and 178–9.

concentrate the entire German population in one republic, but even so the mere fact of the existence of the Autonomous German Republic of the Volga was, as we shall see later, of the utmost importance to some two-thirds of the Germans in the Soviet Union.

Although the tie between nationality and religion may not have been so pre-eminent among the Germans as among other minorities such as, for example, the Jews, the Poles and the Tatars, the fierce Soviet campaigns against religion in the 1920s and 1930s could not fail to have the effect of strengthening the Germans' sense of their national identity.

A factor which had a great influence on the legal-political status of the Germans was the introduction of internal passports for town dwellers on December 27, 1932. The administration now possessed a most powerful means of surveillance, later utilised to the full against the urban Germans (the law did not apply to the rural population). As early as 1934, as a result of the Nazis coming to power in Germany, the Central Committee of the Communist Party decided to have full and accurate data collected on all Germans working in industry and in administrative bodies, and to see to it that this survey should not be publicly known.[4] These 'black lists' were used for the first (partial) deportation of Germans from the frontier regions in the second half of the 1930s.

The Soviet Germans' autonomy.   The autonomy granted Soviet Germans according to the new nationalities policy inaugurated after the Revolution, which remained in being until the late 1930s, took the form of national party and government institutions, which were supposed to be run in the German language, and which were operated by Germans for the speedy sovietisation of the Germans in the Soviet Union.

In April 1918, a delegation of three members of the German Social-Democratic Party in the Volga Region came to Moscow for a meeting with Joseph Stalin, then the People's Commissar for Nationality Affairs. Unlike an earlier all-German delegation, it received a cordial welcome, and the proposal was immediately put before it for a German National Commissariat to be set up under the aegis of the Narkomnats (People's Commissariat for Nationality Affairs, established in November 1917 and dissolved a few years later). In spite of this generous initiative, however,

4 According to the testimony of Dr Evgeniia Evelson, formerly Professor at Moscow University and elsewhere for twenty years, who was employed in preparing the list of Germans. This testimony was presented to the present author in Jerusalem on May 23, 1978.

when the German Commissariat was established it was from the beginning headed not by representatives of the German Social-Democrats in Russia but by two Germans prisoners of war who had passed over to the Communist Party, Ernst Reuter and Karl Petin.[5] Moreover, in October 1918 another prisoner of war, Gustaw Klinger, was sent to Moscow to direct the German department in the Narkomnats.[6] The regulations of the German department, which had already been framed on May 27, 1918, laid down *inter alia* that the German department of the Narkomnats and the Commissariat for the Volga Region Germans were to carry out propaganda in the mother tongue by means of newspapers, literature and radio in order to bring the urban German population closer to communism; advise the central and local administrative authorities on all matters pertaining to the German national minority and take action on its behalf; plan and set up the new institutions of the Autonomous Republic; concern themselves with refugees with the aim of rehabilitating them in their former places of residence; and conduct a campaign against the old German parties, movements and institutions in the German Autonomous Republic.

In the five years of their existence, the German Commissariat and the German department of the Narkomnats came up against numerous difficulties. First, there was a shortage of trustworthy Communists to fill the various posts on the local level. Employing German and Austrian Communists (and even at times German-speaking Hungarians), who were not familiar with the problems of the Germans in the Soviet Union and who tried to 'bring the class war to the German village', only led to increased hatred of the new Soviet régime. Furthermore, many differences of opinion emerged between the Narkomnats and other Commissariats that also dealt with problems of the various nationalities, including the Germans. These differences of opinion hampered the application of the nationalities policy. Moreover, many differences of opinion were also revealed between the German department and the Narkomnats institutions, which aggravated the situation still further.

Despite the limitations on its activity, the German Commissariat succeeded in carrying out some important tasks: it set up the Commune and later the Autonomous German Republic of the Volga; it did in fact help German refugees to return to their former places of residence and promoted education and culture among the Germans. The abolition of

5 *Izvestiia*, April 28, 1918; as quoted in G. Geilke, 'Rehabilitierung der Wolgadeutschen?', *Jahrbuch für Ostrecht*, 1965, vol. VI, no. 1, p. 44.
6 W. Brandt and R. Löwenthal, *Ernst Reuter. Ein Leben für die Freiheit*, Munich, 1957, pp. 106–9.

the Narkomnats in 1923 was therefore undoubtedly a blow to all the extra-territorial national minorities, which thus lost practically their only representation in the central Soviet administrative institutions.[7] A substitute representation, so to speak, was afforded them in the form of the custodial officials (upolnomochennye) who were empowered to act in the name of the national minorities in the administrations of the republics. But this was in the hands of paid officials, which meant that the Germans and others were all the more dependent on the authorities.

Unlike the National Commissariat, which in its first form was still open to representatives of the other socialist parties and to non-party representatives, the national section of the Communist Party comprised party members only.[8] The establishment of the Communist Party German section was closely linked to the phenomenon of the German prisoners-of-war (numbering some 160,000), Austrian prisoners of war and German speakers from other groups. In fact, the section grew out of the Federation of Foreign Groups in the Communist Party, which was set up on April 16, 1918, and the German Group in the Russian Communist Party established on April 24, 1918; at that date it numbered some 400 persons.[9] In 1920, before the return of the most of the prisoners of war to their homes, the German group in the Communist Party consisted of 2,850 members and 720 candidate members.[10] It would appear that there was only a small percentage of Soviet Germans among them, due to the simple fact that the first communist cells in the Volga area were set up only in the second half of 1918 and in other regions only when these came under effective Soviet rule still later.[11] According to the first census of party members carried out in 1922, after the departure of most of the prisoners of war and after mobilization of party members had been speeded up among the the German population, there were only 2217 party members of German origin in the whole of the Soviet Union, comprising .59 percent of all party members in that year.[12] The members of the German section among this total were apparently few, as can be

7 Ibid.; Zhizn' natsional'nostei, 1918, no. 2.
8 See 'Likvidatsiia narkomnatsa', Vlast' sovetov, 1924, no. 1, pp. 129–30.
9 Ia. Sharapov, Natsional'nye sektsii RKP (b), Kazan, 1967. This is practically the only research on the national sections that has been published in the Soviet Union, and it does not deal with the Germans at all apart from giving some statistical data.
10 Oktiabrskaia revolutsiia i proletarskii internatsionalism, Moscow, 1970, pp. 368–9.
11 Die Grosse Sozialistische Oktoberrevolution und Deutschland, Berlin (East), 1967, p. 108; Neues Leben, May 31, 1977.

seen from the fact that even in 1925 there were only 705 members in the German section.[13] There are no data for the later period, but if we take the number of Communist Party members of German origin in 1927, which was 5,561 members and candidate members (i.e. only .49 per cent of all party members)[14] and substract the 1,200 party members in the German Republic who did not belong to the German section, and the 2,000–3,000 party members in the Russian Republic and the other republics who did not belong to the German section either, it is clear that at its peak the German section had no more than 1,500–2,000 members.

The work of the German section among Soviet Germans was limited and met with frequent difficulties, as indicated by the need for a special appeal made by one of the Secretaries of the Central Committee, V. Molotov, to the 'German colonists' that is to say, to the peasants.[15] Like the other national sections, the German section was in fact 'a sort of head without a body', composed of local activists working amid a hostile population that was either banding together against them or at best indifferent to them. Though five study centres existed to prepare German cadres as well as a German department in the University of Western Peoples in Moscow,[16] in the 1920s it was impossible to mobilise any considerable number of workers capable of carrying the heavy burden of communist activity in the German villages.

In drawing up a balance-sheet of the activities of the German section, one must put on the debit side the liquidation of the institutions of the independent community, the liquidation of the non-communist political parties and organisations, the anti-religious campaign, and the destruction of the flourishing village economy, results which would certainly have been achieved without any help from the German section, if more slowly and less efficiently. On the other hand, as we shall see, what was achieved was the establishment of the German Autonomous Republic, an educational and cultural network, and a set of institutions administered in the German language.

12 *Sotsial'nyi i natsional'nyi sostav VKP (b)*, Moscow, 1928, p. 114. It should be pointed out that up to 1917 there were in all 89 Bolsheviks of German origin belonging to the assimilatory stratum of Germans, like Nikolai Baumann and Emmanuel Quiring.
13 *Die Arbeit*, 1925, no. 23 (73), p. 2086.
14 *Sotsial'nyi i natsional'nyi sostav*.
15 *Izvestiia TsK RKP (b)*, 1923, no. 5.
16 *Die Arbeit*, 1923, no. 16, pp. 360–1; no. 18, p. 422; 1924, no. 25, p. 1343.

The first signs that there were to be changes in the Soviet nationalities policy were already visible in the second half of the 1920s. In a letter to Kaganovich and the members of the Ukrainian Politburo in 1926, Stalin warned them against the policy of 'Ukrainisation', which was going too fast for his liking.[17] In 1927 a campaign began to be worked up against 'nationalist deviations'.[18] In 1929, the last year of the existence of the German section, its heads were being accused of nationalism, of concealing the existence of antagonistic social strata in the German village from motives of 'mistaken national solidarity', accepting German kulaks into the kolkhozy, and so on.[19] On January 13, 1930, the national sections in the Communist Party were abolished on the pretext of party reorganisation.[20]

The local-nationality soviets, rural and urban, constituted the central administrative institution of each Soviet national autonomous district. The first of these soviets were already set up in 1924, based on the resolution on nationalities policy put forward at the XII Party Congress in 1923. They were like other soviets in every respect except for the fact, important in itself, that they were administered by the national minority and in its mother tongue. Their main tasks were to promote public health, culture, ties with public bodies and local administration. The difficulties met with by the German soviets resembled those of the German Commissariat and the German section. The main difficulty was the non-existence of German communist cadres and the need to use the services of German prisoners of war or German communist assimilationists, who hardly knew the German language, let alone local conditions.

As Table 1 shows, German soviets spread rapidly in 1925-7:

Table 2.1.   GERMAN SOVIETS IN THE UKRAINE, 1925-35[21]

	1925	1926	1927	1930	1931	1935
National soviets	251	891	990	1,138	1,121	1,076
German soviets	98	228	273	–	254	–

17 I.V. Stalin, Sochineniia, vol. 8, Moscow, pp. 146–51.
18 See E. Girchak, Na dva fronta v bor'be s natsionalizmom, Moscow, 1933.
19 See D. Gitlanskii, 'Leninskaia natsional'naia politika v deistvii', Revoliutsiia i natsional'nosti, 1931, no. 9, p. 41; A. Glinsky, Der greikhengen un felern in der arbet tsvishn di natsionale minderhaiten, Kharkov, 1931, p. 22; Sturmschritt, 1930, nos 2–3, pp. 8–11.
20 Pravda, Jan. 17, 1930; Deutsche Zentralzeitung, March 31, 1930; Partiinoe stroitel'stvo, 1930, no. 2(4), pp. 70–2; no. 6(8), pp. 22–6.

A certain stagnation was observable in the years 1928–32 and a quickening decline after 1935, when the soviets of the national minorities were forced to unite, this being the first step towards their final abolition. The data for the Russian Republic are incomplete, while in Belorussia it is known that there were only two German soviets. There were 550 German soviets in the whole Soviet Union in 1929.[22]

The central administrative body (as distinct from the federative units) was the national *raion* (district), which covered a number of national soviets (thus, for example, 500 inhabitants of the same nationality were enough for the establishment of a national soviet, while 10,000 were needed for a national *raion*). The tasks of the national *raiony* were similar to those of the national soviets, but in the Ukraine, where about half of all the Germans in the Soviet Union (apart from the German Autonomous Republic) were concentrated, the scale of activity and the budgets of the national *raiony* were far larger. There were five German national districts in 1925, seven in 1926 out of a total of 25, and eight in 1931 out of a total of 26. There were still eight German national *raiony* existing in the Ukraine in 1935, which were liquidated, it seems, together with the German soviets in the new administrative division of the Soviet Union in March 1939. In 1929, there were eleven German national *raiony* in the whole of the Soviet Union and sixteen at the start of the 1930s, distributed as follows: eight in the Ukraine, six in the Russian Republic, one in Georgia and one in Azerbaijan.[23] The national soviets and *raiony* could undoubtedly have continued to function for much longer, despite the difficulties they faced, had they not been liquidated in 1939.

The third administrative institution was that of the national courts and the national police stations connected with them. Even though the main task of these courts was to carry on the campaign against religion and against the 'national bourgeoisie', they served as a symbol of national autonomy and played a favourable role by increasing the num-

21 Ia. Kantor, *Natsional'noe stroitel'stvo sredi evreev v SSSR*, Moscow, 1934, p. 22; *Vlast' sovetov*, 1927, nos 44–5, p. 14; E. Pashukanis (ed.), *15 let sovetskogo stroitel'stva*, Moscow, 1930, p. 81.
22 I. Gebgart, 'Perestroit' rabotu sovetov v nemetskikh raionakh', *Revoliutsiia i natsional'nosti*, 1930, no. 1, p. 44.
23 See notes 20 and 21 above and *Vlast' sovetov*, 1926, no. 19, pp. 13–16; D. Mats, 'Spartakovskii nemetskii raion Ukrainy', *Revoliutsiia i natsional'nosti*, 1935, no. 1, pp. 69–71; I. Koslow, *Über den Aufbau in der Krim: Bericht auf dem IV. Vereinigten Plenum des Krimer Gebietskomitees und der Kontrollkommission der KP (b)*, Simferopol, 1931, p. 55.

ber of activities conducted in the mother tongue, including training national cadres for public-political action. Table 2 shows that the biggest increase in the number of German courts took place from 1925 to 1927 (as in the case of the German soviets), with stagnation clearly setting in during the years 1928–34, with a quickening decline from 1935 until the final disappearance of these courts in 1938.

Table 2.2.   NATIONAL COURTS IN THE SOVIET UNION, 1925–34[24]

	Ukraine total	German	Belorussia	Russian Republic	Total
1925	16	5	1	–	17
1926	–	14	–	–	
1927	58	12	10	–	68
1928	81	–	10	1	92
1930	90	–	–	–	
1934	106	11	–	–	

Participation in political and public life. Because of their past history, their social structure and other factors to be further discussed, the activity of the Germans in public and political life in the Soviet Union in the 1920s and the 1930s was fairly restricted as compared with the other European nationalities. We have already seen that there were only a small proportion of Germans in the Communist Party. This was particularly striking in the Autonomous German Republic of the Volga, where there were only 154 Communist Party members in 1922; in 1929 the number of Germans in the party was only 371, which represented 26.9 per cent of the communists in their republic. Not till 1932 was their number as high as 4,538 out of the 400,000 Germans there, and they still constituted no more than 48 per cent of the communists in their republic.[25] In 1925 there were 1,069 Germans in the Communist Party in the Ukraine (out of a German population of 394,000), while there were 3,042 Poles (out of a population smaller by one-third) and 20,306 Jews (out of a Jewish

24 Glinsky, pp. 39–41; Kantor, p. 34; *Der Emes*, Dec. 12, 1925; Dec. 17, 1925; July 26, 1934.
25 *Natsional'naia politika VKP (b) v tsifrakh*, Moscow, 1930; p. 137; S. Dimanshtein, *Itogi razresheniia natsional'nogo voprosa v SSSR*, Moscow, 1936, pp. 15–16.

population of 1,574,000).[26] A similar picture emerges in membership in the Komsomol, the Germans numbering 4,849 members in 1929, while there were 8,276 Poles, and 98,323 Jews.[27]

Scrutiny of the proportion of Germans in Soviet governmental bodies shows the same picture. Thus at the Fourth Congress of Soviets (1927) there were nine German representatives, seven Poles (with a smaller population and without an autonomous republic), 41 Latvians and 60 Jews. In the first Supreme Soviet, elected in 1937, the Germans were represented by nine delegates.[28]

Various conditions contributed to this obvious under-representation of Germans in public and political activity. First, the basic internal elements of Soviet German life discouraged enthusiasm for the new régime; the demographic and social structure of the Germans – mainly rural, with strong attachment to private property – were ill-suited to it. Furthermore, the Germans did not have a broad stratum of intelligentsia with deep revolutionary roots; on the contrary, most of them were still guided by religious belief and tradition. The external situation may also have worked against German participation. Not only were other nationalities with more of a history of socialism – Jews, Latvians, Georgians and Armenians – over-represented, but there was also a desire on the part of the majority nationality in each republic to improve its relative representation, at the expense of the extra-territorial minorities such as the Germans. As against all this, it is hard to prove the existence of any policy of deliberate discrimination against the Germans in this context, although it may be that a policy of this kind did come into being and started to be applied in the second half of the 1930s, due both to distrust of the German 'colonists' and 'kulaks', as they were called, and to Hitler's rise to power.

The Germans' 'statehood' in the Soviet Union. The high point of Soviet nationalities policy towards the German minority was without doubt the setting up in October 1918 of the Workers' Commune of the Volga, and in 1924 its elevation in the Soviet federative hierarchy to an

---

26 *Vlast' sovetov*, 1925, no. 21, pp. 19–20.
27 *Natsional'naia politika*, p. 159.
28 *S'ezdy sovetov v postanovleniiakh i rezoliutsiiakh*, Moscow, 1935, pp. 362, 475; *Vlast' sovetov*, 1938, no. 2, p. 23.

autonomous republic.[29] Unquestionably the favourable policy towards the Germans pursued in the first half of the 1920s was a direct result of an exceptionally propitious conjuncture of internal and external factors and circumstances. In the internal sphere, we have already indicated the desire of the leadership to win over the different nationalities and harness them to international activity. Along with this, the international factor that played a decisive role in this connection was the belief of all the Bolshevik leaders in an imminent German revolution. The Soviet Germans were certainly supposed to play some role in the great events that were expected to unfold; their role would symbolise the future régime of the new Germany and their active mobilisation would help in fulfilling this high mission. The new and improved relations with the Weimar Government, especially after the signing of the Rapallo Pact on April 16, 1922, strengthened these currents still more.

In 1924 the German Autonomous Republic of the Volga covered an area of 25,447 square km. and in 1929, 27,152 square km. Despite the terrible famines of the early 1920s and early 1930s, the population increased from 454,638 in 1922 to about 600,000 in 1938. In 1922 Germans constituted 67.9 per cent of the total population of the republic and 66.4 per cent in 1926; this two-thirds ratio remained till 1938.[30]

The existence of the German Autonomous Republic, despite the limited powers granted under the Soviet Constitution to federative units generally and to this unit in particular was of great significance. It could be seen not only symbolically in the pride of German 'statehood' in the Soviet Union (something that most of the extra-territorial minorities were not privileged to enjoy) but also, and especially, in its practical consequences in the sphere of preserving and disseminating German language, culture and educational institutions, not only among Germans living in the republic but also in all the other Soviet republics.

The actual achievements in these spheres were, however, somewhat limited in practice for objective reasons and perhaps also for some subjective ones – incapacity or unwillingness on the part of the leadership of the republic to take the initiative and act energetically. In the first place, as we have seen, the Volga Germans did not succeed in building up a

29 The decision was taken by the VTsIK and at the Congress of People's Commissars on December 19, 1923. See *Sbornik uzakonenii*, Moscow, 1924, no. 7, p. 20.
30 See S. Sulkevich, *Administrativno-politicheskoe stroenie SSSR*, Leningrad, 1926, p. 136; *Vlast' sovetov*, 1923, no. 3, p. 84; *ASSR der Wolgadeutschen Politischökonomischer Abriss*, Engels, 1938, p. 14.

body of German cadres. Thus it was only in 1933 that they reached a majority (55 per cent) in the Communist Party in their own autonomous republic. In the highest level of the administrative apparatus they were in a minority – 32.58 per cent in the 1920s and 39.2 per cent in 1933.[31] Besides this, it was not easy to apply the use of German in the party and state apparatus, and from time to time it was found necessary to take specific decisions for speedier germanisation in the republic.[32] And in education, culture and research – the sphere of greatest importance for the very survival of the nation as such – the achievements were hardly impressive. The lack of incentive and boldness in the leadership of the republic, the resistance to germanisation on the part of the strong Russian and Ukrainian minorities,[33] budget difficulties and finally, it would seem, the danger of being accused of 'nationalism' prevented the achievement of more satisfactory results.

Demographic and socio-economic processes

Of the first five censuses carried out in the Soviet Union – in 1920, 1923, 1926, 1937 and 1939 – the two first were only partial (the urban population), the 1937 census was cancelled for political reasons, and that in 1939 was published only in part. Thus the most important data are lacking on the German population before the outbreak of the war with Germany.[34] According to the only population census carried out in tsarist Russia, in 1897, there were then 1,790,489 Germans living in Russia, and it is estimated that after the Revolution and the first territorial changes there were some 1,620,000. The 1926 census shows only 1,238,540 Germans, and the 1939 census only 1,424,000.[35] From the

---

31 S. Dimanshtein, *Itogi.*, pp. 39, 157; *Natsional'naia politika* pp. 250–7.

32 *Beschlüsse des 3. Rätenkongresses der Autonomen Sozialistischen Räte-Republik der Wolgadeutschen*, Pokrovsk, 1926, p. 69.

33 It is perhaps of interest that the Germans used to accuse the Russian population of Great Russian chauvinism. See 'Die Soviet-Nationalitäten Politik duldet keinem Chauvinismus', *Wolgadeutschen Pressdienst*, 1931, no. 8.

34 See. L. Starodubsky, *Das Volkszählungswesen in der Union der sozialistischen Sowjetrepubliken*, Vienna, 1938; W. Poletika, *Annulierte Volkszählung von 1937 und Bevölkerungsstand in der Sowjetunion*, Jena, 1937; *Vsesoiuznaia perepis' naseleniia 1926 goda*, Moscow, 1928–9, vols 1–17; A. Bohmann, *Menschen und Grenzen*, Cologne, 1970; F. Lorimer, *The Population of the Soviet Union: History and Prospects*, Geneva, 1946.

35 See note 34.

small amount of data published on the natural rate of increase among the Germans, it appears that in 1927 it was 3.25 per cent,[36] one of the highest among the European peoples of the Soviet Union. This was because of the existence of a prosperous rural population, traditionally interested in large families. Even if we take into account the beginning of the processes of modernisation, which accelerated in the 1930s among the Germans too, and substract about 2 per cent from the annual natural increase of the Germans, it is evident that by 1939 the German population should have reached about 2,250,000. If we take only the period for which we have more accurate data, the years 1926–39, we see that some 137,000 Germans disappeared in the course of these thirteen years. There are many reasons for this, and without embarking on a detailed or exhaustive discussion, we can give some indications. There was loss of life among the German population throughout the period. The Germans in the Ukraine, the Crimea and Siberia were badly hit during the Civil War and also during the great famines of 1921–2 and 1933–4.[37] The German population also suffered severely during the dekulakisation process, with the heavy concurrent losses, and this was the case too in 1936–8 at the time of mass arrests and partial deportation. Besides these population losses, about 25,000 people emigrated from the Soviet Union in 1923–33.[38] Germans also 'disappeared' by changing their declaration of nationality, mainly because of their increasingly grave situation in the second half of the 1930s, and a small part became assimilated to the general population.

In the nineteenth century the process of urbanisation among the Germans was very slow. Thus in 1914 the urban dwellers among them still numbered only 106,000, or only 4.4 per cent of the whole German population. In 1926 there were 184,769 living in towns, constituting around 15 per cent of the German population, while the proportion for the population of the country as a whole was 17.9 per cent. This gap widened steadily, and in 1939 only 19 per cent of the German population was urbanised while for the population of the Soviet Union as a whole it was 32.9 per cent. In other words, the process of urbanisation among the Germans remained slow in the years 1926–39. The question of the integration of the Soviet Germans will be discussed below, but it can be

36 *Natsional'naia politika*, p. 40.
37 B. Bartels, *Die deutschen Bauern in Russland. Einst und jetzt*, Moscow, 1928, pp. 67–8.
38 G. Teich in *Heimatbuch*, 1958, p. 86.

pointed out here that from the point of view of demographic processes – urbanisation, mobility and internal migration – the Soviet Germans were only at the beginning on the eve of the Second World War.

There were a number of basic reasons why the economic situation of the German population worsened steadily after the October Revolution. During the First World War and the Revolution there was a general deterioration of the economic situation, and following this, the long and bloody Civil War brought total destruction to the national economy. Specially severe economic difficulties beset the Ukraine, the Crimea, the Caucasus, and Siberia – regions which, by chance, had large concentrations of Germans. Furthermore, the policy of War Communism (1918–21) was especially damaging to the German population, mainly composed as it was of prosperous and medium peasants linked to the free market, which was abolished completely in those years.

German-owned land in Russia in 1914 was of enormous extent: 14,750,000 hectares.[39] The average holding of a German family was up to 28 hectares. With the changed agrarian policy of the Bolsheviks in 1918, when the coalition with the left Socialist Revolutionaries broke up and village Committees of the Poor (*kombedy*) were created with the declared aim of "bringing the class-war to the village," the situation of the German peasants worsened considerably. Frequent requisitions of agricultural produce accompanied by acts of terror, heavy punishments for those who sold their produce on the free market, and the famine of 1921–2 in the Volga region, the Crimea and the Ukraine, led to the total destruction of the formerly prosperous German village.[40] The New Economic Policy (NEP), which was adopted in March 1921 and continued until 1928, produced a marked improvement in the condition of the German peasants because of the abolition of requistioning, abolition of the ban on employing hired agricultural labourers, the opening of the free market for agricultural produce, and encouragement of private initiative (in accordance with the slogan of Nikolai Bukharin,

---

39 K. Stumpp, 'Leistungen und Bedeutung der deutschen Kolonisten in Russland', *Deutsche in Ausland*, 1939, no. 5, p. 259; A. Vaatz, *Deutsche Bauernarbeit im Schwarz-meergebiet*, Berlin, 1942, p. 10.

40 See P. Rohrbach, *Deutschtum in Not*, Berlin, 1920, p. 388; M. Hagin, 'Beitrag zur wirtschaftlichen und kulturellen Leistung der Wolgadeutschen', *Heimatbuch*, 1967–8, p. 91; K. Lindemann, 'Meine Reise durch deutschen Kolonien Südrusslands und der Krim in den Jahren 1919–1921', *Hammer und Pflug*, 1922, nos 24–5; H.H. Fisher, *The Famine in Soviet Russia*, New York, 1927; 'Volga Region is Emerging from Famine', *New York American*, Oct. 21, 1923.

'*Enrichissez-vous*'). In the first years of NEP the size of the land holdings among the Germans was from 10 to 65 *dessiatins*.[41] If we compare the size of the land holdings among Germans in the Russian Republic with that of the general rural population in 1925, we find that the Germans' situation was far better.[42] Even if the new policy adopted in 1925 regarding the size of land holdings led to a certain decrease in the size of the German peasants' holdings, this was overcome by leasing land from poor peasants who could not or did not want to work their land.[43]

An important quantitative indicator of the degree of prosperity of the German rural population as compared with the general peasantry is the amount of livestock owned by each family. If 35.7 per cent of the whole rural population in the Russian Republic had no work animals at all, the figure among the German Mennonites (the most successful stratum of the Soviet Germans in the 1920s) was only 10.3 per cent; 49.4 per cent in the general population owned one head, 11.2 per cent owned two head, and 3.8 per cent owned more than three, while among the Mennonites 20 per cent were owners of one head, 31.2 per cent owned two head and 38.4 per cent owned more than three head of work animals.[44] The difference is even greater if we compare ownership of productive farm animals. The next quantitative indicator is productivity of the agricultural holdings and this too was far higher among the German rural population. It is important to note, finally, that the Germans knew how to make good use of the cooperative organisations that were widespread in the Soviet Union in the 1920s in the spheres of consumption, marketing and credit. In the German Republic of the Volga, for example, the percentage of workers organised in cooperatives ranged from 19 per cent in 1927 to 38 per cent in 1929, while in the whole of the Soviet Union it rose from 14.5 per cent to 30.5 per cent in this period.

The change for the worse in the situation of the Soviet Germans came with the start of forced collectivisation. Of the four social strata in the village – *batrak* (hired agricultural labourer), poor peasant, middle peas-

41 O. Auhagen, *Die Schicksalswende des russlanddeutschen Bauerntums in den Jahren 1927–1930*, Leipzig, 1942, p. 33.

42 A. Ehrt, *Das Mennonitentum in Russland von seiner Einwanderung bis zur Gegenwart*, 1932, p. 123. Thus, for example, in the Langensalza district of Dzhankoe in the Crimea the average land holding of a Mennonite family was 26 *dessiatins (Krasnyi Krym*, Nov. 4, 1927).

43 It is of interest that the highest prices for land were in the Crimea and in the Republic of the Volga. See Iu. Larin in *Na agrarnom fronte*, 1928, no. 3, p. 22.

44 Ehrt, p. 122.

ant, and kulak (rich peasant) – the Germans belonged mainly to the last two strata. The vagueness of the definition of kulak (a family only needed to have two horses and two cows and to sell its produce on the free market to be called kulaks) gave the authorities a powerful tool for implementing their agrarian policy. According to some estimates, German kulaks numbered around 700,000 out of the 5 million in the Soviet Union, that is 14 per cent while the Germans were less than 1 per cent of the whole population.[45] According to the available data, collectivisation was enforced in the regions with a considerable German population far more speedily than in other regions. In the German Republic of the Volga in March 1930 collectivisation reached 60 per cent and in the Crimea 75.5 per cent, and in July 1931 (after orders from above produced a slackening off) 62 per cent and 50 per cent respectively, while in the whole of the Russian Republic the average was no more than 25 per cent.[46] Even if this was not done solely on grounds of nationality, the factor of nationality undoubtedly had an effect. One of the heads of the Communist Party German section, I. Gebhardt, wrote in 1930: 'There was often a common, widespread opinion that the German village was composed solely of kulaks. This was the source of the over-taxation of the middle German peasants, of their being deprived of their civil rights and finally of some of them undergoing dekulakisation.'[47] It is possible to make a cautious evaluation of the proportion of the Germans who fell victim in the period of dekulakisation. If we reckon that some 4 million peasant farmsteads in the Soviet Union underwent this process and that the Germans were 10–15 per cent of the total, we find that from one-third to half of the German population was destroyed (450,000–625,000 people). The terrible suffering of that time left scars and a trauma that has lasted up to the present day.[48]

From this point of view the fate of the urban German population was less disastrous. Of 184,000 urban Germans in 1926 and 270,000 in 1939, about half comprised part of the working population. We do not have complete data on the occupational distribution of the urban German

45 H. Neusats and D. Erka, *Ein deutscher Todesweg*, Berlin, 1930, p. 32.
46 F. Tsylko in *Na agrarnom fronte*, 1930, no. 5, p. 26; Z. Ostrovskii, *Problemy ukrainizatsii i belorussizatsii v RSFSR*, Moscow, 1931, p. 10.
47 I. Gebgart, p. 44; G. Nabatov, *Respublika Nemtsev Povolzhiia*, Leningrad, 1930; A. Kröker, *Unsere Brüder in Not*, Striegau, 1930; *Nation und Staat*, 1934, no. 4, pp. 200–6; 1935, no. 13, pp. 10–11, 628–33.
48 *Neuland*, 1930, no. 4 (13), pp. 13–16; *Revoliutsiia i natsional'nosti,*, 1930, no. 1, pp. 44–5.

population or its standard of living, and must therefore consider more especially the German population in its own republic. Of the 40,500 Germans in the towns of the Volga Republic towards the end of the 1920s, 58.2 per cent belonged to the working population; by 1936 the number had reached 30,000. In 1926 the percentage of Germans working in non-agricultural employment remained very low: industrial workers (textiles, canning and machines) 6.61 per cent (14,000); officials 3.51 per cent (7.700); liberal professions 0.14 per cent (308); the army 1.6 per cent; industrialists and contractors 0.14 per cent; unemployed 0.51 per cent.[49]

In reaching conclusions on the socio-economic situation of the Soviet German population, it is also important to note their status in higher education and academic studies. In 1927 only 0.61 per cent of the Germans were students (994 in number, compared for example with 23,405 Jews and 1,034 Poles); in 1929 the percentage of German students among the general student body in the Soviet Union was 0.5 per cent, in 1935 0.74 per cent and in 1939 0.8 per cent.[50] The proportion was higher among academics – 254 out of 18,321 (1.4 per cent), while among the Jews, with a population twice the size, it was 13.6 per cent. If we compare this situation with the tsarist period (1913) when the Germans made up 9.3 per cent of all students, the under-representation of the Germans is seen all the more clearly.[51] The main reasons for this state of affairs were the separation of the Baltic Germans from the Soviet Union, the flight of the German intelligentsia from Russia after the Revolution, and the deliberate Soviet policy of discriminating against the prosperous stratum of the rural population. Furthermore, the stratum of the free professions, which also constitutes an important indicator of the extent of modernisation, remained very restricted, and for the same reasons. Finally, urbanisation and collectivisation created a stratum of industrial workers, but even this was limited. The slowness of the process of urbanisation prevented the German population from accelerating the rate of modernisation in this period, while forced sovietisation in many fields between 1917 and 1941 completely devastated the entire social system of the Germans.

49 *Natsional'naia politika*, pp. 42, 49, 128; *Bol'shaia sovetskaia entsiklopediia*, 1e izdanie, vol. 41, p. 518.
50 *Natsional'naia politika*, p. 288; K.E. Bailes, *Technology and Society under Lenin and Stalin – Origins of the Soviet Technological Intelligentsia, 1917–1941*, Princeton, 1978, p. 204.
51 N. Hans and S. Hessen, *Educational Policy in Soviet Russia*, London, 1930, p. 184.

Religion, culture and national identity

The third and innermost circle, the most important of all for measuring
the quintessential national identity of the minority, does not operate in a
vacuum but is profoundly affected by the two outer circles that we have
been considering up to now. We shall try briefly to survey the state of
German religion and culture in the Soviet Union and to assess how the
changes that took place in these fields influenced the sense of national
identity among the Soviet Germans.

Religion among the Soviet Germans. From the inception of German
settlement in Russia, this population was divided among three main
Churches: Evangelical-Lutheran, Catholic and Mennonite. The Baptists
comprised a fourth, small group, numbering some 12,000 in 1920.

In 1909 there were 1,094,344 Evangelical-Lutherans in Russia, 84 per
cent of them Germans, spread over 2,600 congregations.[52] At the beginning of the 1920s they numbered 1,136,000, the Germans constituting
about 70 per cent, while by 1926 their number had dropped to 900,000,
of whom only half were Germans.[53] This drastic decline stemmed from
emigration and the shrinking of Soviet territory – mainly the cutting
off of the Baltic region where many Evangelical-Lutherans were concentrated. The loss of life in the Civil War and the great famine also had its
share in the decline. The position of the clergy was already difficult in the
1920s; their number fell from 190 in 1900 and 114 in 1927 to 45 in 1934
and only eight in 1936.[54] The opening of the Theological Seminary in
Leningrad under Bishop A. Malmgren in 1925 did little to retrieve the
situation. The First Synod of the Evangelical-Lutheran Church in the
Soviet Union was held in Moscow in June 1924, with 56 delegates
participating, headed by the two leading personalities in the Church,
Bishops A. Malmgren and T. Meyer. It laid down a new structure for
the Church in accordance with the regulations that had been prepared.[55]

52 H. Römich in *Heimatbuch*, 1961, p. 82.
53 W. Kolarz, *Religion in the Soviet Union*, London, 1961, p. 249; W. Kahle, *Geschichte
  der evangelisch-lutherischen Gemeinden in der Sowjetunion, 1917–1938*, Leiden, 1974,
  p. 249.
54 K. Stumpp in *Die Kirchen und das religiöse Leben der Russlanddeutschen*, Stuttgart,
  1969–72, p. 277. Kahle, on the other hand, gives somewhat different data. According to him, there were 183 clergy in 1917; 84 in 1927, 34 in 1934 and 10 in 1936. W.
  Kahle, pp. 326–7.
55 See R. Stupperich, *Kirchenordnungen der evangelisch-lutherischen Kirchen in Russland*,
  Ulm-Donau, 1959.

The Soviet Union was divided into regional synods (*Bezirkssynoden*) under elected councils and a General Synod in Moscow. Fourteen of the seventeen synods set up were German.[56] The Second Synod of the Church took place in Moscow in the 1928 with 43 delegates and the Third (which was also the last) in the fall of 1933. With the death of Bishop Meyer and the departure of Bishop Malmgren – he left the country on a visit in 1936 and the Soviet government refused him permission to return – the Church went to pieces, and in the course of the 1930s all organised activity came to an end. In the 1920s it had still been possible to work among the faithful and even to distribute religious periodicals: *Unsere Kirche* appeared from 1927 till 1929, as did a *Kalendar* in the town of Pokrovsk. The Mennonites, for their part, published *Unser Blatt* and *Der Praktischer Landwirt*. This community will be discussed later). The Baptists also succeeded in bringing out *Familien Freund* in 1925–8.

The Catholic Church in 1918 numbered 1,600,000 believers mainly Germans and Poles, members of 1,195 Churches.[57] The war on the Catholic Church, which was waged fiercely in the first stage of the establishment of the Soviet Union, reached its peak in the big show trial of 1922. The expulsion of the heads of the Church from Soviet territory made it impossible to organise the congregations, and the closing down of the Theological Seminary in Saratov caused further difficulties. It was only in 1926, with the arrival in the Soviet Union of the Papal delegate Michel d'Herbigny, that there was any possibility at all of taking steps to reorganise the Catholic Church, by dividing the country into regions headed by priests in the absence of bishops. The regions with a considerable German population came under Bishops August Baumtrog, Johannes Roth and A. Frison. In 1926 there were still 30 of the former 36 priests officiating in the Volga area, and 64 priests in the Black Sea area (the Crimea and part of the Ukraine).[58]

In 1917 there were some 110,000 Mennonites in Russia, organised in 365 villages in the Ukraine, the Crimea, the Caucasus, Siberia and Central Asia; losses in the Civil War and emigration halved their number. The Mennonite Church organisation was one of the very few in the 1920s which the new régime failed to shatter in the first years –

56 H. Maurer, 'Die evangelisch-lutherische Kirche in der Sowjetunion, 1917–1937', *Kirche im Osten*, 1959, vol. 2, pp. 74–6; Kahle, p. 111.
57 P. Mailleux in R. Marshall Jr. (ed.), *Aspects of Religion in the Soviet Union*, Chicago, 1971, p. 364.
58 *Die Kirchen und das religiose Leben der Russland Deutsche*, pp. 33–4.

the result of a rare combination of strong religious faith and a solid economic, social and educational base, all in one rural-community setting. In the period 1922–6 the Mennonite Church held three conventions, and the 1925 convention even had the boldness to address the authorities with specific demands – something very exceptional in the Soviet context. These were formulated in eight points, which included the right of free religious assembly, religious education both for children and young people (forbidden by law), the holding of Bible classes and exemption from military service.[59] The existing favourable constellation in those years made it possible for the Mennonites to receive satisfaction in part.[60]

The anti-religious campaign in the years 1918–39 can be divided into a number of periods: 1918–20, 1921–3, in 1924–8 and 1929–39. In the first period, despite the enactment of outright anti-religious legislation, the campaign was relatively restricted. The new régime was not firmly in the saddle, and the first priority was the fight to the death against other political parties and organisations. The worst blow was the confiscation of Church property and restriction on religious education. In the second period, after the final liquidation of the opposition parties, religion was the principal remaining obstacle to the spread of communism, and accordingly a war of unparalleled ferocity was fought against religion on a great variety of fronts. There was ceaseless, blaring propaganda in all the media, mobilisation of propagandists from among the different nationalities, war on the religious festivals, closing down of individual churches and arrests of clergy. In the third period, with the application of the NEP and relative liberalisation in other spheres, a considerable improvement took place in the situation of all the Churches. However, it was precisely in this period, in 1925, that the most extreme anti-religious organisation was created, the 'Union of the Godless', headed by E. Iaroslavskii, of which membership rose from 87,033 to 138,402 between 1926 and 1927.[61] While only six nationalities participated in this organisation in 1927, there were 97 doing so by 1931. The number of German members was only 2,000 in 1929, when the number of Jews in it was already 200,000.[62] The low German participation

59 Ehrt, p. 142.
60 See F. Epp, 'Mennonites in the Soviet Union' in Marshall, p. 291; *Bundesarchiv, Koblenz* R–57 neu 1123 (*Bericht des Rates über seine Tätigkeit seit der letzten V.V.*, May 18, 1925 – Dec. 23, 1927).
61 *Voinstvuiushchie bezbozhniki v SSSR za 15 let*, Moscow, 1932, p. 346.
62 *Natsional'naia politika*, p. 325.

can be explained by the small extent of secularisation among them and by their political passivity.

The organisation waged war on religion on two fronts: 'scientific' propaganda according to Marxist-Leninist principles, directed mainly at the educated urban population, and strident propaganda against religious festivals and the clergy. Special newspapers were published with nothing but anti-religious propaganda, such as the German-language *Neuland* and *Der Gottlose an der Drehbank*. General and literary newspapers also devoted a great deal of space to the anti-religious campaign. Nevertheless, it seems that in the German regions their influence was fairly limited. Thus, for example, in the six German national districts in the Ukraine, with a population of 140,000, subscribers to these papers numbered only 324.[63] In 1928 the main German-language anti-religious paper, *Neuland*, appeared in 1,200 copies, in 1929 in 1,400 copies and in 1932 in 10,000.[64]

Organising in the German villages was also tardy (as we have said, it was felt only in the years 1931–2). One of the original means used for anti-religious propaganda among the Germans was arranging artistic performances that were intended to compete with the religious holidays.[65] The biggest danger to the Christian Churches in this period was the attempt made by the authorities to found a competing church, named the 'living church', with the help of priests loyal to the régime. We know, for example, that this attempt failed miserably among the Germans in the districts of Ufa and Samara.[66] In 1929–39, which were unquestionably the worst years of all, the anti-religious campaign combined both strategies complementing each other. The mass propaganda was kept up in all its forms in the light of day, while the secret police went to work clandestinely arresting hundreds of priests and lay people active in the congregations. Most of the churches that still remained open at the beginning of the 1930s were now closed down and leading Church figures were accuseed of collaborating with the White forces and with Nazi Germany, organising emigration from the Soviet Union, and so on. Of the 246 Evangelical-Lutheran churches still open in 1932 only an isolated few remained in 1939; 89 senior

63 *Deutsche Zeitung*, April 12, 1931, as quoted by Kolarz, p. 204.
64 W. Kahle, p. 289.
65 R. Martel, *Le mouvement anti-réligieux en URSS (1917–1932)*, Paris, 1932, p. 190.
66 W. Kolarz, p. 254. According to A. Gross, in 1926 there were 4,000 members of the 'living church' who 'conquered' 48 German villages.

clergymen in this Church were arrested.[67] The destructive work of the Organisation of the Godless reached its height in this period, membership growing from 465,498 in 1929 to five and a half million in 1932. In the German Republic of the Volga, however, there were no more than 4,600 in 1938.[68]

German culture in the Soviet Union.   German culture in Russia before the Revolution was closely bound up with religion. The political changes and the anti-religious campaign were directed at cutting this link, both formally and in content. Sovietisation in the sense of russification, which was imposed with increasing vigour in the 1930s, had the effect of speeding up the process of replacing other languages. More and more Germans became familiar with the Russian language and culture, if not as part of assimilation processes then certainly as open acculturation.

In this context we shall note the changes that occurred in the educational system, and in literature, the press, art and scientific research.

EDUCATION   Before the Revolution, despite the heavy pressure of russification on the national minorities, an extensive educational network existed among the Germans in the German language. This included elementary and secondary schools, vocational schools and teacher-training, commercial and agricultural colleges.[69]

Statistical data available on German schools in the Soviet Union in the 1920s and 1930s are only partial and often conflicting. In the German Republic of the Volga in 1919 there were 236 German schools; in 1921 there were 336 and in 1922, after the great famine, their number dropped to 327, with 41,878 pupils.[70] From 1922 to 1927 there was a growth of 23 per cent, the number of schools reaching 396 with 53,642 pupils.[71]

67 *Bundesarchiv*, R-41 1/138 (Büro des Reichspräsidenten und Reichskanzlei); R-43 1/140; *Die Kirchen*; A. Reinmarus, 'Mennonity'; *Anti-religioznik*, 1938, no. 1, pp. 48–53; W. Birenbaum, *Christenheit in Sowjetrussland – Was wissen wir von ihr?* Tübingen, 1961; W.J. Ciszek, *L'espion du Vatican*, Paris, 1966.
68 *Antireligioznik*, 1938, no. 12, p. 56.
69 In 1914 in the Volga region alone there were 61,000 pupils studying German; in the Crimea and the Eastern Ukraine 42,140, and in the Caucasus 1,955. Thus in Russia without Bessarabia, the Baltic regions and part of the Ukraine, there were about 105,000 pupils. *Deutsche Post aus den Osten*, 1938, nos 6–7, pp. 8–12.
70 I.P. Trainin, *Der Verband der Sozialistischen Sowjetrepubliken*, Hamburg, 1923, p. 108; *ASSR der Wolgadeutschen*, p. 43.
71 *Wolgadeutsches Schulblatt*, 1929, no. 1, p. 5.

The percentage of German children studying in these schools in 1927 was 98.2 per cent, and in the Russian Republic 84.2 per cent.[72] The number of German pupils in the German Republic of the Volga increased to 68,085 in 1934 and 89,484 in 1936, a relatively low rate of increase considering the growth of the population and the passage of the 1931 law on compulsory education. In 1937–8, when German was taught (in German) only in the Volga Republic, there were 421 schools with 126,000 pupils.[73] The number of teachers in 1922 was 771; in 1938 it was 3,326.[74] Institutions of higher training in the German Republic of the Volga did not expand as foreseen, and their number was limited: in 1938 there were four teacher-training colleges, three medical schools, three agricultural colleges and one music academy. A university in the full sense was not set up – largely, it would seem, owing to the lack of initiative and the inaction of the leaders in the republic. It is important to note that Germans also came to study in these various colleges or institutes from outside the republic and precisely therein lay their national importance. We have only scattered data on schools in the Russian Republic, with its German population of approximately 400,000. In 1922 there were 434 German schools there,[75] but in 1928 only 249 with 13,630 pupils.[76] This was largely because the Russian Republic followed a different policy regarding its extra-territorial national minorities from that of the other republics, especially the Ukraine and Belorussia. An important role in teacher-training was played by the German Central Pedagogic Institute, founded in Odessa in 1922. The Universities of Saratov, Moscow, Leningrad and other cities offered *Germanistik* studies.[77]

Outside the Russian Republic, there was an extensive network of German schools in the Ukraine, where there were 576 schools in 1924, 564 in 1925 and 609 in 1926 with 33,168 pupils, or 70 per cent of all German pupils. A decisive increase took place in the 1927–32, so that in 1929–30 the number of schools was 628 with 61,075 pupils, and

72 *Narodnoe prosveshchenie v RSFSR k 1927–1928*, Moscow, 1928, p. 211.
73 *Deutsche Zeitung*, Sept. 1, 1938.
74 ASSR der Wolgadeutschen; Bohmann, pp. 62–3; *Bolshaia sovetskaia entsiklopediia*, vol. 41, pp. 599–600.
75 *Zhizn' natsional'nostei*, 1922, no. 3 (9); *Wolgadeutsche Monatshefte*, 1923, nos 15–16, p. 222; R.J. Ballig, 'The German Schools in Southern Russia', *The Catholic University of America*, 1931, vol. VI, no. 2, pp. 3–21.
76 *Narodnoe prosveshchenie v RSFSR k 1929–1930*, Moscow, 1930, p. 83.
77 *Zur neuen Schule*, 1925, no. 45, p. 80; *Wolgadeutsches Schulblatt*, 1928, no. 3, pp. 585–7.

although the number of schools had dropped in 1931–2 to 571, pupils had increased to 63,670.[78] From 1933 on, a decline set in visibly in the numbers of both schools and pupils (451 schools and 55,623 pupils[79]). In 1934–8, there was a notable move to unite the schools of the national minorities with the Russian or Ukrainian schools as an intermediate step towards their final liquidation. Indeed, in 1938–9, there does not appear to have been a single German school remaining anywhere in the Soviet Union except in the Republic of the Volga, and those were abolished with the deportation of the Germans in August 1941.

Higher studies in the German language were limited in the Ukraine, where three teachers-training colleges played an important role, one in Prishib, another in Khortitsa and the one already mentioned in Odessa, founded earlier than the others.[80]

When the German schools were set up, they, like those of other national minorities, were faced with many difficulties and managed only in part to overcome them. There was a permanent shortage of good teachers who could also be trusted politically; constant pressure from the local authorities had a demoralising effect; and there was a shortage of buildings, laboratories, teaching equipment and, especially, textbooks, some of which were still imported from Germany in the 1920s. Finally, some parents opposed sending their children to German schools, whether on religious grounds or because of the low standards of the German schools compared with the Russian ones. However, it seems likely that most of these difficulties could have been overcome and the German educational network maintained had it not been laid low by the axe of total liquidation.

PUBLISHING AND LITERATURE   From 1918 till 1921, German book and newspaper publishing was in a chaotic state. The old German papers – *Deutsche Stimme, Saratower Deutsche Zeitung, Der Advensbote, Deutsche Rundschau* – were already shut down in 1918, while the *Christliche*

---

78 *Vlast' sovetov*, 1926, no. 19, p. 13; nos 44–5, p. 16; Gitlanskii in *Revoliutsiia i natsional'nosti*, 1931, no. 5, p. 43; D. Mats in *Revoliutsiia i natsional'nosti*, 1935, no. 6, p. 60.

79 S. Dimanshtein, *Itogi*, p. 200.

80 The number of students in the Pedagogical Institute in Odessa was 76 in 1928, 201 in 1931. In 1938, 77 students completed the course in this Institute (16 in history, 20 in philology and literature, 19 in natural sciences, 8 in geography and the rest in other departments). *Deutsche Post aus dem Osten*, 1938, no. 7, p. 28; Dimanstein, p. 201. Interview with Dr J. Schnurr, Stuttgart, 1978.

Familienkalendar was closed in 1920. A few non-communist papers belonged to the Churches, as we have seen, and these were also closed by the end of the 1920s. In these years 24 communist or pro-communist papers appeared, published by prisoners-of-war. They would seem to have had little influence on the German population. A third type of paper was published in this period under the influence of the German prisoners of war but edited by and intended for the Soviet Germans. There were nine of these papers, the most important being *Der Rote Fahne* (1919–22) and *Zum Kommunismus* (1919–20). In the period 1919–22, the publication of German papers was stabilised both in quantity and quality. In the Volga region eleven newspapers and periodicals appeared, the main organ being *Nachrichten*, which was published in Pokrovsk from 1919 until 1941.[81] Thirteen other papers and periodicals appeared in other places, among them the *Deutsche Zentral Zeitung*, published in Moscow from 1926 to 1939 and the official paper of the German section of the Communist Party until the section was closed down in January 1930.[82] In the third period (1930–41) there was in fact a rise in the number of periodicals published, but the additions were mainly technical publications, translated from Russian, with very little German national content. In 1930 sixteen German papers and periodicals appeared; in 1933 there were 41 (printing 197,515 copies) and 40 in 1935. Then in 1935–9 many of the German papers were closed down, most of them in the Ukraine, where the number dropped from fourteen to six.[83] Thus only 21 German papers were still appearing in 1939, mostly in the German Republic of the Volga. In terms of their content, these papers were just like the Soviet papers in Russian and other languages; the German national issues which they dealt with became fewer and fewer in the 1930s as a result of the changed policy on nationalities and the general atmosphere of terror in the country.

In all matters concerning the publication of German books a dis-

---

81 F.P. Schiller, *Literatur zur Geschichte und Volkskunde der deutschen Kolonien in der Sowjetunion für die Jahre 1764–1926*, Pokrovsk, 1927, pp. 51–5; *Neues Leben*, January 9–30, 1980.

82 Apparently this is not a complete list and has been put together from Soviet publications such as Schiller (see note 81) and *Gazety i zhurnaly SSSR, 1917–1960*, Moscow, 1970–6 (vols I-IV); L. Guseva, *Spisok saratovskikh periodicheskikh izdanii, 1917–1967*, Saratov 1969, pp. 178–82.

83 Sturmschritt, 1931, no. 2–3, p. 8; Dimanshtein, pp. 216–17; *Revoliutsiia i natsional'nosti*, 1936, no. 6, p. 85; Bohmann; p. 63.

tinction must be made between those not specifically meant for the Soviet German population (although this population could of course benefit from them) and those written by and for Soviet Germans. For this reason it is hard to get accurate data on the different categories.[84] In 1918–21, the principal books published were the classic Marxist-Leninist works and the writings of the Soviet leaders. From 1923 on, the list of technical text books begins to lengthen. In 1927, 197 and in 1928, 319 German books were published. In 1913, before the outbreak of war, there had been 717. In the years of 1929–32 there was a considerable rise in the number of German books published: in the Russian Republic alone there were 1,385 and in the Ukraine in 1930, 450. But thereafter (see Table 3) an uninterrupted decline set in in German book production as in other spheres, stemming from the changed nationalities policy.

Table 2.3.   GERMAN BOOKS PUBLISHED IN THE
SOVIET UNION, 1933–39[85]

1933	1934	1935	1936	1937	1938	1939
531	508	512	413	319	303	270

In the 1930s, as a general rule, there was a steady increase in the number of original Soviet German books as well as in the number of translated works, technical literature and textbooks. There were fewer and fewer books on the history, literature and culture of the Germans, while the works of the fathers of Marxism waxed exceedingly.

Until 1934 German writers had their own unions, mainly in the Russian Republic and the Ukraine, as part of the overall system of writers' organisations. They worked out of newspaper editorial offices and concerned themselves with German literary periodicals. The German section in Moscow was set up as early as 1922 and in the Ukraine only in 1930. The first convention of German writers in the Soviet Union – which also turned out to be the last – took place on

---

84 According to M. Buchsweiler, about 1,000–1,200 out of the total of 6,000 German books that appeared in the Soviet Union in 1917–41 were written by Soviet Germans. M. Buchsweiler, *Volksdeutsche in der Ukraine am Vorabend und Beginn des Zweiten Weltkriegs – ein Fall doppelter Loyalität?*, Gerlingen, 1984, p. 183. The Soviet source gives the number of books published in German in 1917–67 as 4390 original and 1308 translated works: *Pechat' SSSR za 50 let*, Moscow, 1967, p. 172.

85 Gitlanskii, p. 44; Dimanshtein, pp. 209–11; Buchsweiler, p. 173.

March 21–26, 1934. There were 35 delegates, twelve from the German Republic, eleven from Moscow, seven from the Ukraine and five from Leningrad.[86] The first attack on German literature in the country came at the end of the 1920s, when some of the most eminent German writers were severely criticised for being apolitical and infected with 'petit-bourgeois ideology' and 'nationalism'. Among the writers most harshly attacked were F. Bach, J. Jansen, E. Kufeld, P. Sinner and A. Rothermel.[87] It is important to note that Soviet German literature began to be controlled in the 1930s by German communists who arrived in the Soviet Union as refugees from Germany, and who were joined by communists from Hungary, Austria, Rumania and elsewhere. Not a few of these were Jews, a fact exploited to the full by Nazi propaganda.[88]

In summing up it can be said that the artistic level of German literature was not high, although a number of interesting works were written in the 1920s, such as those of G. Luft, D. Schellenberg, E. Kufeld, F. Bach, and others.

Theatre. The art of the theatre was not developed or widespread among the Germans before the Revolution, although numerous choirs existed in the German villages, mostly connected with the churches. Many German theatrical troupes were founded in the 1920s – there were 26 in the Ukraine alone in 1926[89] – but the Germans had to wait for a genuine professional theatre until 1933, when one was founded by the government of the German Republic of the Volga in Pokrovsk, with the help of the theatre in Odessa and of German performing artists and producers who had emigrated to the Soviet Union.[90] In 1934 new German immigrants founded Der Deutsche Theatre Kolonne Links, and helped strengthen the German theatre group in Dnepropetrovsk. In 1936 the leading anti-fascist German theatre was founded in Moscow with the participation of the outstanding producers E. Piscator, A.

86 A. Ritter in *Akzente*, 1975, no. 1, p. 51; H. Huppert in *Internationale Literatur*, 1934, no. 3, pp. 134–41.

87 *Sturmschritt*, 1930, no. 2–3, p. 10; 1932, no. 8, pp. 14–16.

88 J.B. Becher, E. Weinert, H. Huppert, F. Leschnitzer, W. Bredel, F. Wolf, A. Hotopp, A. Kurella and others.

89 P. Zaitsev in *Vlast' sovetov*, 1926, no. 19, p. 16.

90 H. Haarman, L. Schirmer and D. Walach, *Das Engels Projekt: ein anti-faschistisches Theater der deutschen Emigration in der UdSSR (1936-1941)*, Worms, 1975, p. 27; 'Das deutsche Theater in Odessa', *Heimatbuch*, 1966–7, p. 155.

Granach, C. Trepte, M. Vallentin and B. Reich,[91] who also made a decisive contribution to raising the level of the Soviet German theatre as a whole. For objective reasons such as the shortage of Soviet German plays and the general prevailing political situation, the repertoire of the German theatre was drawn from the classical German dramatists, Schiller and Lessing, from modern communist or progressive writers such as F. Wolf, or else from translations from the Russian (the works of Maxim Gorki, Chekhov, Pushkin, Korneichuk and Mdivani) or from world classics (mainly Shakespeare, Molière and Ibsen). For some reason the plays of Brecht were not put on in the Soviet German theatre, apart from *Die Gewehre der Frau Carrar* in Odessa.

Besides the theatre groups, there were radio broadcasts in German directed towards the Soviet Germans, mainly in the German Republic of the Volga, giving musical and artistic programmes from the German repertoire. Very little is known of the works of Soviet German musical composers, painters or sculptors.

Research. In the sphere of scholarly research on their own history or their present socio-political position, the Soviet Germans were seriously hampered by their failure to establish universities in their republic or any kind of academic institute in other republics, as was done, for example, by the Jews and the Poles. Research was done by isolated individual researchers such as Professors V. Schirmunsky (University of Leningrad), G. Dinges (Saratov) and A. Ström (Odessa)[92] on German philology and Soviet German folklore. P. Sinner, F. Schiller and G. Sawatzky were active in the field of literary research. As for historical research, we can point to only one work on the history of German settlement in Russia, that of D. Schmidt.[93] A number of essays appeared in the field of religion, but on the purely propaganda level as part of the anti-religious campaign. Attempts to reform and simplify the German language, according to the views of B. Bartels (in 1925) and A. Ström (the early 1930s), were rejected on the 'internationalist' grounds of the damage that would be done to the ties between the Soviet Germans and their fellow-nationals in Germany and elsewhere and thereby by extension to communist

91 A. Ritter in *Europäische Ideen*, 1976, no. 14–15, p. 126; *Das Wort*, 1936, no. 5, pp. 58–64; M. Liebermann, *Aus dem Ghetto in die Welt. Autobiographie*, Berlin (East), 1979.

92 Volksliederarchiv (Leningrad); Zentralstelle für die Mundartforschung; Das deutsche Zentralmuseum (Engels).

93 D. Schmidt, *Studien über die Geschichte der Wolgadeutschen*, Pokrovsk, 1930.

propaganda and its power to influence Germans outside the Soviet Union. What in fact decided the matter was the overall policy of the administration, for the arguments about possible harm were baseless: the first reform in the 1920s, with latinisation of non-Latin alphabets and the similar cyrillisation in the 1930s did not harm links with the 'outside' peoples in their homelands with well-rooted and widespread culture.

The Germans' sense of national identity

This important subject will be treated more fully in the last chapter (pp. 136 ff.) where long-term influences can be taken into consideration. Here we shall examine how the processes of sovietisation and modernisation influenced the Soviet Germans in the years 1917–41.

The number of Germans who 'disappeared' – that is, who did not declare their German nationality in the population censuses – appears to have been low in the 1920s because of the absence of any impending threat on account of their German nationality. However, the situation at the time of the 1939 census, when the Germans were beginning to suffer very serious consequences due to their national origin, was completely different. It is hard to estimate the number of Germans who disappeared, since we do not know the precise rate of natural increase in 1926–39, nor how many Germans died in the collectivisation and the famine that came in its wake.

The processes of accelerated sovietisation that directly affected the German villages in the 1930s certainly influenced the Germans' attitude to their national identity in the direction of acculturation to the Russian or Ukrainian language and culture. The general processes of modernisation of the traditional family and society worked in the same direction through the increase in social mobility, internal migration and urbanisation. However, we saw earlier that in the 1930s these processes were still only beginning, so at that time their effect on the sense of national identity was limited.

There are a number of quantitative indicators that can assist us in assessing the changes that took place in the essential strength of German national identity in the Soviet Union: mixed marriages, use of the German language, and migration (in the sense of escape) away from the Soviet Union. As we have seen, the German village community was built around a traditional national-religious congregation, immured against outside influences. Thus the number of mixed marriages was very low. This state of affairs changed as a result of the revolutionary events of 1917–21 and the increase in the number of Germans living in urban centres, which even before this date had been a more open society in which mixed marriages were more likely to occur. In 1925 in the European part of the Russian Republic, of every 100 German men who married, 15.32 made mixed marriages (among Jews the figure was 18.83, Latvians 70.8 and Poles 80.5); in 1926 the figure was 10.94 and in 1927 14.09 (that is, an annual average of 13.5). Among German women who married, on the other hand, the percentage of mixed marriages was lower: 7.52 in every 100 in 1925; 8.44 in 1926 and 11.43 in 1927.[94] The picture was different in the Ukraine: for every 100 men who married in 1925, 11.63 made mixed marriages, in 1926 12.97 and in 1927 12.1, while for every 100 German women marrying, 10.99 made mixed marriages in 1925, 11.08 in 1926 and 13.35 in 1927.[95] We have no data on this for the 1930s, but this process must certainly have been speeded up, if we take as indicator the lists drawn up by the Nazis when they occupied the Ukraine. These showed, for example, that in 1942 in the Dnepropetrovsk *oblast*, where 824 families remained, 265 of the 483 German men were married to Russian or Ukrainian women. In the Zhitomir *oblast*, 82 out of 209 Germans had made mixed marriages, while there had been only six mixed marriages in the whole *oblast* in 1914. As against this, in the Kronau district with its rural population, out of 2,857 families only 65 had made mixed marriages. That is to say, the proportion of mixed marriages was higher in the urban centres and in areas far removed from concentrations of Germans.[96]

In 1926, 94.9 per cent of all the Germans in the Soviet Union declared German as their mother tongue, when in the same year among the Jews 71.9 per cent declared Yiddish and among the Poles only 42.9 per cent declared Polish.[97] Unfortunately, the data under this head in the 1939 census were not published, and we cannot therefore draw any conclusions on the russification of the Germans under the influence of the overall processes and more specifically of the russification policy that reached its peak in 1938, when it became obligatory to teach Russian in all the schools of all the Soviet nationalities. If, however, we take into account, that in 1959, after twenty years without any visible trace of

94 *Natsional'naia politika*, p. 41.
95 *Ibid.*
96 *Bundesarchiv*, R-617 (Reichsministerium für die besetzten Ostgebiet); *Kölnische Zeitung*, Jan. 27, 1943.
97 *Natsional'naia politika*, p. 36.

German culture, 75 per cent of the Germans declared that German was their mother tongue, it is clear that in 1939 the percentage must have been nearer 90 than 75. In everything relating to acculturation – in the sense of adapting oneself to the foreign culture and expressing oneself in the foreign language (mainly Russian) without loss of the sense of national identity (as against assimilation) – this process would appear to have been just at its beginning in the late 1930s. It was at a more advanced stage only among the educated urban population and especially among members of the liberal professions, the intelligentsia and the skilled workers, whose relative numbers were still low.

The desire to leave the country where you were born and have lived all your life and to migrate to another country stems of course from many factors – some 'negative' like repudiation of the existing political and economic state of affairs, and others 'positive' like the pull of the country you want to go to. The rapid survey which we have already given and the analysis that will be given more fully later together indicate that the situation of the Soviet Germans was certainly deteriorating in the 1930s, but already in the 1920s many had wanted to leave the Soviet Union. Two to three thousand Germans left in 1918–22, 18–20,000 in 1923–8, and over 6,000 in 1929–33.[98] In 1923–4 and 1929–32 Germany's economic situation was extremely poor, so that one can reasonably conclude that the dominant factor in emigration was opposition to the Soviet régime, as well as the impossibility of preserving German religion and culture as had been done before the Revolution.

The imminent catastrophe

Given the focal point of this study, it has not been possible to consider the influence of external factors on Soviet nationalities policy in general or regarding the Germans in particular. Nonetheless, in concluding this chapter we are bound to point out the way in which Hitler's rise to power affected the situation of the Soviet Germans.

We have already seen that as early as the 1920s the Germans in the Soviet Union suffered during the famines and the collectivisation because

---

98 Ehrt, p. 159; Auhagen, p. 76; Political Archives of the Federal German Ministry of Foreign Affairs, Bonn (hereafter 'PA AA') IV, Russland; PA AA Russ Pol 25 (German Embassy, Moscow).

of their specific socio–economic situation. The national factor may well have been at work here, as well as their 'colonising and kulak past'; however, there is no doubt at all that in 1933–41 and of course after 1941, the official relationship towards them was profoundly affected by the external factor. The Soviet leadership feared that the Soviet Germans would not remain steadfastly loyal to the Soviet Union in the event of a war with Germany. This is why lists of Germans were drawn up as early as 1934: then and in the following years all those who had ever had any connection with their families in Germany, by receiving letters and parcels or in any other way whatever, were in danger of arrest.[99] In 1935 there was a complete break in contacts between the Soviet Germans and the outside world (in this respect the situation of other nationalities was no better).[100] In 1936–8, the years of the massive purges, most of the German communists were very hard hit, both in the German Republic of the Volga and elsewhere throughout the country.[101] Many journalists and editors, writers and artists connected with German culture were arrested;[102] scientists, doctors and engineers too were not spared. Arrests of Germans continued in 1939, despite the general let-up in the use of mass terror that began in that year.[103]

Reports that Germans were not called up for service in the Red Army as early as 1936 are inaccurate – there was only a limitation on the

99 Bundesarchiv, R-6/109 (*Behandlung der Volksdeutschen in Russland*; Dr. Rempel, *Die Bodenfrage in den deutschen Siedlungen in der Ukraine*); R-104 (*Handakten Ministerialrat Dr Maurer über das deutsche Volkstum im Osten; Briefwechsel Gebhardt-Maurer*).

100 Among those arrested for connections with the Germans were also Jews and members of other nationalities. An interesting case was the arrest of 30 engineers who had been sent to Germany on extension courses in 1934–5 and on their return were accused of spying for the Nazis. See interview with Mrs Ass, whose husband, of Armenian origin, Armen Gudashsazian, was one of this group. Interview with Mrs Ass by E. Evelson, Tel-Aviv, May 17, 1978.

101 A clear indication in this direction can already be found in an article by one of the leaders of the German Republic of the Volga, A. Welsch, in *Revoliutsiia i natsional'nosti*, 1936, no. 1, p. 57.

102 In the very first stage, 1933–5, newspaper editors were dismissed from their posts and there were also arrests of writers. See J. Schnurr in H. Bachmann, *Durch die deutschen Kolonien des Beresaner Gebietes*, Stuttgart, 1974, p. xiii.

103 K. Stumpp, *Die Russlanddeutschen Zweihundert Jahre unterwegs*, Freilassing, 1964, p. 33. Two big trials of Germans were held in February and August 1939 on accusations of spying for the Nazis, German nationalism, etc, National Archives (Washington) DAI (*Komando Dr Stumpp*) LOC, 151 and LOC, 153.

mobilisation of new recruits and close surveillance over those already in the army.[104] A campaign of defamation started in 1934 and 1935 against the Mennonite, Protestant and Catholic clergy of German origin, many being arrested and deported.[105] The first extensive wave of deportations of Germans from the rural regions was carried out in May and June 1936, when some 18,000 Germans and Poles were deported.[106] Deportations continued at a greater rate in 1937 and 1938, when at the same time German cadres and cadres of the other extra-territorial minorities were systematically liquidated: the national soviets, the national regions and the courts were all abolished, and teaching of the German language in the schools was banned except in the German Republic of the Volga.

The signing of the Molotov-Ribbentrop Pact on August 23, 1939, and the further German-Soviet agreements of November 16, 1939, and September 5 1940,[107] were bound to affect the situation of the Soviet Germans. Stalin could not continue pursuing an open anti-German policy inside the Soviet Union at a time when 'friendship' with Nazi Germany was the order of the day, despite the Nazis' practice of exploiting the existence of the *Volksdeutschen* as part of their expansionist purposes under the pretext of defending Germans everywhere in the world. The direct, immediate consequence of the agreements signed was the transfer of 395,750 Germans from the areas annexed by the Soviet Union to the regions occupied by the Germans;[108] there must have been some Soviet Germans among them, though probably not a large number. As against this, there was no change at all in the legal-political status of the Germans in the Soviet Union in 1939–41. The change for the better from their point of view was that there were fewer arrests and the deportations stopped. The agreements may also have saved the Volga Germans for at least two years from deportations like those suffered by their fellow nationals in the Ukraine. This did not mean that the Soviet

---

104 Bundesarchiv (Koblenz), R-6 (Auswanderung und Ansiedlung); A. Weissberg, *Conspiracy of Silence*, London, 1952, p. 348; *Freundschaft*, Feb. 14, 1970; May 12, 1970; May 14, 1970.

105 National Archives (Washington), T-454 R 20 RMO.

106 A. Bohmann, p. 70. On earlier arrests, in 1935, see Chapter 3.

107 All the documentation on the German-Soviet, pacts is in the archives of the Federal Ministry of Foreign Affairs, Bonn. See *PA AA*, *Moskau Kult*, B; PA AA, *Moskau Pol.* 2 no. 1; *PA AA*, *Moskau* 198/2. In English, see *Nazi-Soviet Relations, 1939–1941*, New York, 1948.

108 I.W. Brugel, *Stalin und Hitler-Pakt gegen Europa*, Vienna, 1973, p. 197.

Germans were no longer suspect. On the contrary, suspicion against them increased, but it was not expressed in public.[109]

Another result of the German-Soviet agreements was that all propaganda against Nazism and fascism was completely halted, which meant a clear worsening of the situation of German anti-Nazis who had found refuge in the Soviet Union. Stalin's eagerness to curry favour with Hitler was such that in an act of unparalleled baseness refugees who had just escaped from Nazi death camps were handed over to the Gestapo, among them a number of Jews.[110]

There was a certain slackening off in the liquidation of German culture in the Soviet Union that had been going on throughout the late 1930s, but the staging of anti-Nazi plays was of course stopped. The plays *Doktor Mamlock* and *Familie Oppenheim* were dropped from the repertoire on August 23, 1939, the day the first pact was signed. Soviet German writers, artists and scholars apparently realised that, despite the breathing-space it afforded them, the 'great friendship' with Nazi Germany would not last for long and that the day of wrath for the German nationality in the Soviet Union was approaching.

---

109 A Swiss journalist who visited the Soviet Union at this time described how Germans were attacked in the places where they worked, and so on. P. Werner, *Ein Schweizer Journalist sieht Russland*, Olten, 1942, pp. 64–5.

110 See M. Buber-Neumann, *Als Gefangene bei Stalin und Hitler*, Stuttgart, 1968; G. Herling, *Welt ohne Erbarmen*, Cologne 1953, p. 70; Brugel, p. 189.

CHAPTER THREE

'OPERATION BARBAROSSA' AND THE DEPORTATION

Ingeborg Fleischhauer

The deportation of a large part of the Soviet German minority and its settlement beyond the Urals came as a prompt Soviet reaction to the German invasion of the Soviet Union on June 22, 1941. The proceedings concerned have been discussed repeatedly in reports of personal experiences,[1] data supplied by the refugees' organisations,[2] general descriptive works[3] and historical research.[4] For all that, consideration has seldom been given to the more general problem of the internment, evacuations and forced deportations of those minorities or minority groups whose loyalty to their Soviet fatherland or host-country was questioned.[5]

1 See, *inter alia*, K. Stumpp, 'Die Schicksalsjahre 1941–1945 für einen Grossteil der Russlanddeutschen. Dazu einige Erlebnisberichte', in *Heimatbuch der Deutschen aus Russland* (hereafter *Heimatbuch*), 1966, pp. 23–34.

2 A. Mergenthaler, 'Unsere Landsleute unter dem Sowjetregime und in der sowjetschen Verbannung', *Heimatbuch*, 1957, pp. 117–31.

3 See A. Solzhenitsyn, *Arkhipelag Gulag*, vol. I, London, 1974, pp. 555–79, as well as W. Leonhard, *Die Revolution entlässt ihre Kinder*, Cologne, Berlin, 1955, p. 94, and S. Leonhard, *Gestohlenes Leben*, Frankfurt/Main, 1956, p. 384.

4 The historical coming to terms with this question, after Khrushchev's speech at the XX Congress of the CPSU, put an end to the memory gap even if in a somewhat compressed form (see Robert Conquest, *The Nation Killers: The Soviet Deportation of Nationalities*, London, 1970, p. 67). In the secret speech, the question of the national minorities in the Soviet Union deported during World War II was presented for the first time but without mentioning the German and other relatively large minorities. See, for example, V. Kolarz, *Die Nationalitätenpolitik der Sowjetunion*, Frankfurt/ Main, 1956; G. Vvedensky, 'The Volga Germans and other German Groups', in *Genocide in the USSR: Studies in Group Destruction*, series I, no. 40, Munich, 1958, pp. 49–54; R. Conquest, *The Soviet Deportation of Nationalities*, London, 1960; R. M. Levine, 'The Russian Germans' Reaction to German Invasion', *Survey*, 23 (1977/8), no. 4 (150); M. Buchsweiler, 'Ethnic Germans in the Ukraine towards the Second World War: A Case of Double Loyalty?', Tel Aviv, 1980 (English abstract of dissertation in Hebrew).

5 In World War II, where the treatment of resident citizens of enemy states or citizens of enemy origin was concerned, the principle of reciprocity largely held good, although proportions varied greatly. On the German side, all former Russian and Soviet citizens were kept under close observation, with the Ukrainian nationalist collaborators with the Germans held under 'honorary arrest' (*Ehrenhaft*) by the Gestapo (Cf. *Ereignismeldung UdSSR*, no. 15, July 17, 1941, p. 1); the entire Russian

And it was too often beclouded by inaccurate figures based on specula-
tion or guesswork.[6] Despite much research, we still lack a critical analysis,
comparing the various relevant sources, of the displacement of the
German population on Soviet territory following the German attack on

---

emigration in Germany, including monarchist groups, was put into the custody of
Himmler's SS (cf. R.C. Williams, *Culture in Exile: Russian Emigrés in Germany
1881–1941*, Ithaca, NY-London, 1972, pp. 331–62), along with 19 former German
repatriates from the Soviet Union and with Soviet citizens interned in Vienna
(*Ereignismeldung UdSSR*, no. 6, June 27, 1941, p. 1).

But it will also be recalled how Japanese Americans in the United States and
German political *émigrés* in Britain were interned. As for the Soviet Union,
there was already the precedent from the First World War: the evacuation of what
were considered politically unreliable national minority groups, mainly Germans and
Jews. Between the autumn of 1914 and early 1915, the Russian military authorities
had German settlers evacuated from the Russian-Polish *gubernie* to central Russia,
Siberia and Central Asia. During the great German-Austrian offensive in the spring
of 1915, the Russian High Command found itself constrained to have some 70,000
Germans evacuated from the Volhynia theatre. And with the enemy advance in the
following months, the military authorities ordered the evacuation of 10,000 German
colonists from the Kiev *guberniia*, some 20,000 German settlers from the Podolia
guberniia and northern Bessarabia (up to the end of 1915), and 11,500 Germans from
Chernigov *guberniia* (up to February 1916). Furthermore, German colonists from
two villages as well as numerous nationalist-minded German Balts were deported to
the east from the Baltic front zones. Simultaneously, the small group of nationalistic
intellectuals from the German colonies in southern Russia and the Volga region were
sent to Siberia as a preventive measure. The memoirs written by these circles make it
clear that the decisions of the Russian military authorities were not determined
arbitrarily by hysteria but by realism and the actual state of affairs.

It is more difficult to answer the question of the legitimacy of the forcible
expropriation of some 500,000 hectares of German-owned land in the Russian
frontier zones as well as of some coastal stretches on the Black Sea and the Sea of
Azov, as part of Russian wartime legislation (1915–17). All the same, these expro-
priations affected only a small fraction of the German-owned land in Russia.

It is interesting that in 1939 the *Great Soviet Encyclopaedia* condemned the 'barbaric measures of the tsarist regime' carried out against the Germans in Russia in
World War I as a form of national oppression, and at the same time praised the
'boundless devotion of the working-class of the Volga German Autonomous Soviet
Republic to the cause of Communism'.

6 Thus Bohmann starts from the assumption that 'about 900,000 *Volksdeutsche*' were
banished to regions on the further side of the Urals (A. Bohmann, *Menschen und
Grenzen. Strukturwandel der deutschen Bevölkerung im sowjetischen Staats – und
Verwaltungsbereich*, vol. 3, Cologne, 1970, p. 71), while American research inclines
today towards a figure of about 600,000 Germans deported (see Conquest, *Nation*,
pp. 64, 66).

the Soviet Union.[7] A comparative analysis of this kind is called for after extensive work on the abundant relevant documents,[8] all the more so now that new facts have recently come to light.

As other writers have already noted,[9] one is dependent in this kind of research mostly on published and unpublished material from the pens of Nazi office-holders, which, precisely with regard to this question, is founded on two sorts of mythologising falsications. The displacement of population on the Soviet side, with all the undoubted human misery it caused, was grotesquely distorted on national lines for Nazi propaganda purposes in a way that barely veiled the naked tactical interest in this national group and its power-political exploitation. Reporting by the Nazis on the Germans who were found, seized and registered in the regions occupied by the German and Rumanian troops was marred by the racial-biological and racial-political criteria applied to these so-called *Volksdeutsche*,[10] as well as by an obsession with large numbers and the mania of the competing Kommandos to 're-germanise' parts of the local population. Finally, investigation is hampered by the obscurity that surrounded the westward treks of civilians towards the end of the war and the disintegrating German troop formations that were brought up to strength with forcibly drafted *Volksdeutsche*. The Soviet drive for compulsory repatriation of former Soviet citizens after the end of the war also extinguished many traces.

In spite of these difficulties, the whole subject is worth tackling for two reasons. On the one hand, the German minority in the Soviet Union provides a characteristic example of Stalinist nationality policy in an extreme situation, in this case war. On the other hand, the way this policy was enforced during the Second World War – seen against the

7 Again the viewpoint of the refugee organisations: G. Teich, 'Entwurf der personellen Verluste der russlanddeutschen Bevölkerung aus der UdSSR in Kriegs- und Nachkriegszeit bis 1950' in *Heimatbuch*, 1958, pp. 82–94; and K. Stumpp, 'Folgenschwere Auswirkungen der russischen politischen Entwicklung auf das Deutschtum in Russland' in *Heimatbuch*, 1966, pp. 5 ff.

8 See my study *Das Dritte Reich und die Deutschen in der Sowjetunion*, Stuttgart, 1983.

9 R. Hoffmann, 'Das Ende der volksdeutschen Siedlungen in "Transnistrien" im Jahre 1944', in H. Boberach/H. Booms (eds), *Aus der Arbeit des Bundesarchivs. Beiträge zum Archivwesen, zur Quellenkunde und Zeitgeschichte*, Boppard am Rhein, 1977, p. 448.

10 In National Socialist terminology, the word *Volksdeutscher* (ethnic German) signified a person of German stock living abroad who was not a German citizen (i.e. *Reichsdeutscher*). From its very beginning, the Hitler *Reich* proclaimed itself to be the legal protector and representative of the *Volksdeutsche* all over the world. The Soviet Germans are referred to as *Volksdeutsche* in this chapter.

background of events in the First World War – also throws light on how the Russian German minority was inevitably affected by these conflicts since it was, rightly or wrongly, considered a potential instrument of the German *Reich's* appetite for expansion, albeit a distant one. The wider causal connection is the burden of this chapter: the Germans of the Soviet Union were not so much the direct victims of Stalin's incalculable nationality policy, as has hitherto been argued in the literature, as indirect victims of the eastward drive of the Third Reich.[11]

Piecing together the facts

Soviet population censuses have a rather special history.[12] Only the census of 1926 can be considered reliable where the Germans in the Soviet Union are concerned.[13] The incomplete 1939 Census[14] gave the figure of 1,423,545 Soviet citizens of German nationality, but without any key as to their region of domicile.[15] The 1926 Census, however, did include regional distribution, as follows: Russian Republic 806,301; (Russian) Ukraine 393,924; Transcaucasia 25,327; Belorussia 7,075. In the

11 They escaped this fate in the German drive to the east in World War I thanks only to the wait-and-see attitude of the Tsar and the resistance offered by the liberal and left parties in the Duma. See I. Fleischhauer, 'The Tsars' Nationalities Policy Reconsidered – The Case of the Russian Germans', *Journal of Modern History*, 53, 1 (1981), 1065–90.

12 I. Starodulsky, *Das Volkszählungswesen in der Union der Sozialistischen Sowjetunion*, Jena, 1937.

13 *Vsesoiuznaia perepis' naseleniia 17ogo dekabria 1926 g. Kratkie svodki*, Moscow, 1928. For a German evaluation see E. Stieda, 'Die Volkszählung in der Union der Sozialistischen Sowjetsrepubliken vom 17. Dezember 1926', in *Allgemeines Staatsarchiv*, 17 (1928), pp. 157–63; 19 (1929), pp. 437–50. And regarding the German minority: K. Stumpp, 'Das Deutschtum in Russland nach der Volkszählung von 1926', in *Heimatbuch*, 1957, pp. 103–6.

14 See *Izvestiia* (Moscow), no. 99, April 29, 1940, for the results of the 1939 census.

15 The assumption made by the German Institute for Foreign Policy Research when the Russian campaign was being planned that almost half a million Germans would be found in the Ukraine was an optimistic maximum estimate: 'The German national group with almost $\frac{1}{2}$ million holds the fourth place among the nationalities [of the Ukraine]. The Ukraine is that area of Russia where most of the Germans are settled. Of the 1.4 million [Germans] who, according to the last census, are to be found in Russia more than three-fifths(?) live in the Ukraine. The rest are in the Volga Republic, Transcaucasia, and the Semipalatinsk area, etc. The Germans live primarily number of districts in the Kherson, Ekaterinoslav and Tavrida provinces.' *Materialen für Neuordnung. Nur für den Dienstgebrauch! Die Ukraine. Im auftrag des Auswärtigen Amtes bearbeitet vom Deutschen Institut für aussenpolitische Forschung*, Berlin, 1940.

Russian Republic itself, the share of the Ural and Trans-Ural regions was 149,527 Soviet citizens of German nationality, but the share of the European part, which concerns us here, was 656,774. These last resided mainly in the Lower Volga region (439,105) and the Middle Volga region (24,364), in the Northern Caucasus (93,915), in the Crimean Peninsula (43,631), in the Leningrad-Karelian region (30,470), in the central industrial zone (15,123) and in the central black earth zone. In 1926, therefore, in the whole European part of the Soviet Union, including the Transcaucasian Federation, there were about 1.08 million Germans (which does not include Germans who preferred not to list themselves as such).

Given the vicissitudes of life in the 1920s and 1930s, it is not surprising that the German population of the Volga Republic showed a below-average population growth, from 379, 930 in 1926 to 398,000 in 1938.[16] Added to this, the waves of deportations and banishments poured chiefly into the trans-Ural regions. In the European part of the Soviet Union, the German population in 1941 must therefore have been between 1 and 1.1 million, but nearer, it would seem, to the million mark.

The movement of the German population after the start of the German Russian campaign

It seems clear, looking back at events following the implementation of Operation Barbarossa, that the Soviet administration had made a prior decision to evacuate the entire population of German origin in the event of a German invasion. As this would cover all regions where the German army might advance, it meant, in practice, the entire European part of the Soviet Union. In spite of this decision in principle, the Soviet leadership presumably found itself constrained by economic and technical-military considerations to carry out the evacuation in a series of stages rather than all at once. These considerations can presumably be traced back, first to the need to put the population of German origin too to work protecting and saving the agricultural and industrial inventory in the zone of the German advance or else making it unusable by destroying machines, tractors, all kinds of vehicles, cattle and so on; and secondly to the need to be able to use the German population to operate natural defence systems (ramparts, tank-traps, trenches and so on) and above all to bring in the harvest. Yet a further consideration relates to the speed of the German

16 See the Report of A. Heckmann, *Deutsche Zeitung* (Moscow), Nov. 19, 1938.

advance on the different sectors of the front, with all the imponderables involved, which the Soviet military leadership could only evaluate with difficulty and for the immediate future.

It corresponds logically with this state of affairs that only the first stage of the evacuation of the Germans from the zones where enemy troops had penetrated with unexpected speed should have been implemented, while the evacuation was proceeding on a larger scale and more rapidly in the regions further east and other sectors still free of fighting. According to a report of the *Reich* Ministry for the Occupied Eastern Regions, 'The further eastwards one pushes, the greater the damage that has been done – beyond the Dnieper were German villages in which all life had been extinguished.'[17]

Of all the occupied areas, the regions of the Soviet Union that were most thickly settled with Germans lay in the zone of operations of the Army Group South. These were the former New Russian *gubernie* of Kherson, Ekaterinoslav and Tavrida as well as the Crimea and the Caucasus, where German colonists had been settled for some 150 years. There were also the more distant regions of the Western and Central Ukraine, parts of the former *gubernie* of Volhynia, Podolia and Kiev, where German peasants had established themselves in the second half of the nineteenth century. In the chronological order set for evacuation, these parts of the Western Ukraine were the first to be affected by the measures planned. In 1935 a border strip 100 km. wide had been totally cleared of all the Germans in the town and village communities. The first affected of all these were the thickly settled districts of Pulin (Okrug Volynsk) and Novograd-Volynsk (in German, Zwiahel). The Germans and the Jews living there had also been forcibly evacuated in the First World War in 1915. The first days of 1935 (January 1–7) saw the arrest of large numbers of men, who were all imprisoned in Zhitomir within a few hours; on January 28 police units surrounded the German inhabitants' homes, and those who had remained behind and the families of the arrested men were given 24 hours to prepare for deportation. Their cartloads of belongings were sent to Zhitomir, where the families were re-united, and from there all the families were taken by train to Murmansk.[18]

---

17 See German Records (= GR), World War II Records Division, National Archives, Washington, DC, Microfilm T. 454, R 20, F 498 ff. 'Die Vernichtung des Schwarzmeerdeutschtums' (Here: F 501).

18 K. Stumpp, document no. 3, 29. 8–7.9. 1941, GR T 81, R 599, F 5 386 542.

In the other regions with a partly German population, the Nazi advance led to control points (electric power-stations, bridges, the newly-constructed high watch-towers and so on) being transferred to Ukrainian hands. The villages were subjected to strict guard and night patrols. Individuals were investigated, Germans were arrested, and in some places the German language was banned.[19] As a first step in the general evacuation, all German men from town and *kolkhoz* aged 16–60 (in the case of Ukrainians the age bracket was 20–50) were sent off east with the cattle and the moveable equipment of the collective farms. German women and girls in these age-groups were put to digging defensive trenches (3 × 6 metres), as the second step in the withdrawal.[20] The third and final measure was to start the evacuation of all the remaining German population, mainly women, children and old men, who were loaded on freight trains and trucks and sent east.

In some instances the speed of the German advance prevented deportation. In one region where a special staff from Rosenberg's ministry hoped to find some 80,000 *Volksdeutsche* there were only a little over half that number remaining – some 47,000, settled together in two districts: 5,000 in the General District (to use the German designation) of Volhynia and 42,000 in the General District of Zhitomir.[21] The population and age-group structure of these Germans was also characteristic of those remaining in other parts of the Ukraine: two-fifths were children under 14, two-fifths girls and women, and one-fifth youngsters over 14 and men.[22]

The only part of the Ukraine where, even in the first stage of evacuation, the men aged 16–60 were never deported was the region between the Dnestr and the Bug, which had been the western part of the former *guberniia* of Kherson – that part of the Black Sea region handed over to Rumanian sovereignty under the German-Rumanian Convention of Tighina (August 30, 1941) and briefly named 'Transnistria'. The German and Rumanian troops advanced swiftly from the south-west and reached the Dnestr on July 18 (though Odessa fell only on October 16), which prevented even the first steps of the deportation from being put

19 'Akten D. Karl Stumpp', in *Akten des Deutschen Auslandsinstituts Stuttgart*, Manuscript Department, Library of Congress (= DAI-LC), Box 150.
20 DAI-LC, Box 149.
21 GR T 454, R 105, F 1103: Reichsministerium Ost, Führungsstab Politik, Hauptamt I, Ie (Rassenpolitisches Referat), March 1943.
22 G. Wolfrum, *Das Schwarzmeerdeutschtum, Geschichte und Charakter*, Posen, 1944, p. 4. ff.

into effect. Consequently, the population structure of the Germans encountered there was a more natural one, the relatively small number of the men reflecting losses in earlier arrests and banishment: of the 128,949 Germans there, 34,248 were men over 14, 46,076 women over 14, and 48,625 children under 14.[23]

Deportation also remained relatively limited in the neighbouring districts between the Bug and the Dnieper east of 'Transnistria' as well as within the whole of the Dnieper bend.[24] True, here as in other parts of the Ukraine, all the men from 16 to 60 had been evacuated east (the first stage). Still, the registering staff recorded the presence of another 30,000 Germans in the 'General District' of Nikolaev and 70,000 in the 'General District' of Dnepropetrovsk (formerly Ekaterinoslav).[25] Nevertheless, mass displacements 'by lists', together with shootings, took place here when the war overtook the area.

In the regions east of the hard-fought Dnieper, deportation of the German population was almost complete. For this reason, only a few Germans remained behind, for example in the Zaporozhe-Mariupol-Melitopol triangle, 'because organisation broke down and the necessary means of transport were often lacking'.[26] In September 1941, sixty German villages there, with some 50,000 inhabitants altogether, were almost totally evacuated. On September 4, 1941, NKVD personnel who had been brought in sent off the male population aged 16–60 of the villages of Heidelberg (in Russian, Zhuravlevo[27]), Grüntal, Neu-Montal

23 Wolfrum, *Schwarzmeerdeutschtum*, p. 6. On Nov. 14, 1941 the '*volk*-specialists' of *Einsatzgruppe* D were still talking about a German national group numbering 'approximately 175,000 people' (*Ereignismeldung UdSSR*, no. 133, p. 36). Towards the end of the war, there eventually trekked westwards from 'Transnistria' between 134,000 (entry by SS-Hauptsturmführer Berg on Feb. 3, 1944, concerning information from SS-Obersturmführer Dr Wolfrum: Akten des Persönlichen Stabes Reichsführer SS, Bundesarchiv [= BA], NS 19, neu 2656) and 135,000 people (P. Bamm, 'Der grosse Kriegstreck 1944', in GR T 81, R 294, F 2419140–46).

24 GR T 454, R 20, F 153–7, Panzergruppe, 1, Abt, Qu., Gr. H. Qu. 14.9.1941. In the western bend of the Dnieper, the Nikopol/Zaporozhe/ Krivoi Rog area, uniformly German settlement areas were found, some 50 villages with altogether about 50,000 Germans. They were reported to have welcomed the German soldiers enthusiastically and have been receptive to hatred of Communists and anger against Jews as exponents of Bolshevism.

25 GR T 454, R 105, F 1103.

26 *Ereignismeldung UdSSR*, no. 156, Jan. 16, 1942, pp. 51–3.

27 The Russian names of settlements or villages given here conform to *Die deutschen Siedlungen in der Sowjetunion. Ausgearbeitet und herausgegeben von der Sammlung Georg Leibbrandt (Sonderausgabe, nur für den Dienstgebrauch!)*, part 7: Gesamtverzeichnis, Berlin, 1941.

and Andersberg in columns of 200 men at a time on foot in the direction of Stalino (today Donetsk)-Kharkov. The 273 men aged 16–60 from the villages of Marienheim (Perekrestovo), Alexanderheim (Aleksandrovka), Friedrichsfeld and Kornfeld were sent on foot towards Kharkov by way of Pologi and Lazovaia. Some 7,000 men from the villages of Neu-Nassau and Hochstädt (Vysokoe) were put on to freight trains and transported east by way of Voronezh and Penza. A man who escaped from these trains saw how some trains carrying about 3,000 German women and children were bombed from the air near the railway station of Mitrofanovka and a large part of the evacuees were killed. In Millerovo the same witness saw several trains with Germans from the Crimea, the Caucasus and the Stalino district. Between September 22 and 25, 1941, 2,300 men from the villages of Kostheim (Konstantinovka, Krechmonov), Tiefenbrunn, Waldorf, Karlsruhe and Reichfeld were summoned to the War Commissariat and then sent in a body on foot to Rostov.

This triangle of towns was totally evacuated on September 28–29, 1941. Thus, 6,000 persons from the settlements of Hochstädt, Friedrichsfeld and Rosental (among others) were brought to Stalino in freight trains and from there transported to an unknown destination. Two thousand inhabitants of the villages of Tiefenbrunn, Blumental, Tiefenhagen and Petershagen (Petrovskoe, Solodkaia, Balka) were assembled at the railway station of Tokmak but were surprised by German troops before they could be taken away.

The German Mennonites from one of the ten villages comprising the settlement region on the Grishino-Stalino route, some 40 km. northwest of Stalino, were deported in the same stages: on August 31, 1941, men fit for military service were sent to work on fortifications, and on October 5–7, the rest of the population was sent in freight trains towards Tomsk. On September 3, Germans in leading posts in these villages were taken to Stalino and shot, along with other Germans already held there.

Analogous procedures were followed with the Mennonite colonies on the Molochna and in the district around Grunau (Aleksandronevsk) near Mariupol. In villages with 500–600 inhabitants at the beginning of the war it was seldom that more than three or four people who were either sick or remained in hiding. Here too in most cases the men were mobilised for work on fortifications or charged with driving the herds of cattle east. In the absence of the men, the women were assembled in the railway stations, often believing that they were going to follow their husbands, and were then transported east in freight trains.[28] A man who escaped related that the total evacuation of the Germans from these villages north of the Sea of Azov took place in September; the destination was Kazakhstan.[29] It was learned later that from the settlement regions north-east of Melitopol, especially in the area around Halbstadt (Molochansk) where there had been about 15,000 Germans before the war, the population that still remained there after 15–20 per cent had been evacuated to work on fortifications received an order on October 1, 1941, to move within two hours to the assembly point, taking along provisions of clothing and food. From there they were brought together in the larger railway stations (Prishib, Molochna) and on October 3, put into open train wagons. They were told that anyone who stayed behind or tried to escape from the transports *en route* would be shot, and the order for departure was given.[30]

It was in this area north of the Sea of Azov that an *Einsatzkommando* of *Einsatzgruppe* D, charged with registering and 'taking care of' the *Volksdeutsche* as well as exterminating Jews, finally realised that evacuation of Soviet citizens of German nationality was then being carried out with great precision: 'If we compare the times of the transports with the data on the advance of the German troops, we can hardly reckon on still finding Volksdeutsche'.[31] This prognostication was confirmed when the *Einsatzkommando* arrived in Taganrog. The men of the German colonies in the environs of that town had been taken away on September 17, and sent to an unknown destination, and nearly all the remaining Germans had been put on to trains and sent north. The only Germans exempted from deportation were those married to Russians.[32]

Special expectations had been nursed by various Nazi agencies concerning the ethnic German groups living in the strategically important regions of what the Nazi ideologues referred to as the 'Gothic' Crimea and the Caucasus. In the preparations for the planned germanisation of the Crimean Peninsula, the starting point was the assumption that some 49,000 Germans were to be found there;[33] there was even talk of there

---

28 Bericht des SS Sonderkommandos der Volksdeutschen Mittelstelle über den Stand der Erfassungsarbeiten bis zum 15 März 1942; GF T 175, R 68, F 2 585 161 ff.
29 Cf. *Aussendeutscher Wochenspiegel* (Stuttgart), I, 41, Nov. 19, 1941, 41/33.
30 *Ereignismeldung UdSSR*, no. 134, Nov. 17, 1941, pp. 5 ff.
31 *Ibid.*, p. 7.
32 *Ibid.*, no. 141, Dec. 3, 1941.
33 Cf. M. Luther, 'Die Krim unter deutscher Besatzung' in *Forschungen zur osteuropäischen Geschichte*, 3 (1956), pp. 28–98. Here p. 39.

being 51,000.[34] However, the troops entering the Crimea found it empty of *Volksdeutsche*,[35] and according to reports of prisoners of war and eye-witnesses, the German settlements in the Crimea had all been completely evacuated on August 16 and 17, 1941,[36] in great haste. Thus, for example, the German inhabitants of Delizerberg, 5 km. west of Feodosiia, were ordered at 1800 hours on August 17 to be ready for a transport within 3 hours, leaving their possessions behind. At 2100 hours they were sent by train to Kerch and from there transported further to Kazakhstan and Karaganda.[37] On August 16, the inhabitants of Rosental (Shaban-Oba) were ordered to report in 3–4 hours, ready to leave and with a maximum of 50 kilos of luggage per person. They were brought in carts to the railway station, where there was complete chaos on account of the numerous now ownerless transport animals and wagons. From here they were taken by train to the northern and southern districts of the Caucasus, most of them in the region of Voroshilovsk (today Stavropol again) and Ordzhonokidze (formerly Vladikavkaz). In the Caucasus district they were spread out among the different *kolkhozy* to help bring in the harvest. According to eye-witness accounts, men aged 17–55 were partly mobilised and transported to the region of Poltava in the Ukraine to dig tank-traps and defensive trenches.[38] When the harvest was in, the remaining Germans from the Crimea, together with the German inhabitants of the Caucasus districts, were taken to regions beyond the Urals.

The hope that a good number of Germans would be found in the towns of the Crimea[39] also soon proved deceptive. The *Sonderkommando* 11a of *Einsatzgruppe* D, having completed the registration of the *Volksdeutsche*, was therefore obliged to report among other things: 'In Evpatoria there are 74 families, part of them with an infusion of German blood, of whom only 20 persons are of pure German descent.'[40]

34 *Meldungen aus den besetzten Ostgebieten*, no. 4, May 22, 1942, p. 8.
35 Testimony of Field-Marshal von Manstein in *Trial of the Major War Criminals before the International Military Tribunal* (Nuremberg, Nov. 14, 1945–Oct. 1, 1946), Nuremberg, 1948, vol. 20, p. 640.
36 *Ereignismeldung UdSSR*, no. 132, Nov. 12, 1941.
37 *Ibid.*
38 Report of eye-witness Thomas Antoni, in K. Stumpp, 6. *Bericht*, GR T 81, R 599, F 5 386 521.
39 *Ereignismeldung UdSSR*, no. 142, Dec. 5, 1941, p. 8.
40 *Ibid.*, no. 149, Dec. 22, 1941, p. 14.

After the Crimean experiences, the scientific research staff of the Waffen-SS Battalion zbV operating in the Ukraine and Crimea[41] were left to reach the inevitable conclusion:

Stalin's deportation order . . . affects . . . practically the whole of *Deutschtum* in the European part of the Soviet Union. In the settlement regions that are not yet under the protection of the German armies as they storm ahead, the NKVD apparatus begins to function. It now appears that preparations were already made long before hand, and all *Volksdeutsche* were registered and kept under observation. In the Crimea we have been able to ascertain the exact nature of the deportation. Not only *Volksdeutsche* but also married foreign nationals were taken – a total deportation carried out 99.5 per cent. The only people who got away are completely isolated individuals who were able to escape or those who lost their nationality long before. As a rule the NKVD drew up the deportation lists according to 'Blood Law' and did not take into account membership in the CPSU or political opinions. There were only a very few Party members among the *Volksdeutsche* . . . but the Bolsheviks did not trust even them . . . The Crimean Germans were taken first to the Caucasus to bring in the harvest there. They were sent on to Siberia at the beginning of the winter and their fate after that is not yet known.[42]

Before the beginning of the Russian campaign, as the starting-point for estimates of the number of Germans in the Caucasus region, the military-geographical experts of the Third Reich had to take the latest known figure, namely about 60,000. Of these people 40,000 were in the northern Caucasus and 20,000 in rural Transcaucasia as well as in the towns, among which Tbilisi in particular possessed an old German colony.[43] In mid-1942 it could be stated: 'The 50,000 Germans who were in the Caucasus in the [First] World War have been as good as wiped out.'[44] The Germans were deported from the Caucasus late in

---

41 This was the Waffen-SS Battalion zbV with the *Sonderkommando* of the Foreign Ministry (Sonderkommando Künsberg), to which belonged such leading historians as Scheibert, Karasek and Remes.

42 GR T 354, R 184, F 3 838 693 ff. 'Das Deutschtum im Spiegel des Sowjetschrifttums', pp. 103–28 of the brochure of the SS-Battalion zbV, *Meldungen vom Einsatz in der Ukraine und Krim*. This is the first historical indication that lists were used for the deportation proceedings.

43 *Militärgeographische Angaben über das europäische Russland. Die Volgagebiete, Textheft, Generalstab des Heeres, Abteilung für Kriegskarten und Vermessungswesen (IV Mil. Geo.)*, Berlin, 1941, p. 24.

44 *Meldungen aus den besetzten Ostgebieten*, no. 13, July 24, 1942, *Anlage* 5, p. 6.

1941,[45] especially in October and November.[46] From reports in the letters of the deportees, it was possible to reconstruct their route: it led via Salsk, Baku, Krasnovodsk, the Caspian Sea (a crossing that lasted about 26 days, in hard winter conditions – on one ship alone some 775 people died of cold), Ashlabad, Tashkent, Alma Ata, Semipalatinsk, Novosibirsk, Tatarsk, Omsk, Petropavlovsk to Sokhotin in Siberia. The whole journey took about three months in conditons made even more harsh by an early and exceptionally severe winter. In one train alone, 400 children died in the cattle cars on the journey.

On arrival in Siberia, men of 17–50 were mobilised in the labour army (*trudovaia armiia*, shortened to *trudarmiia*). They were put into the mines and other places of hard labour and treated as prisoners. The rest of the deportees – women, children and old men – were not as a rule taken into the collective farms but were placed in so-called 'special settlements' on the bare, frozen earth. (These *spetsialnye poseleniia* – shortened to *spetsposeleniia* were fenced-in settlements with watch towers, where the deportees lived under close NKVD supervision.) Many died of hunger and cold after selling or bartering their last pieces of clothing.

The most numerous ethnic German group totally displaced in the Soviet Union, the Germans of the Autonomous Volga Republic, experienced the deportation in its 'model' schematic form. The National Socialist 'East Planners', especially the *Reich* Minister for the Occupied Eastern Territories, Alfred Rosenberg, had already included this German group pre-emptively in their grandiose planning for the 'New Order for the Eastern Area'. Their hopes evaporated at the beginning of September 1941, when the Presidium of the Supreme Soviet of the USSR decreed the forced deportation of the entire German population of the Volga Republic. Measures, corresponding to those in the overall planning referred to above, for deporting Germans of the Volga region had indeed already been initiated a good deal earlier. They appear to have

---

45 Cf. GR T, R 646: *Bericht über den Kaukasus* (Aug. 28, 1942), RMVP Abt. Ost.: 'All the Germans . . . were already evacuated to Siberia, Turkestan and Kazakhstan a year ago. One only finds occasional Germans, mostly women who were able, through their marriage to Russians, Kalmyks and members of other ethnic groups, to camouflage themselves. Only some are singled out for concentration in special territories; the children are for the most part racially unacceptable. The people are spiritually broken. There are hardly any German men. It is interesting to note that various German families who were, for example, evacuated from the Crimea in the past year got stuck in the north Caucasus.'

46 *Meldungen aus den besetzten Ostgebieten*, no. 34. Dec. 18, 1942.

been begun about a month after the German attack,[47] that is in the second half of July. The first large-scale measure was taken at the end of July – the clearing and evacuation of the republic capital, Engels (previously Pokrovsk), and of the principal towns of the *raiony*. But already in the first half of July, armed detachments of the NKVD had been sent into these towns where they occupied public and administrative buildings. All the streets were guarded, and inhabitants leaving the town risked the death penalty. The entire communications network was cut off and contact with the outside world became impossible. Transport was at a standstill. All Germans holding leading positions were arrested and disappeared (which generally meant that they were shot), and their positions were taken over by NKVD personnel.[48] With the top stratum of leaders eliminated, preparations were made for liquidating other sectors and carrying out the deportation. Thus on July 28, 1941, 80 prison officials were sent to Engels from Kursk 'to shoot part of the Volga Germans there on the spot'.[49] On the same day a commando unit of 600 men and a few days later one of 900 Communist Party members were sent to the Volga Republic from Kursk to take over the farms of the evacuated Germans.[50]

According to some eye-witness accounts, the mass deportation of the Germans began in parts of the Volga Republic in July;[51] according to those from other areas it took place in August.[52] The population was ordered to be ready to leave within a short time, usually two hours. Immediately after large parts of the Volga region were cleared, streams

47 Vvedensky, 'Volga', *Studies*, Munich, p. 50. Immediately after the German attack there had already been mass shootings of Volga Germans interned in the north Russian and north Siberian penal camps. The writer was informed by Prof. S. Frenkin, now living in Jerusalem, that in his camp in the Komi Autonomous Republic, on the first night of the German Soviet campaign, the Volga Germans were called together and shot against a wall in the camp, among them a friend of his named Grimm. On the deportation of the Volga Germans, see too G. Geilke, ' "Rehabilitierung" der Volgadeutschen' in *Jahrbuch für Ostrecht*, 6 (1965), 1, pp. 35–9, and A. Sheehy, 'The Volga Germans: Soviet Treatment of some National Minorities' in American Historical Society of Germans from Russia, *Papers*, 1973, 13, pp. 1–9.
48 Vvedensky, p. 50.
49 According to statements by a Communist Party member, a prisoner of war of the Germans, who took part in this operation: *Ereignismeldungen UdSSR*, no. 169, Feb. 16, 1942, p. 11.
50 *Ibid*.
51 *Volja*, Munich, 1953, pp. 19–24.
52 *Sotsialisticheskii Vestnik* (New York/Paris), 1946, no. 1, pp. 18–19.

of refugees flowed in, mostly from Rumania (here especially from Bessarabia), and directed to the empty villages. They found themselves in places and houses that had been abandoned in extreme haste, the tables still laid with half-eaten meals. Bellowing cattle, untended for hours or days, completed the spectacle of hasty abandonment of hereditary homesteads.[53] V. Volzhanin, sent to take care of the cattle left behind in a former German Volga colony, reported that tens of thousands of these animals had to be slaughtered.[54]

In August 1941 provocations were staged on a large scale, planned either as tests of the Volga Germans' loyalty or else to provide grounds for convictions; these resulted in more mass shootings and deportations.[55] Planes with German markings painted on them dropped on to some of the Volga colonies parachutists in German uniforms who asked the Germans living there to take them in and hide them for some hours as the vanguard of the German army. Wherever they were taken in, the villages concerned were immediately liquidated. In the course of these actions numerous house-searches took place; swastika flags were found in the lofts or granaries of many houses (at the time of the Molotov-Ribbentrop Pact they had been distributed as part of the preparations for a planned visit by Hitler to the Volga colonies) and their residents too were liquidated. German Communist Party leaders in the regions concerned were held responsible for what occurred and also executed;[56] as German traitors (or as their accomplices) they were shot according to martial law. In a Decree of the Supreme Soviet dated August 28, 1941, published in the *Supreme Soviet Gazette* of September 2,[57] the measures that had already been taken and completed were codified and legitimised:[58]

53 Dr Ada Steinberg of Jerusalem, then a refugee from Kishinev, was directed in a stream of refugees to the ghost-like empty quarter of Engels. She recounted how the refugees made the shattering discovery that the Germans had been deported only a few hours or days before their arrival.

54 Vvedensky, pp. 50–1.

55 It can be assumed that the planning and execution of this operation, as well as the entire deportation of the Germans from the Volga region was the responsibility of General Serov, for many years head of the NKVD. Maia Kaganskaia, a former resident of Kiev now living in Jerusalem, informed the author that a member of the Ukrainian Communist Party Central Committee, known to her, took part in the planning and execution of the parachute operation. Details of it were given to the author by Dr A. Ludmirskii of Jerusalem, among others, who learned of these events during a work sojourn in the region to which the Germans concerned were deported.

56 *Sotsialisticheskii vestnik* (New York-Paris), 1946, no. 1, pp. 18–19.

57 *Vedomosti Verkhovnogo Soveta SSSR*, no. 38 (153), Sept. 2, 1941.

58 Cited here according to the certified copy of the translation of the Reich Ministry for the East in GR T 454, R 20, F 420 (with minor corrections).

Re the evacuation of the Germans living in the Volga region:
According to trustworthy information received by the military authorities, thousands and tens of thousands of saboteurs and spies among the German population living in the *raiony* of the Volga Republic were awaiting a signal from Germany in order to carry out disruption in the *raiony* of the Volga region settled by Germans.

None of the Germans living in the *raiony* of the Volga region informed the Soviet authorities of the presence of so large a body of saboteurs and spies among the Germans of the Volga region, whence it follows that the German population conceals in its midst enemies of the Soviet people and the Soviet government.

If there are subversive activities which German saboteurs and spies in the German Republic of the Volga region and neighbouring *raiony* are plotting on instructions from Germany and which lead to bloodshed, the Soviet government, in accordance with the wartime laws, is obliged to take punitive action against the whole German population of the Volga region. In order to avoid such undesirable shootings and prevent grave bloodshed, the Presidium of the Supreme Soviet has found it necessary to evacuate the entire German population living in the *raiony* of the Volga region to other *raiony*, with the provision that the evacuees have land allotted to them and State assistance to establish themselves in the new *raiony*.

Raiony in the regions of Novosibirsk and Omsk, of the Altai, Kazakhstan and other contiguous localities possessing abundant cultivable land are indicated for the re-settlement.

The Committee of State Security is hereby instructed urgently to carry out the evacuation of all the Germans of the Volga region and to distribute land and equipment in the new *raiony* to the Germans evacuated from the Volga region.

Chairman of the Presidium of the Supreme Soviet of the USSR
M. KALININ

Moscow, the Kremlin   *Secretary of the Presidium*
28.8.1941   A. GORKIN

At the end of August 1941, combined NKVD units arrived in all parts of the Volga to carry out the total deportation. Nearly 400,000 people were assembled, entained and transported in extremely harsh conditions,[59] and the conditions which the Germans found at their

---

59 Edward Crankshaw, as a foreigner, was able to witness the despatch of the Germans from the Saratov district: 'It was very much like any other mass deportation in Eastern Europe under emergency conditions: long-settled families suddenly ravished from their homes and driven in draggled, dazed procession to the railway, there to be herded into sealed freight cars with no room to lie down, no apparent sanitary

destination were also extremely hard.[60] Besides the 'special settlements' and the labour army, many of the men deported reached the dreaded Vorkuta coal mines.[61] Germans from the Volga region who were living in other parts of the Soviet Union were also deported to the east at this time.[62]

The independent press of the world reacted to the draconian measures taken against such a 'harmless little people'[63] with consternation;[64] nevertheless it was well understood even in neutral countries such as Switzerland that the Soviet government was at that very moment exert-

---

arrangements, and with, to say the least, inadequate food. The weaker would probably die where they stood on the interminable journey into Asia, with the wait at every siding an instalment of eternity. To all appearances, these unfortunates were indistinguishable from Russian peasants. They might have been a trainload of dispossessed kulaks being taken away to the mines. It was extremely cold: the winter of 1941 began too soon. But there was no lamentation. The Volga Germans had learned that much from the plain. They stood wedged in their vans, the fortunate ones gazing out impassively through the bars in the top of each door, and waited like Russian peasants, because there was nothing else for them to do' (*Russia and the Russians*, London, 1947, p. 38).

A subsequent Instruction for the execution of the Decree of Aug. 28, 1941 (cited in Stumpp, *Auswirkungen*, p. 7), stipulated that the families must be brought to the station for entraining in carts, but that then the heads of families must be separated. The men must then be entrained in separate trains, made ready beforehand, presumably for the purpose of their transfer to the labour army. 'Nothing must be said about the above-mentioned separation from the head of the family.' See, too, the report of a prisoner of war on the deportation of the Germans from the Volga region in: GR 77, R 1028, F 6 500 735 ff. *Abteilung Ausland/Abwehr*, WF ST/W Pr, July 9, 1942.

60 See the report of a prisoner of war over the treatment of Germans from the Volga region in Siberia in GR T 454, R 17, F 545 ff. *OKW und SS-Sonderkommando*, *Reich* Ministry for the Occupied Eastern Territories, Jan.–May 1943.

61 DW 47, 288 596–8 Fremde Heere Ost (IIb), no. 1506/44 secret March 3, 1944, to: Vertr. d. AA b OKH (Gen St dH): 'Excerpt from . . . hearing: In June 1942, 15,000 Volga Germans (men 15–50 years old) were carried off to Vorkuta. They were put to work in the coal mines . . .'

62 W. Carroll, a journalist accredited to Moscow at this time, reported that simultaneously with the deportations of the Germans from the Volga region, 'the Volga Germans were weeded out of Moscow. Many diplomats and journalists had employed Volga Germans as servants. They were clean, industrious and efficient. Now the police ordered them to take provisions for two weeks and to go immediately by train to Siberia. Soviet citizens of Finnish descent were also weeded out' (*We're in This with Russia*, Cambridge, Mass., 1942, pp. 83 ff.).

63 *National-Zeitung* (Basel), Sept. 15, 1941.

64 *Neue Zürcher Zeitung*, Sept. 29, 1941.

ing itself to the utmost to defend the Dnieper line – the last strategic protection of the Donets basin – and would balk at no sacrifice to stop Hitler's armies from reaching the approaches to the Urals, the country's second-largest supply base for the armaments and war industry. If the Donets basin were lost, the concentration of German-settled areas of the Volga region round Saratov and Kuibyshev (previously Samara), joined on the south by the German settlements round Stalingrad and to the east by numerous German settlements in the regions from Orenburg (from 1938 to 1957 (Chekalov) to Ufa, represented the way forward to the vital industrial and energy centres of the southern Ural region.

In Germany the authorities concerned were thoroughly shaken.[65] Rosenberg, on learning of the Decree of August 28, 1941, laid down 'Guidelines for radio propaganda on the banishment of the Volga Germans to Siberia',[66] in which he made the Jews of the occupied territories in the east the victims of his impotent fury.[67] These Guidelines included the following:

It is proposed that in radio broadcasts to the USSR, England and the USA, the outrageous crime of the Bolshevik rulers against the Volga Germans be denounced in the harshest terms. In these broadcasts it must be made unmistakably clear that if the scheme announced by the Bolsheviks for deporting the Volga Germans is carried out, Jewry in the regions under German control will pay for this crime many times over. It must be affirmed that infamous Jewish deeds have up to now been expiated only in single instances, but that Jewry as a whole still enjoys far-reaching rights in the areas under German control. With the implementation of the proceedings announced by the Bolsheviks against the Volga Germans, the Jews of Central Europe will likewise be deported to the most easterly of the regions under German administration. If the crimes against the Volga Germans are carried out, then Jewry will have to settle the account for these crimes many times over.

65 See *Frankfurter Zeitung*, Sept. 11, 1941: 'Terror an der Wolga'.
66 GR T 454, R 20, F 375 ff., Berlin, Sept. 13, 1941, with a covering note from Dr G. Leibbrandt, Head of the *Hauptabteilung* I (Political) of the *Reich* Ministry for the Occupied Eastern Territories, to O. Bräutigam: 'On the instructions of the minister, I request that you bring to the attention of the Führer immediately through his adjutants the following ''Guidelines for radio propaganda on the banishment of the Volga Germans to Siberia'' and, if he agrees, pass it on immediately to the *Reich* press chief.'
67 This is just one instance of the deadly link between the fate of the Soviet Germans with that of Central and East European Jewry. This link was programmed organisationally by the Nazi planning staffs.

These sentences were framed in the *Reich* Ministry for the Occupied Eastern Territories at a time when hundreds of thousands of Jews in the occupied eastern regions had already been isolated or else systematically liquidated by the *Einsatzgruppen* (mobile action units) of the *Sicherheitspolizei* and the *Sicherheitsdienst*: by the end of September 1941 *Einsatzgruppe* D, operating in the zone of Army Group South alone, had already killed 35,782 persons in the southern Russian zones concerned, mainly Jews, some Communists and some *Volksdeutsche* regarded as unreliable.[68] Furthermore, at this same time preparations were already in full swing for the Wannsee Conference on the 'Final Solution' of the Jewish question (January 20, 1942), where the head of the Political Division, G. Leibbrandt, would take part as the representative of the *Reich* Ministry for the Occupied Eastern Territories.[69] The Guidelines were thus nothing but a propaganda bluff intended to cover up the real facts and shift the Third Reich's guilt for the terrible fate of the *Volksdeutsche* on to the Jews of Central Europe, whose deportation and liquidation had begun long before.

The removal of the Germans from the Volga region had been completed by the end of September 1941.[70] An enactment of September 7, 1941,[71] abolished the Autonomous Volga Republic and its *raiony* were annexed to other administrative units. These measures showed that the Soviet government regarded the deportation of the Germans from the Volga region as final. To obviate or forestall eventual protests inside and outside the country, a show trial was held in Moscow on October 8, 1941, when a German from Saratov with the well-chosen name of Preuss was condemned as a spy in the service of Germany,[72] as a kind of retrospective legitimation of the measures already implemented.

Practically complete evacuation had also been carried out in the other regions of the Soviet Union conquered by the German Wehrmacht. In the northern sector of the zone of operations of Army Group South, the

---

68 See H. Krausnick and H.-H. Wilhelm, *Die Truppe des Weltanschauungskrieges. Die Einsatzgruppen der Sicherheitspolizei und des SD, 1938–1942*, I: H. Krausnick, *Die Einsatzgruppen vom Anschluss Österreichs bis zum Feldzug gegen die Sowjetunion. Entwicklung und Verhältnis zur Wehrmacht*, Stuttgart, 1981, p. 202.

69 See *Besprechungsprotokoll des Wannsee-Konferenz mit Teilnehmerliste*, NO-2586, Eich 74; Reproduction in *Encyclopaedia Judaica*, Jerusalem, 1971, vol. 16, p. 263.

70 *Aussendeutscher Wochenspiegel* (Stuttgart), Oct. 1, 1941 (Suppl. 34) cited a report from Bern stating: 'The transportation of the Volga Germans has been completed.'

71 *Vedomosti Verkhovnogo Soveta SSSR*, 1941, no. 40.

72 *Neue Zürcher Zeitung*, Oct. 10, 1941.

Einsatzkommandos of *Einsatzgruppe* C discovered that 'the greater part' of the Germans settled there had been 'carried off to the interior of Russia' in the autumn of 1941.[73] In the contiguous regions to the east, Poltava and Kharkov, *Einsatzkommando* 4b of *Einsatzgruppe* C still found a few remnants of the former colonist groups: some 800 Germans in the district round Berdiansk and some 3,200 in Chernikovka; 600–700 Germans who had remained behind were registered in the towns of Slaviansk, Kramatorskaia, Konstantinovka and Artemovsk, and just 87 in the district of Poltava.[74]

The findings were similar in the zone of operations of Army Group Centre. Only a small workers' colony on the outskirts of the city of Minsk, former Volga German peasants who had fled in 1928 from deku-lakisation and compulsory collectivisation, had escaped deportation. It comprised several thousand families.[75] Furthermore, the number of Germans registered in the towns east and west of the upper Dnieper very seldom reached even 200[76] (Borisov, Bobruisk, Vitebsk) or in some cases 100 (Smolensk, Mogilev, Orsha). In the region east of the Dnieper, the population had 'long before already been evacuated according to plan'.[77] In the region north-east of Chernigov, the Germans had been 'arrested at the outbreak of the war and carried off to the interior of Russia'.[78] The ten or fifteen German families of Briansk had migrated from the Volga region like the Minsk Germans: they were put on freight cars in mid-September and 'forcibly deported to an unknown destination'.[79] The same was true of some fifteen Volga German families in Ordzhonokidzegrad and for the Germans from Iasma. These facts led to the conclusion that, 'the Bolsheviks have also recently evacuated every single *Volksdeutsche* from the present zone [of war operations]'.[80] In the districts east and north of Smolensk hardly any Germans were still to be found. 'As regards Bolshevik measures against *Volksdeutsche* in the Red Army, it can be affirmed that all of them were taken out of a red construction battalion in September and transported in an unknown direction.'[81] Finally, 133 persons presented themselves in Pskov 'at the

73 *Ereignismeldung UdSSR*, no. 187, March 30, 1942, p. 10.
74 *Ibid.*, no. 187, p. 9 ff.
75 *Ibid.*, no. 176, March 4, 1942, p. 5.
76 *Ibid.*, no. 194, April 21, 1942.
77 *Ibid.*, no. 133, Nov. 14, 1941, p. 4.
78 *Ibid.*, no. 107, Oct. 8, 1941.
79 *Ibid.*, no. 133, p. 10.
80 *Ibid.*
81 *Ibid.*, no. 145, Dec. 12, 1941.

proclamation calling on persons of German origin to register, mainly impelled by the hope of financial support. A third had German parents, a third German fathers, a sixth German mothers.' Of these, 66 were children under the age of sixteen and about four-fifths were women; half the persons registered were over sixty years of age.[82]

In the zone of operations of Army Group North, a German population had for nearly two centuries been concentrated in the district around Leningrad. All the men of military age from these old artisan colonies had been taken out and sent to 'labour units in other parts of Russia', their 'whereabouts unknown' in all instances.[83] The first registration produced 1,644 persons of German descent in the Leningrad colonies (353 men, 680 women and 611 children under fifteen).[84] By the time of the transfer to the resettlement camps by the Third Reich, their number had increased to 2,800.[85] Some 1,000 Germans from the Ingermanland district were transported together with them to the West.

As for the fate of the more than 20,000 Germans estimated to be inside the city of Leningrad, it was known that 'numerous *Volks-deutsche* are crowded together in utter isolation in the small former German colony of Petrovskaia Slavianka. They are not allowed to leave the settlement and contact with them is completely forbidden'.[86] These German inhabitants of Leningrad were finally deported to Siberia on March 16, 1944, after the end of the blockade.[87]

The deportation figures

With the exception of the Volga area, the numbers of Germans in the different regions affected by the Soviet deportations can only be ascertained indirectly, that is by comparing the figures of Germans registered on the German side. This method is unreliable and inaccurate insofar as many of the German figures were grossly exaggerated from the beginning of the registration,[88] especially with the introduction of the German

82 *Ibid.*, no. 189, Apr. 3, 1942, p. 5. The proclamation had been issued by the occupying German army.
83 *Ibid.*, no. 151, Jan. 5, 1942, p. 7.
84 *Ibid.*, p. 6.
85 *Ibid.*, no. 181, Feb. 27, 1942.
86 *Ibid.*, no. 170, Jan. 18, 1942, p. 4.
87 Conquest, *Nation*, pp. 107–8.
88 See criticism by Dr R. Korherr, Himmler's executive statistician, of the figures of the ethnic Germans and their re-germanisation by the Ethnic German Liaison Office (Vo Mi); G. Reitlinger, *The SS: Alibi of a Nation, 1922–1945*, Melbourne, 1956, p. 221.

National List (*Deutsche Volksliste*) and analogous procedures. According to German data, the treks of the *Volksdeutschen* leaving Russia at the end of the war brought some 350,000 persons[89] to the west:[90] 72,000 from the districts of Kherson, Nikolaev, Nikopol, Kharkov, Zaporozhe, Kiev, Krivoi Rog, Melitopol, Mariupol, Khortitsa and the Melitopol region (the 'Russian Operation'); 73,000 from Grunau-West (Aleksandrovsk), Halbstadt (Molochansk), Gronau, Kherson, Nikopol, Dnepropetrovsk, the Zaporozhe region on both sides of the Dnieper, the Nikolaev region (the 'Black Sea Operation'), 44, 600 from the districts around Zhitomir in the western Ukraine; and 135,000 from 'Transnistria'. Along with this so-called 'Great Trek' leaving Russia when the German Eastern Front collapsed, small groups of Germans from the districts under the German military government had already been sent off to the West before: 3,800 from the former German colonies around Leningrad and Ingermanland and 11,500 from the combat areas of the Northern Caucasus, the Donbass and the Kalmyk steppe. Another 10,500 Germans were evacuated to the West from the White Russian districts around Minsk before the advance of the Soviet troops.

This total of some 350,000 persons who left the Soviet Union also included 'germanisable' aliens (*eindeutschungsfähige fremdvölkische*), 're-germanisable' people of German or partly German origin (*wiedereindeutschungsfähige deutschstämmige*), and 'alien' (*fremdvölkische*) relatives of *Volksdeutsche*. If one takes this figure into account, unverifiable as it is, then our assumption that there were 1 to 1.1 million Germans in the European part of the Soviet Union at the outbreak of the German-Soviet war suggests the conclusion that a maximum of 750,000[91] Germans, but probably between 650,000[92] and 700,000,[93] were deported from the European to the Asian part of the Soviet Union.

89 These were the figures for 1944. Compared with them, according to the first registrations of Vo Mi (up to Feb. 15, 1942) and before the systematic implementation of the German national lists and analagous procedures, only 185,408 Germans were registered: 43,377 men, 67,273 women and 73,208 children under 14; see *Bericht des SS-Sonderkommandos der Vo Mi*, GR T 175. R 68, F 2 585 161 ff.

90 Given here according to the compilation of P. Bamm, *Kriegstreck*; see also Office of Strategic Services, Research and Analysis, no. 1611: *Population Movements of Black Sea Germans according to German Sources*. Nov. 13, 1944.

91 Even A. Mergenthaler while casting doubt on this figure, made use of it himself (*Landsleute*, p. 123).

92 This was approximately the figure reached by Stumpp as well, and it was adopted by A. Giesinger, *From Catherine to Khrushchev: The Story of Russia's Germans*, Winnipeg, 1974, p. 307.

93 Mergenthaler (*Landsleute*, 123) has said that this figure could be close to the truth.

The question of the deportation lists

The question arises of how the NKVD succeeded in carrying out this deportation operation with such precision and in such a relatively short time, despite the extraordinary confusion of the war and in front zones that were being fought over.

It is a revealing fact that eye-witnesses occasionally refer to previously prepared lists of the Germans in the districts concerned. Hermann Maurer's dramatic account was also based on these eye-witness reports: 'Murder-lists were drawn up, whole districts had to be rooted out. This was prevented only by the swift advance of the German troops. But large units of population in the settlements beyond the Dnieper were carried off – the 51,000 Germáns from the Crimea packed off headlong in trains for the Far East in August 1941. 380,000 Volga Germans . . . were driven from their homeland and exposed to annihilation . . . 250,000–300,000 were the pitiful remnant remaining between the Dnieper and the Caspian Sea.'[94]

In fact one has to start from the realisation that without some list containing the names of German inhabitants of the different villages, locations and cities in these vast spaces, a deportation of this nature would hardly have been possible. Given this assumption, the question arises of when such lists were drawn up.

That gap in our knowledge can now be considered filled, thanks to the personal testimony of Professor Evgeniia Evelson, a jurist who practiced law in Moscow for many years. Living in the West today, she does research on what are called economic crimes in the Soviet Union. While a student in Moscow, Evgeniia Evelson took part in planning and drawing up the lists. The last quarter of 1934, she says, was when this was done, a dating which appears justified in the light of German-Soviet relations at the time. In October 1933 Rudolf Nadolny, an advocate of closer relations with the Soviet Union, took over from R.von Dirksen as ambassador in Moscow. He sought to inform the Foreign Ministry and Hitler of the barrier of mistrust and fear which had existed in Moscow since Hitler took power and that had tended furthermore to become worse during his posting there. Nadolny's removal after less than a year in Moscow (Count Schulenburg took his place in October 1934) deepened the Russian mistrust. According to German diplomatic reports, Moscow lived in fear of war, and the dynamics of the Soviet Union's current foreign policy (joining the League of Nations, Anthony Eden's

94 GR T 454, R 20, F 546-608, as well as T 454, R 20, F 498 ff.
95 The statement was made in Russian, and has been edited by the author of this chapter.

visit to Moscow, mutual assistance pacts with France and Czechoslovakia) showed clearly that the government's main concern in its foreign relations was to be prepared for a German attack. So the neutralisation of potential sympathisers with the enemy – about a million Germans – would be a natural precautionary measure and a matter of foresight. A characteristic measure in this direction was the total evacuation of the Germans from a band of territory 100 km. wide on the Volhynian frontier. Begun on January 1, 1935, an ominous date for legislative and administrative measures, this deportation, inspired by fear or foresight regarding the future war, was the first act foreshadowing the deportations carried out in the summer and autumn of 1941.

Professor Evelson put together the story as she remembers it in a document, written in September, 1979, which she has generously placed at our disposal:

If the Soviet press talks of Hitler's attack on the Soviet Union as unexpected and says that there were no data to be had [inside the Soviet Union] concerning the Germans, I can only say this is untrue. Leaving aside the question of secret service intelligence and the political aspects . . . I shall describe something that occurred when I was young in connection with my work, something which I witnessed and where I was an executive agent. To be admitted to a university in Russia at that time, one was expected to submit a practical piece of work. I had been working for three years in a pencil factory in Moscow, the Krasin Works. As was the fashion in those days, I was suddenly transferred from the factory to the administration [the *apparat*] of the then National Commissariat of Local and Light Industry (in the building of the National Commissariat for Heavy Industry on Nogin Square). The National Commissar was then a simple worker at the tramways depot, a veteran Bolshevik and former underground fighter, Konstantin Konstantinovich Strievskii. As for me, I was appointed deputy head of the Schools Administration and Study/Distribution Division. At the same time I was taking evening courses at the P. Stuchka Institute for Jurisprudence.

At some time late in 1934 (that is, after Hitler came to power in Germany) an invitation arrived addressed to me (but as 'Mr') to appear at a particular time before the Central Committee of the CPSU on a given day and hour. I took my identity card and went along. The room I entered contained a group of people. Sitting at the table was a small man with thick glasses, who turned to me and said, 'Who is it you are looking for?' I gave the name. 'Well, well, so Strievskii is collecting a kindergarten?' I said: 'Do you mean I can leave?' – He answered: 'No, stay!'

This man was Boris Stepanovich Revskii, G. Malenkov's representative on the Industry Division of the Central Committee of the CPSU and Head of its Accounts Section. Before this he had worked with L. Kaganovich in the Ukraine, and in the administrative apparatus of the Central Committee of the

CPSU. Revskii told the gathering that they had been called to consider a very important matter, so important that all present were bound to the strictest secrecy. He told us that the Central Committee was interested in receiving information on people of German nationality – where and in what positions they were employed in the whole country. (I remember that this occurred after Hitler's take-over!) 'How can we manage it so that every official, every National Commissar, knows every last German and all about him as well? [And this in such a way] that no one suspects that the Central Committee of the CPSU, as well as all the relevant institutions, is interested in the matter? . . .'

A lot of senseless suggestions were put forward. I sat there in despair, still bristling at the way I had been received. Then I stood up, and these veteran workers and party cadres gaped to see such a young woman, also the only Jewess at this extraordinary session. I said that the Supreme Council for Agriculture was soon going to be divided into two National Commissariats and that these Commissariats did not yet possess any exact allocation, not only of personnel but also regarding the operations they would be given to carry out. For these reasons I would propose an enforced 'passportisation' of the whole of industry [registration of individual certificates or identity cards]. There should be a review of the available basic capital, and the entire size of the worker-leadership cadres should also be re-examined along with the technical and engineering personnel. Then these postings should be allocated in quotas according to nationalities, so that it would not appear that interest was being concentrated only on people of German nationality. When I had finished stating my proposals, the assembled 'hard core' cadres gazed at me in astonishment. Revskii got up and said, 'Where did Strievskii dig out this pearl?' A group was accordingly set up to work out a scheme for 'passportising' industry; Revskii himself was involved in it, as were the head of the Cadres Division of the National Commissariat for the Forestry Industry – a certain Dynin (a Communist Party member, naturally) – and myself. . . . My scheme covered the whole of industry and all the leading positions in it according to nationality. It was intensive work, and my scheme was applied throughout the Soviet Union. I certainly cannot say how the Germans were registered on the spot in the Soviet institutions, the party organs, and the German Volga Republic. But of this I am certain: by the end of 1934 *every German* born in Russia or brought there temporarily or permanently as a worker in the wide field of Soviet industry in the country *was individually registered to the fullest extent* regardless of what branch of industry he belonged to, and this in each and every National Commissariat, and also *all personnel data* were listed and collected by the Central Committee of the CPSU.

The work was completed in due time and in the strictest secrecy, though the 'Secret' stamp was not always used, to avoid drawing attention to the so-called 'passportisation'.

At the end of 1934 *all the lists of all the Germans working in industry*, irrespective of their position or function, were presented to the Central Committee of the CPSU. Thus there was no longer a single corner in the whole Soviet Union that was not completely covered by the registration, nor were there any longer Germans whose official employment and family size were not known. As for Revskii, with whom I remained on good terms right up till I left the Soviet Union [in the mid-1970s], I know that when Malenkov was removed from the Central Committee of the CPSU, all his favourites were got rid of, and Revskii was then pensioned off by the Party. . . .

On instructions from the Central Committee of the CPSU, the following Special Mention was entered on my service record: 'For completion of special tasks of the Central Committee of the CPSU, thanks are attested to E.A. Evelson. She is to be paid a double month's salary and sent, journey and expenses paid, to the sanatorium in the city of Kislovodsk.'

The Germans (my acquaintances) know nothing of this part of my biography; they do not know that I was able to pinpoint every German employed in the whole of Soviet industry together with his family. Nor could they have known that in the war the Germans would kill my husband and leave my daughter fatherless. I was not married at the time. My address then was: Moscow, Kropotkin St., 28, Apartment no. 11.

To sum up, I repeat: at the end of 1934 the Central Committee of the Communist Party of the Soviet Union had before it the most precise data on the numbers and occupations of all the Germans living in the USSR.

All the secret service work and repressions carried out later were guided by the data we collected and arranged.

I completed my studies in the Institute and, thank God, was accepted into the programme for a doctorate, as otherwise . . . [my fate would have been the same as that of Strievskii].

K.K. Strievskii, a fine man who lived right up till the end in his modest house at the tramway depot, was shot in 1937. The same fate befell his successor, the Mayor of Moscow, K.V. Uchanov.

CHAPTER FOUR

THE ETHNIC GERMANS UNDER NAZI RULE

Ingeborg Fleischhauer

Nazi documents touching on the question of the Soviet ethnic Germans give the impression that this group, which had been well assimilated since its first arrival at the time of Catherine the Great, had only fallen slightly short of the expectations and plans of the German occupation forces during the Second World War.[1] But, as various historians have pointed out (Lucy Dawidowicz, for instance), the Nazi documents themselves do not provide a reliable basis for the drawing of historical conclusions. Unfortunately, there is a scarcity of other material that would give the scholar a complete all-embracing picture of Soviet German life under Nazi occupation. For the Western researchers, Soviet sources, especially those of the local and regional archives, constitute almost totally unknown territory, and in any case are not made available. Objective eye-witness reports are limited in number as well as in accuracy. However, useful supplementary information is to be found in reports of the legal investigations into Nazi crimes, collected under the rubric of National Socialist Crimes of Violence (*Nationalsozialistische Gewaltverbrechen* – NSG) in the Central Collective Office of the Federal Legal Administration[2] in Ludwigsburg, Germany. The most relevant materials here are the depositions taken in the course of the prosecution of crimes committed by the *Einsatzgruppen* (mobile action units)[3] and of the *volksdeutscher Selbstschutz* (the ethnic Germans' self-defence units), which add valuable information to the relevant investigations made in

1 The National Archives in Washington, DC, hold the most complete collection of the Captured German War Documents ('German Records') in microfilm. The majority of the originals have by now been handed back to West Germany and are available in various archives there. A small part of Captured German Documents, still in the original, can be studied in the Manuscript Division of the Library of Congress, and a still smaller part is in the Hoover Institution, Palo Alto.

2 Zentrale Stelle der Landesjustizverwaltung in Ludwigsburg/Württemberg, also called Zentrale Stelle zur Ermittlung Nationalsozialistischer Gewaltverbrechen.

3 On the *Einsatzgruppen*, see H. Krausnick and H.-H. Wilhelm, *Die Truppe des Weltanschauungskrieges. Die Einsatzgruppen der Sicherheitspolizei und des SD, 1938–1942*, 2 vols, Stuttgart, 1981; A. Streim, 'Zum Beispiel: Die Verbrechen der Einsatzgruppen in der Sowjetunion' in A. Rückerl (ed.), *NS-Prozesse nach 25 Jahren Strafverfolgung*, Karlsruhe, 1971, pp. 65–106.

preparation for the Nuremberg Military Tribunal, especially in relation to the *'Einsatzgruppen* case'.[4] These additional materials make possible a closer understanding of Nazi expectations, the behaviour of the occupation forces, and the ethnic Germans' response.

The German occupation forces in the Soviet Union did much to make the ethnic Germans in the occupied areas part of the German Master-Race of Eastern Europe. But, although there were clear cases of voluntary collaboration, Nazi efforts on the whole failed. The majority of the ethnic Germans in the Soviet Union did not either embrace National Socialism as an ideology, or act in the way a member of the 'German race' was expected to act in the East European dumping ground. Instead of becoming active supporters of the Nazi occupation agencies, the ethnic Germans themselves became, in part, victims of the ill-fated Nazi eastward expansion and, in particular, of Himmler's machinery of destruction of the East European nations.

This may seem surprising for, as we saw in chapter 2, these Germans had suffered greatly under successive Soviet measures against religion, against the kulaks, and against national and social cohesiveness within the national minorities.[5] Liquidation, deportation and other forms of social and economic repression had left their mark on these communities, together with the considerable losses in the years of the great hunger that followed forced collectivisation. By the end of the 1930s the fate of the Soviet Germans had become desperate. The short spring in Soviet-German relations during the first year after the Molotov-Ribbentrop Pact did not essentially alleviate their situation; it rather enhanced the hope that they would be allowed to leave their historic areas of settlement and emigrate, if not to Germany, then preferably to Canada or South America.

The German invasion of the Soviet Union on June 22, 1941 changed their existence dramatically. When the less indoctrinated units of the German Wehrmacht arrived in their villages, enthusiasm was shown in some places. But traditional offerings of bread and salt were made to the Wehrmacht in the first weeks of the eastern campaign not only by ethnic Germans – representatives of other national groups, from the Baltic

---

4 *Trials of War Criminals before the Nuremberg Military Tribunals*, vol. IV: 'The Einsatzgruppen Case' and 'The RuSHA Case', Nuremberg, Oct. 1946-April 1949, Washington, DC, 1950.

5 These questions will be addressed in the forthcoming large-scale study: B. Pinkus and I. Fleischhauer, 'Die Deutschen in der Sowjetunion. Geschichte einer nationalen Minderheit im 20. Jahrhundert'.

nations to the Ukrainians, were equally relieved to see an end to the traumatic experience of Stalinism. Their mood and situation changed drastically with the arrival of the SS troups. In fact, the ethnic Germans' relation to the SS is the main key to understanding their role and behaviour under German occupation.[6] For if high SS functionaries claimed that 'the European East belongs to the *Schutzstaffel* [SS],' this was most true of all in the case of the ethnic Germans in the occupied parts of the Soviet Union. After an intense struggle between the appropriate Nazi agencies, the Soviet Germans were placed within the competence of Himmler's units and became objects of their colonisation and germanisation plans for Eastern Europe.[7] A long series of developments led to the eventual control of the ethnic German's fate by the SS.

In the earliest days of its existence, the Nazi Party showed very little interest in the Soviet Germans. This was true too of its leader, Adolf Hitler. Moreover, what Hitler knew of Russia he had learned partly from his confidant Alfred Rosenberg, himself a half-educated man, and partly from reading treatises on Russia written by members of the Pan-Germanic League. Since these informants were mainly people of Baltic German descent whose meagre knowledge of Russia proper was often distorted, Hitler's notions of Russia tended to be vague, simplistic and irrelevant. The former Russian Germans, he held, had been either massacred or bolshevised and in the latter case were useless for the furthering of German plans in the East. In addition to this, where the starving and suffering national minorities in Soviet Russia were concerned, he held that the German *Reich* and its soldiers would not be tied to any humane attitude, nor would it wish to appear in the sentimental pose of philanthropic liberator.

However, with Hitler's rise to power, some Russian German *émigrés* in Germany began to act on behalf of their 'brethren in distress' (*Brüder in Not*). In trying to influence the Nazi attitude in

6 An autobiographical account by a South Russian Mennonite describes this experience: Susanne Toews, *Trek to Freedom: The Escape of Two Sisters from South Russia during World War II*, Manitoba, Canada, 1976. The foundations of an understanding of these processes have been laid by a number of valuable works: G. Reitlinger, *The SS: Alibi of a Nation, 1922-1945*, Melbourne, 1956; G. Reitlinger, *The House Built on Sand: the Conflicts of German Policy in Russia*, London, 1960; A. Dallin, *German Rule in Russia, 1941-1945: A Study in Occupation Policies*, London, 1957; M. Buchsweiler, *Ethnic Germans in the Ukraine towards the Second World War: A Case of Double Loyalty?*, Tel Aviv, 1980.

7 J.Ackermann, *Heinrich Himmler als Ideologe*, Göttingen, 1970; I. Kamenetsky, *Secret Nazi Plans for Eastern Europe*, New Haven, 1961.

favour of the Soviet Germans, they concentrated their efforts mainly in three directions:
— the Foreign Policy Office of the National Socialist Party under Alfred Rosenberg,[8] with his political adviser Georg Leibbrandt (this later became the *Reich* Ministry for the Occupied Eastern Territories, led by Rosenberg);
— the Anticomintern, a body for ideological struggle against Soviet socialism within Josef Goebbels' *Reich* Ministry for Propaganda;[9] and
— semi-scientific and semi-academic institutions, such as the German Foreign Institute (Deutsches Auslandsinstitut) in Stuttgart.[10]

While more or less convincingly displaying a National Socialist outlook and mode of behaviour, the Russian German *émigrés* within the competent Nazi agencies showed some solid knowledge, combined with an often geniune willingness to profit from the present political conjuncture in order to improve the lot of their co-religionists and former fellow-countrymen now suffering under Stalin's rule. But the efforts of these people were never to bear fruit fully, and by the time Hitler declared war on the Soviet Union they had lost any real influence, and were used mainly as informants for SS agencies. By then, the SS had all the power over ethnic German affairs in its hands.

In 1936 Himmler created the Ethnic German Liaison Office (*Volksdeutsche Mittelstelle* – Vo Mi), an SS agency of chameleon-like character which only began to reveal itself in its true colours at the beginning of the war.[11] At its head was party and SS veteran Werner Lorenz, who after a ruthless struggle succeeded in concentrating most of the control over ethnic Germans abroad in his own hands; by 1939 most of the other relevant agencies, especially those of former Russian Germans *émigrés*, had been liquidated or left with practically no functions.

In October 1939, after the successful conclusion of the Polish campaign, Himmler's role as master of the East was further enhanced by his appointment as *Reichskommissar* for the Strengthening of

8 R. Bollmus. *Das Amt Rosenberg und seine Gegner. Zum Machtkampf im national-sozialistischen Herrschaftssystem*, Stuttgart, 1970.

9 On the '*Antikomintern*' see W. Laqueur, *Russia and Germany*, London, 1965, chapter X.

10 On the German Foreign Institute, see E. Ritter, *Das Deutsche Auslandsinstitut in Stuttgart 1917–1945. Ein Beispiel deutscher Volkstumsarbeit zwischen den Weltkriegen*, Wiesbaden, 1976; and A. Smith, *The Deutschtum of Nazi Germany and the United States*, The Hague, 1965.

11 On the significance and activity of the Vo Mi see *Trials of War Criminals before the Nuremberg Military Tribunals*, vol. V, pp. 140 ff., Washington, DC, 1950.

Deutschtum.[12] In this capacity, he created a second office for ethnic German affairs to compete with Werner Lorenz's Vo Mi: Ulrich Greifelt's Main Staff Office of the Reichscommissioner for the Strengthening of *Deutschtum* (*Stabshauptamt* of the RKF). From then on, these two intimates of Himmler shared, used and abused their power over the ethnic Germans in Eastern Europe – very often to their detriment. In particular, they saw in the Soviet Germans the raw material for Himmler's dreams of germanisation and colonisation in the East, human material that could in various ways be arbitrarily settled, resettled and employed by the process known as '*Menscheneinsatz*' in the Germans' '*Lebensraum*' in Eastern Europe.[13]

But before using them as tools in the colonisation machinery, these Germans had to be screened and selected by means of the so-called German National List (*Deutsche Volksliste* – DVL). It divided the ethnic Germans in Eastern Europe into four categories:

– Racially pure Germans with German (i.e. National Socialist) consciousness;

– Racially pure Germans without German consciousness, but considered capable of becoming true National Socialists (people in groups 1 and 2 were entitled to apply for German citizenship and become '*Reichsdeutsche*' immediately);

– People with predominantly 'German blood', considered capable of being 're-germanised' by means of the re-germanisation procedure (*Wiedereindeutschungsverfahren* – WED) (those in group 3 were entitled to apply for temporary German citizenship, after which they would have to live for ten years under racial-political surveillance before becoming *bona fide* members of the German ethnic community);

– Persons with only some 'German blood' or those who were assimilated to other nations, were unwilling to become German citizens or were considered unable to be 're-germanised'. They could be, and in many cases, were, handed over to the Gestapo and eventually sent to a concentration camp or liquidated on the spot.

12 R.L. Koehl, *RKFDV. German Resettlement and Population Policy, 1939–1945. The History of the Reich Commission for the Strengthening of Germandom*, Cambridge, Mass., 1957.

13 Two of the most revealing documents of the Himmler staff were: *Der Menscheneinsatz. Grundsätze, Anordnungen und Richtlinien. Herausgegeben vom Reichskommissar für die Festigung deutschen Volkstums. Stabshauptamt*, Berlin, 1940; and *Generalplan Ost* (cf. H. Heiber, 'Generalplan Ost', *Vierteljahreshefte für Zeitgeschichte*, 6 (1958), pp. 281–325).

The task of screening the local Germans and deciding their fate was – despite some administrative disguise – entirely in the hands of the SS and of Heydrich's security police.

Ethnic Germans in the zone of military advance

With the advance of the German Wehrmacht into Soviet territory, the conquered areas were first placed under military administration before being handed over to the civil power. Within these regions, immediately following on the heels of the regular German army units, Heydrich's mobile killing and action units (*Einsatzgruppen der Sicherheitspolizei und des SD*) carried out their programme of cleansing the East of undesirable elements: Jews, commissars, aliens and partisans. At the same time they were to register the ethnic Germans and carry out the first constructive measures (*Aufbauarbeiten*) ensuring their privileged status. This twofold goal of activity – the destruction of Jews and undesirable aliens on the one hand and the construction of a prosperous ethnic German community on the other – was the product of Hitler's far-reaching plans of a new ethnic order (*völkische Ordnung*) in the whole of occupied Europe. It also expressed Himmler's programme of building up a strengthened *Deutschtum* at the expense of inferior nations, a programme that did untold damage to the role and fate of local Germans.

As the first 'constructive measure', the *Einsatzgruppen* registered previous German losses through deportation and forced resettlement by the Soviet authorities. They then 'cleansed' the German settlements of various kinds of aliens and undesirable elements. They appointed a German as mayor and ordered him to recruit men between 18 and 45 years of age to form the so-called *Selbstschutz*. The *Selbstschutz* received its initial military training from the *Einsatzkommando* of the respective *Einsatzgruppe*. Its role consisted first of all in assisting the *Einsatzkommando* in various tasks: protection of local Germans from partisan activity and against Rumanian soldiers; searching for communists, commissars, escapees and partisans; and purging the settlements and their surroundings of Jewish residents and escapees, which was usually carried out in the following way.

The head of each *Einsatzkommando* stationed in a German village asked the newly-appointed German mayor to draw up a list of all Jewish families and individuals living there. Having received the list (in most cases disguised as a 'resettlement list'), the *Einsatzkommando* ordered the

German *Selbstschutz* to round up the Jews and bring them to a central collection place such as a school, a cellar or a stable. There they were held, sometimes overnight. *Selbstschutz* members had to watch over them and prevent escape; beating and shooting of those who attempted escape were considered normal. When all the Jews designated for 'execution' (the Nazi term for this kind of murder) had been collected, the local Germans were asked to bring a wagon, load it with the victims (the term here was *Judenfuhren*, or 'Jew loads') and take it to a place on the outskirts of the village (a silo hole, for example, or an empty river bed). Here the men of the *Selbstschutz* had to dig deeper, hollowing the place out to the necessary depth. They had to translate the orders of the *Einsatzkommando* to the arriving Jews: to undress and kneel in front of the pit. The men of the *Einsatzkommando* did the actual shooting, but it is said that some of the Soviet Germans volunteered; on other occasions the *Einsatzkommandos* asked them to do the shooting and they refused. In most of the cases later reported, the local Germans were said to have assisted unwillingly and with feelings of guilt towards their Jewish neighbours. Some mild forms of protest were reported, but shame seems to have been the dominant feeling in the local German population. The apparently more or less general disapproval of what 'the Germans' did in their village might be seen as a continuation – in changed circumstances – of their attitude towards the terror and liquidation carried out under Stalin.

In every German village from which reports are extant some ethnic Germans were killed as well, sometimes together with the Jews. These were former officials, schoolmasters, teachers, mayors, commissars, *kolkhoz* leaders, party members or simply victims of personal revenge or denunciations. The Rosenberg ministry calculated the 'human scrap' to be eliminated within the ethnic German communities at 10–15 per cent. Germans who were married to Jews and refused to dissociate themselves from their partners were killed together with them and their children. People of mixed German and Jewish descent were liquidated as well.[14]

After six to eight weeks of action, the *Einsatzkommandos* left the

14 The indiscriminate liquidation of various kinds of so-called '*Mischlinge*' had its basis in the 'special Jewish notion for the East', defined by the Wannsee Conference on the Final Solution of the Jewish Question in Europe (Berlin, Jan. 20, 1942) and its subsequent sessions. See among others G. Reitlinger, *The Final Solution: The Attempt to Exterminate the Jews of Europe, 1939–1945*, London, 1953.

German villages and moved further east. Many of the villages, especially those where some religious belief had been retained, were left in a state of trauma.

Ethnic Germans under Rumanian administration ('Transnistria')

Because of the rapid joint German-Rumanian advance into the Black Sea region, Germans living in this area were not subjected to forced evacuation by the Soviet authorities. About 130,000 Germans were registered in the territory between the Dnestr and the Bug Rivers which fell under Rumanian civil administration and came to be known as 'Transnistria'. When the Rumanians took over in the autumn of 1941, the commandos of *Einsatzgruppe* D operating there had to leave, to be replaced in mid-October by SS *Sonderkommando* R (Russia) of the Vo Mi under SS-*Brigadeführer* Horst Hoffmeyer. It thus became the ruling authority for the Germans living in 'Transnistria'. The task of the Commando consisted in completing the actions of the *Einsatzgruppe* as well as in strengthening the *Deutschtum* of the local Germans by giving them a special privileged portion in the local economic and social life. One of its first actions was to concentrate the Germans living in villages where the settlements were scattered into some main command centres of settlement (*Kommando-bereiche*). This served two goals: to isolate the Germans from their neighbours of other national groups for reasons of racial-political separation and security; and to bring them under the exclusive control and guidance of the SS. In these German concentrations the men of Hoffmeyer's SS units entrenched their programme of military and economic guidance, and laid the foundations of a kind of special SS-order state.

On the military side, the SS continued to build up the German self-defence units, but now on a much larger scale. In the spring of 1943, at least 20,000 ethnic Germans of the Black Sea area were members – either already active or still undergoing training – of these paramilitary formations. Their field of activity widened as well: instead of assisting the mobile killing units of the SS in shooting the relatively few Jewish residents of their villages and settlements, they were now ordered to assist the men of the Vo Mi *Kommando* R in liquidating tens of thousands of Rumanian and South Russian Jews.

Since Rumanian officials usually refused to kill Jews, large groups of Jews were directed to the German settlement areas where the German SS would exterminate them. Large extermination pits were dug by the

Selbstschutz, close to some of the German settlements, and with its help
formations of thousands of half-starved, half-frozen Jewish men, women
and children were prepared for killing. Again it was the firing squads of
Sonderkommando R of the SS that did the shooting – assisted by men of
the local *Selbstschutz*, who then had to set fire to the bodies. The possessions of the murdered Jews were distributed: clothing and shoes to the
local Germans, gold, jewellery and money to the SS. Between 50,000
and 70,000 Rumanian and 'Transnistrian' Jews were murdered in this
way by the SS *Sonderkommando* assisted by the German *Selbstschutz*. The
German population of the surrounding settlements became increasingly
aware of the mass murder of innocent people that was going on. Seen in
retrospect, its reaction ranged from embarrassment to deep moral distress. In some cases there seems to have been strongly expressed criticism
against local Germans who had voluntarily assisted in the slaughter.

The economic guidance of the SS consisted of placing more land at the
disposal of the local Germans at the expense of Russian and Ukrainian
villages, arranging a special marketing system that favoured German
producers and consumers, and establishing special shops and warehouses
for Germans. Under *Menschenführung* (human guidance), the SS first
divided the population according to the guidelines in the German
National List, and then took over the political and ideological activation
of the rather passive, backward, mainly Catholic German colonists.

Ethnic Germans under German civil administration

About 200,000 ethnic Germans living in the other parts of South Russia
had not been deported and now came under German civil administration
in the *Reichskommissariat Ukraine* (RKU). The entire civil administration of the East was part of the Ministry of Occupied Eastern Territories,
and thus Rosenberg was nominally in charge. In reality, however,
control was strongly contested between the various agencies with
entirely different and often contradictory plans and programmes for the
ethnic Germans of the RKU. The *Reich* Ministry of the Occupied
Eastern Territories favoured some liberty in religion, culture and economic matters so as to make the local Germans an economic and cultural
élite in the occupied East; reprivatisation of land factories and real
estate and decollectivisation of agriculture were the first priorities. But
in all its plans and initiatives tending in this direction Rosenberg's

Ministry was strongly opposed by Göring's economic agencies and Himmler's colonisation planners.

Rosenberg's representative on the spot, *Reichskommissar* Erich Koch, had his own conception of the Ukraine as a colonial territory; but he considered the local Germans to be of poor racial quality, and not to fit his scheme for the germanisation of the Ukraine. In his view, they needed a long period of training and education to become worthy members of the German race; he preferred to use the Polish Germans and the auxillary personnel from Germany proper and the Netherlands to build up the local strata of overseers of agricultural, industrial and other enterprises.

From the summer of 1942, Himmler's agencies, attacking the Rosenberg Ministry for its 'total failure' in ethnic German questions, gradually took over the whole complex of the ethnic Germans' education, economy and military training. They now applied the same pattern in the RKU which they had used successfully, as they saw it, towards the 'Transnistrian' Germans. But little time was left. With the withdrawal of the German Wehrmacht, the SS ordered the Soviet Germans to take their movable goods and move West. Under dramatic conditions, about 350,000 Germans trekked in groups for thousands of kilometres, mainly to the 'Warthegau' (the Poznan area in what had been Polish territory between the wars). Here they were parted from their possessions and cattle and concentrated in camps, administered by the Vo Mi, which were the recruiting ground for various Nazi agencies: the Wehrmacht, the Waffen-SS, the SA, the *Arbeitsdienst* and many others. During the great Soviet offensive of the winter of 1944–5, most of these Germans were either in the camps on the eastern periphery of 'Greater Germany', or still on the move. Relatively few had succeeded in finding shelter in Germany proper, and of those a large proportion were soon tracked down by Soviet repatriation officers and forcibly repatriated to the Soviet Union under the regulations of the Yalta agreement.[15]

At least 200,000 Soviet Germans were overtaken by the Red Army on its way to Berlin. They were immediately rounded up, put into sealed freight cars and sent to the trans-Ural region where they were kept in 'special settlements' for Germans. The loss of life on the way ranged between 15 and 30 per cent. From Germany proper some 80,000

---

15 On the repatriation see J. Epstein, *Operation Keelhaul: The Story of Forced Repatriation from 1944 to the Present*, Old Greenwich, Conn., 1973; and N. Tolstoy, *The Victims of Yalta*, London, 1978.

Germans from the Soviet Union were sent back by way of 'repatriation' under Allied auspices and joined their fellows in the special settlements for Germans. Forced labour and NKVD surveillance were the conditions of their existence until the mid-1950s. Only about 70,000 Russian Germans survived the treks and the German camps, succeeded in reaching German soil and by going into hiding managed to escape repatriation. They alone remained in the West, and many of them emigrated to Canada and South America soon after the war. The entire Russian German community paid the price for Hitler's eastward expansion with the permanent loss of their historic home.[16]

---

16 A more detailed description of their historic fate is given in I. Fleischhauer, *Das Dritte Reich und die Deutschen in der Sowjetunion*, Stuttgart, 1983.

CHAPTER FIVE

THE GERMANS IN THE SOVIET UNION SINCE 1945

Benjamin Pinkus

In a general study of the Soviet Germans since the end of the Second World War – from the legal, political, economic and cultural points of view – the long-term significance for the Germans of events in the war years has to be taken into account. Their subsequent fortunes were mostly a direct result of what happened to them in 1941–5 and the image they acquired then.

Earlier, both in tsarist and Soviet times, they had been thought of as a 'quiet', hard-working, not problematic group which preserved its national-cultural identity while maintaining an unqualified loyalty to the host country. The Nazi invasion and ensuing events gave rise to a feeling that at least some of the Soviet Germans were disloyal; this was rein-forced by the prolonged discriminatory treatment meted out to them in the Soviet Union. In recent years, however, examination of the policy of deportation has encouraged a view of the Soviet Germans as innocent victims of a largely arbitrary Stalinist policy, which affected not only them but other national groups as well. On their side, the ethnic Germans, after all the tribulations of the Stalinist years, can at best have the most complex feelings toward the country which has been their homeland for over two centuries.

The effects of the deportation orders of the early 1940s lasted for decades, and in some important aspects they have lasted up to the present. There are three distinct periods in the history of the Soviet Germans in the post-war era. The first ten years after the war can be classified as the deportation régime; from 1955 to 1964 covers the road to rehabilitation, and since 1965 we can see the results of rehabilitation.

The legal-political status of the Germans

In 1945–6, when the deportation ended, there were about 1,250,000 Germans in the Soviet Union (there had been 1,543,000 in 1941). About 650,000 lived in the northern regions of the Russian Republic (for example in the Altai and the areas of Omsk, Novosibirsk, Kamerovo,

Krasnoiarsk, Tomsk), about 530,000 in Kazakhstan (in Karaganda, Kustanai, Tselinograd, Pavlodar, Semipalatinsk, Kokchetav, Dzhambul) and about 70,000 in Kirgizia (Frunze, Tokmak) and in Tajikistan (Dushanbe).

Although much research has been published in the Soviet Union, and in the West since the 1950s about the 'Gulag Archipelago', very little is known of the legal status of the deported German and other nationalities. For 1941–55, therefore, we must examine first the legal basis for the deportation and the régime according to which it was conducted.

The 1941 decree of deportation not only did not cover all Soviet Germans, but it did not even state the Soviet laws on which it was based and the principles whereby the deportees' existence was to be regulated. Nor did it state how long the deportation was to last. However, the second decree (of November 26, 1948), which was never made public at all in the Soviet Union (a Soviet custom maintained up to the present), did clarify a number of important points. It stated *inter alia* that the people concerned had been deported permanently, without the right to return to their previous places of residence. For violations of the rules established for the special settlements or of travel procedures, they were threatened with imprisonment or hard labour for up to twenty-five years. Sentences were handed down by the MVD Special Board (*Osoboe Soveshchanie*. Aiding and abetting or harbouring an offender was punishable by five years' hard labour.[1]

But here too there is no explanation of what the deportation régime consists of or on what legal foundations it is based. We therefore have to turn to current Soviet legislation to find the missing legal foundations. It is clear from the deportation decree that the Presidium of the Supreme Soviet based itself on sections 1(a), 1(b) 1(c) and 1(d) of clause 58 of the Soviet Criminal Code of 1926 (as amended in 1929 and 1934) concerning treason against the fatherland, and clause 19 of the same Code concerning 'intent to commit treason' and 'preparation' to do the same. The punishments specified were imprisonment for 10–25 years or, in aggravating circumstances, the death penalty.[2] As we shall see later, however, these clauses were invoked in arrests and trials of only a small number of cases. The Forced Labour Code of the Russian Republic of August 1, 1933, established three types of labour camps: those for industrial and

1 See *German Samizdat*, A.S. no. 1776, p. 6; and A. Nekrich, *The Punished Peoples: The Deportation and Fate of Soviet Minorities at the End of the Second World War*, New York, 1978.
2 *Ugolovnyi kodeks RSFSR*, Moscow, 1935, pp. 22–26.

agricultural forced labour (clause 33); for severe régime forced labour (clause 34); and for special severe labour (clause 35). Clause 8 laid down that persons sentenced to forced labour by a court of law or by the decision of an administrative body (that is, by a Special Board of the NKVD) could be sent to forced labour camps. It is important, finally, to see how Soviet legal literature defines the phenomenon of deportation (*ssylka*) based on the legislation enumerated above. The *Legal Encyclopaedia*, which appeared in 1953, refers to 'the obligatory removal of the condemned from a given locality to be compulsorily settled elsewhere for a period of time laid down in the verdict'.[3] Any individual sentenced under clause 36(*b*) of the Forced Labour Code can be deported for a period of three to ten years and an additional penalty of one to five years. The punishment of deportation may not be imposed on minors under the age of sixteen.

This brief description of the Soviet law shows quite clearly how uncertain was the legal basis for the deportation of the Germans, both in the sphere of general legislation and in that of specific laws. Solzhenitsyn was certainly justified in writing: 'The penal code was one thing, but the deportation of hundreds of thousands of people – that was another thing. It was the personal decree of the monarch.'[4] In the first place, the accusation of treason was a collective one, contrary to Soviet law; no sentence was passed by any judicial body whatever nor even by an administrative board, as required by Soviet law; the length of the period of deportation was not fixed at the outset but only after some eight years had passed; and finally, the prohibition against deporting children under the age of sixteen was ignored.

We will now examine the nature of the deportation régime and the way it was conducted until its final abolition in 1955. First, deportation and the operation of the deportation régime led immediately and automatically to deprivation of all civil rights. However limited the rights of the individual in the Soviet Union, especially in this period, their absolute removal unquestionably had serious consequences. The Soviet Germans were thereby deprived of any possible defence and became permanent victims of the arbitrary will of the bureaucracy and of general public hostility. They lost their representation on all the soviets from the

---

3 *Iuridicheskii slovar'*, Moscow, 1953, p. 651. It should be noted that at the time of the enactment of the 1933 Forced Labour Code the correct terminology was OGPU, the NKVD having been established in 1934. Subsequent changes in nomenclature explain the variety of terms used here for the internal security organs.

4 A. Solzhenitsyn, *Arkhipelag Gulag, 1918–1956*, Paris, 1973, vol. 1, p. 90.

highest level to the lowest. They were discharged from all the institutions of the Soviet civil service. A paradoxical situation was created in this respect: due to the war, certainly, Germans and members of other deported nationalities were not expelled from the ranks of the party, in spite of their loss of civil rights.[5] The ending of mobilisation of Germans into the army, by an order issued in July 1941, and the withdrawal of veteran officers and soldiers of German nationality in the early months of the war, had a significance which is still evident today.[6] Secondly, the deportation régime caused increased splitting up of families beginning, as we have seen, at the time of the deportation itself. This was exacerbated in 1942–5, when the men and a large part of the women were taken for service in the labour army, and in this way very many children lost their parents and were put into orphanages or adopted by Russian families – who did not always treat the children of 'traitors' properly. There were many tragedies for children who lost track of their parents permanently.[7]

Further, deprivation of freedom to travel and to correspond was especially serious, not only in the civil-political sphere but also economically and culturally. For this purpose, the Germans received the special identity cards given to all deported national minorities in 1941–5. They

5 Nekrich gives some interesting details that illustrate this paradox. Thus Chechen members of the Communist Party were taken in closed cars, with police escort, to meetings of the regional party in the places to which they were deported. *Ibid.*, p. 119. See Robert Conquest, *The Nation-Killers: The Soviet Deportation of Nationalities*, London, 1970, p. 109.

6 These instructions were very hard to obey because the Germans were dispersed in many units and because of the renewed chaos that prevailed in the army in this period. Moreover, some commanders did not want to carry out the instructions for various reasons, and asked the Germans in their units to change their names and appear as Russians and even as Jews. Various reports have been written about this in newspapers, in Soviet German literature and even in Russian literature. See especially E. Petrus, *Euer Heim ist meine Burg*, Alma Ata, 1969; D. Wagner, *Ritter ohne Furcht*, Alma Ata, 1973; K. Simonov, *Soldatami ne rozhdaiutsia*, Moscow, 1964; V. Vladimirov, *Chto zhe skazat' komissaram*, Alma Ata, 1975. We have compiled a list of 46 Germans who stayed on and served in the army or in the partisan forces: 21 of them in different army units, 17 in partisan units and 8 in a special unit mobilised in January 1943 to act behind the enemy lines on the Leningrad front. As many as 5 among these few combatants were privileged to receive the decoration of Hero of the Soviet Union (cf. Moldavians 2, Estonians 9, Kirghiz 12, Tajiks 15).

7 Soviet German literature still dwells on this painful subject, without of course blaming the Soviet authorities who were in fact responsible. Since the 1950s there have always been special columns in the Soviet German papers headed 'Search for Missing Relatives'.

had to report to the NKVD institutions and the militia twice a month in the first stage, once a month in the second stage, and from 1954 on, once a year.[8] To maintain close and constant surveillance over the millions of people categorised as deportees, a special section was established in the NKVD called the Main Directorate of Deportations (*Glavnoe pereselencheskoe upravlenie*), with representatives in every town and village and an officer posted in every enterprise and large office. Its methods were the same as those used in other areas – the use of volunteer workers and informers, obtaining reports about suspicious activities, and so on.[9]

Finally, the new status accorded to the deported Germans, placed them outside the educational network of secondary and higher education and even partly of elementary education and led to the almost total obliteration of their national culture.

Although the important changes that took place in the Soviet administration after Stalin's death had little effect on the legal status and the economic and cultural position of the Soviet Germans, these changes of course constituted the background for rehabilitation. Only a few Germans were covered by the general amnesty decreed on March 27, 1953, and they were those serving light sentences (less than five years' imprisonment). For the Germans the change in the nature of the deportation régime was much more important. It was not abolished but made less harsh; as already mentioned, the Germans were required to report only once a year, surveillance was less close, and infractions of the régime were not severely punished as before.[10]

When the situation of the Germans is compared with that of other deported national minorities and with life under similar deportation régimes, it emerges that their early rehabilitation was directly influenced by an outside factor. Until the end of 1954 there was, in fact, no change at all in Soviet policy towards West Germany,[11] but from January 1955 feelers were put out from the Soviet side regarding the establishment of diplomatic relations between them.[12] Before the West German

8 On this, see Nekrich, p. 119. *German Samizdat.* A.S. 1776, p. 10; A. Fisher, *The Crimean Tatars*, Stanford, 1978, p. 174.
9 Piotr Deriabine, at that time a KGB officer in the Altai, describes KGB methods among the deported nationalities. See P. Deriabine and F. Gibney, *Policier de Staline*, Paris, 1966, p. 65.
10 On this see *German Samizdat*, A.S. no. 1776, 2811–6.
11 V. Baras, 'Stalin's German Policy after Stalin', *Slavic Review*, 1978, no. 2, pp. 253–67.
12 The ending of the state of war with Germany by the decree of the Presidium of the

Chancellor, Adenauer, visited the Soviet Union in September 1955, he prepared proposals for negotiation, and among them the return of German citizens from the Soviet Union and the situation of Soviet Germans had an important place.[13] However, when the talks between the two delegations began, they hit a snag right away when the question of emigration was put on the agenda. The Soviet head of government, Marshal Bulganin, contended angrily that there were no German prisoners of war in the Soviet Union, but he was later prepared to admit that there were 9,678 German war criminals who had been condemned by Soviet tribunals.[14]

Khrushchev fanned the flames when he began to describe the atrocities committed by the Germans in the Soviet Union, to which Adenauer retorted that the hands of the Red army were also dripping with blood. A breakdown of the negotiations seemed unavoidable, but the vital interests of both parties proved decisive and a compromise formula was found, whereby prisoners of war would be returned, and the repatriation of civilians would be discussed when a list of names was submitted for this purpose. The situation of Soviet Germans would be raised only in general terms, since it was an internal Soviet matter. However, the Soviet authorities apparently decided that they would make a gesture, and on September 17, 1955, a decree of the Presidium of the Supreme Soviet was published, 'Regarding an Amnesty for Soviet Citizens who Collaborated with the Occupying Authorities during the War in the Years 1941 to 1945'.[15] Clauses 1–3 of the decree laid down that prisoners serving sentences of up to ten years' imprisonment under clauses 58/1, 58/3, 58/4, 56/6, 58/10 and 58/12 would be released, and the sentences of others reduced by half. The amnesty did not apply to those sentenced for murdering Soviet citizens or for assisting in murder. An additional decree supplementing this amnesty was published on September 20,

---

Supreme Soviet on January 25, 1955 should have symbolised this about-turn, but ratification of the Treaty of Paris by West Germany on January 27 froze these first contacts for a number of months. See Keesing's Research Report, *Germany and Eastern Europe since 1945*, New York, 1973.

13 In his memoirs Adenauer points out that he put this question (and the return of more than 100,000 Germans) at the top of the agenda. Adenauer, *Erinnerungen, 1953–1955*, 1, Stuttgart, 1966, p. 492.

14 For the negotiations, see *Pravda*, Sept. 10, 11, 12, 13, 1955.

15 *Vedomosti Verkhovnogo Soveta SSSR*, 1955, no. 17.

16 *Ibid.*, no. 19. The decree also appears in *Sbornik zakonov SSSR, 1938–1967*, 2, Moscow, 1968, pp. 629–31.

1956,[16] Neither of these decrees did anything to solve the central problem of the deported Soviet Germans, and a special decree was issued for this purpose on December 13, 1955, 'Regarding Abolition of the Restrictions on the Legal Status of the Germans and their Families under the Deportation Régime'.[17] Nothing was said in the preamble to this decree about annulling the accusation of treachery or cancelling the August 28, 1941, decree of deportation. The 1955 decree stated: 'In consideration of the fact that the restrictions on the legal status of the Germans and their families in the different regions of the state are no longer necessary, they are hereby abolished.' Absolutely no amends were made for the injustice done to the Germans by the liquidation of their republic, their deportation and the expropriation of their property.

This was far from amounting to full and final rehabilitation, in the moral-legal or in the political-material sphere. The new situation now created was absolutely contrary both to the Constitution and to Soviet laws ensuring freedom of movement and free choice of place of residence. It cannot be ignored, all the same, that the restoration of civil rights was of great importance to the Germans, since this freed them from being subject to special surveillance. They could now search for relatives who had been dispersed in different places, correspond with relatives abroad, change their place and type of work, send their children to secondary schools, and be eligible for service in the army.[18]

In a discussion of the rehabilitation of the deported nationalities, the central question of why some of them were fully rehabilitated and others only partly is a complicated one. The answer to it depends on how decisions were reached in the Soviet administration in 1955–7. Although, as we have seen, the external factor played a role in moves towards the rehabilitation of the Germans, it was not decisive in their case because internal considerations carried far more weight; hence the Germans did not receive rehabilitation.[19]

Next one cannot overlook the distrust felt towards the Germans and the

17 It is characteristic of Soviet policy that this decree was not published in the press or included in the Collections of Soviet Laws and Decrees. It was published in *German Samizdat*, A.S. no. 1776.

18 According to Conquest, Germans already began to be called up for the army in 1954, but conversations with Germans who were repatriated to West Germany indicate that this is not accurate and that the call-up began only after the publication of the decree of December 1955. See Conquest, p. 109.

19 H. Carrère d'Encausse, *L'empire éclaté*, Paris, 1978, pp. 35–6, 196–203; A. Fisher, *Crimean Tatars*, pp. 174–9.

Crimean Tatars, backed as it was by fierce hatred from the surrounding populations. Also it was judged that to return the Germans and the Tatars to their former homes was likely to harm the Slavic population and weaken the Russian and Ukrainian republics while the return of other deported nationalities appeared desirable since it would weaken the Caucasian and not the Slavic republics. Further, the large size of the German population, and its economic importance in its new homes, unlike, for example, the Chechens and the Balkars, also influenced the decision taken. The decisive factor, however, was apparently the lack of fight shown by the Germans at this time compared with the struggle put up by the Chechens to return to their homeland.

In 1964, as in 1955, it was again an external factor that pressed the Soviet authorities into taking a new step on the long road to the rehabilitation of the Soviet Germans. After the years of tense relations between the Soviet Union and Germany as a result of the Berlin crisis, Khrushchev decided to take a new line, and for this purpose sent his son-in-law, Adzhubei, to Bonn in July 1964 to prepare the way for a visit he himself would make to Germany. To buttress this mission with a significant gesture, the Presidium of the Supreme Soviet issued a decree on August 29, 1964, 'Regarding the Introduction of a Change in the Decree of the Presidium of the Supreme Soviet of August 28, 1941 relating to Transfer of Germans Residing in the Volga Regions'. The fact that this decree was published in the official gazette only on the December 28, 1964,[20] and in the Soviet German paper *Neues Leben* only on January 20, 1965[21] illustrates the vacillations of Soviet policy towards the German minority and the extent to which foreign policy considerations influenced it both before and after Khrushchev's fall in October 1964. The lengthy preamble to the decree stated: 'Life has shown that mistaken and unfounded accusations were the result of arbitrary action in the conditions of Stalin's cult of personality.'[22] That was as much as to say that only the 'personality cult' was responsible for the terrible wrong done to a whole people, for which no amends had been made even ten years after Stalin's death. No less important than this disclosure about the guilty party, however, was a historical affirmation of significance for

---

20 H. Lehmann, 'Moskau führt deportierte Völker zurück', *Das Parlament*, 1957, no. 13, p. 6.

21 It is noteworthy that this decree was not published at all either in the principal papers such as *Izvestiia* or in the local press, so that its very existence is not known to the Soviet population to this day.

22 *Sbornik zakonov*, p. 165.

the Soviet Germans in 1964: 'During the war years, the decisive majority of the German population together with the Soviet people contributed in fact by its toil to the victory of the Soviet Union over Nazi Germany, and since the war the Germans have actively cooperated in communist construction.'[23] It should be noted that the decree refers not merely to the German population of the German Autonomous Republic of the Volga but to all Soviet Germans, and – what is especially important – rescinds the accusation of treachery and collaboration with the enemy which had been applied to the whole German population.[24] The preamble closed by enumerating all the blessings the Soviet administration had bestowed on the Germans, who had taken root in their new places of residence and enjoyed all Soviet civil rights.

The Presidium of the Supreme Soviet accordingly cancelled the decree of August 28, 1941, while leaving the Germans in their new places of residence. At the same time, it extended assistance to them for their economic and cultural development, taking account of their specific national interests. So it is clear that this decree did not mean a fundamental change in the rehabilitation of the Soviet Germans in that it did not order the reconstruction of the German Republic of the Volga. Nor did it grant the Germans the possibility of returning to the places they were deported from or payment of compensation for the property of which they had been deprived at the time of their removal. All the same, the decree is of undoubted importance since it brought moral-political rehabilitation through formal cancellation of the collective accusation of treachery and collaboration with the enemy administration and by offering the possibility of developing a national cultural life.

The last decree to deal with the rehabilitation of the Soviet Germans, which changed their political-legal status formally at least, was issued by the Presidium of the Supreme Soviet on November 3, 1972. The full title of the decree was 'Regarding Abolition of the Restrictions on Choice of Place of Residence that were Imposed in the Past with Regard to Various Categories of Citizens'.[25] Clause 1 of the decree reads: 'It has

---

23 *Ibid.*
24 Soviet German authors make much of this point. E.g. in a play by A. Saks, one of the heroines, the child Hilda, hears the decree read out and says, 'But we came from the Ukraine,' and Viktor replies, 'The decree refers to us too.' The head of the family sums up, 'This is political rehabilitation for all Soviet Germans.' A. Saks, 'Friedrich Bauer und die Seinem', *Neues Leben*, Mar. 15, 1978.
25 This decree has not been published in the Soviet Union. Even if non-publication of Soviet legislation is common practice, it is illuminating all the same on the reasons

been decided to abolish the restrictions in the matter of choice of place of residence that were laid down in the degree of the Presidium of the Supreme Soviet of the USSR on December 13, 1955 with regard to Germans and members of their families and in that of September 22, 1956, with regard to former Greek and Turkish citizens and persons of enemy nationalities without civil status.'[26]

Clause 2 was the most important in its substance. It explained that Germans with Soviet citizenship had the same right as all other Soviet nationalities to choose their place of residence anywhere in the Soviet Union, in accordance with the legislation in force on work arrangements and the regulations relating to identity certificates. Clause 3 stated that it was the duty of the institutions concerned (the Ministry of Justice and the Ministry of the Interior) to supervise the implementation of the decree; a directive to this effect was in fact issued by the office of the Procurator on November 9, 1972.[27] However, there is a fly in the ointment. The Soviet authorities can use administrative means to prevent implementation of the decree, that is by withholding permission to register in the new place of residence (the famous *propiska*) or by not giving work. Although there were quite a number of such instances, the existence of the decree undoubtedly helped many Germans to move to the European republics, mainly the Baltic republics.

Even though it is clear that this too was surely not full rehabilitation, there is not doubt that it was of great importance to the Soviet Germans and led to substantial changes in every aspect of their life. Leaving aside for a moment the economic, social and cultural changes, we will now briefly discuss how this rehabilitation led to the integration of the Germans in public and political life.

We have seen that for historical, demographic and economic reasons the Soviet Germans had taken only a restricted part in Soviet political life, although in the 1930s German representation in Soviet administrative institutions developed widely and significantly. The publication of the rehabilitation decree of December 1955, and the start of military service for the ethnic Germans from the beginning of 1956, ought to have led the Soviet authorities to consider it necessary to bring the Germans into both the Communist Party and the Soviet administrative

---

why it is precisely this decree or law and not another that is not published. See *Khronika zashchity prav v SSSR*, New York, 1975, no. 12, pp. 50–1.

26 *Ibid.*

27 Instructions of the Chief Procurator of the USSR, *Prikaz general'nogo prokurora*, no. 54.

institutions. We will now examine the place of the Germans in the Party and its institutions on the one hand and, on the other, their representation in administrative institutions, such as the soviets on the various governmental levels.

The Germans in the Communist Party. We have already noted the paradoxical situation that came into being regarding membership of the Communist Party: how the deported nationalities, while deprived of all civil rights, nevertheless remained members of the party. It is certain however that in 1941–5 no new members were accepted in the party or the ranks of the Komsomol from among the Soviet Germans. There has been no data at all published up till now concerning the number of German Communist Party members: we can do no more than try to reach an estimate indirectly, with the help of only partial data.

The factors that cause the various nationalities to be over- or underrepresented in the Communist Party are many and complex – and often contradictory. Our lack of knowledge of how and when decisions are taken in this field makes analysis even more difficult. First, the 'historical' factor still has an important place – in other words the existence of certain nationalities which for a variety of reasons were more heavily represented in the party than others, such as the Georgians, the Jews and the Armenians. Secondly, there is an advantage in belonging to one of the Slav nationalities which, apparently for political reasons, are given preference in certain spheres. Thirdly, if there is a wide stratum of officials belonging to a given nationality, this will affect that nationality's representation in the party. Fourthly, the proportion of the population which is urbanised and the general socio-economic structure are also important. Fifthly, the existence of a federative unit and its level in the entire system have a significant effect on representation in the party and in the administration. And finally, there are many elusive subjective factors such as party policy *vis-à-vis* one or another national minority at different periods under the influence of outside factors, and the attitude of the national minority to Soviet rule.

In reviewing these factors, we immediately realise that the Soviet Germans have no 'historic past' in the party, do not belong to a Slav nationality, do not posses a wide stratum of officials, are still more than 50 per cent rural, do not have a federative unit, and to their great misfortune belong to the deported nationalities, which still remain under deep suspicion despite the rehabilitation. Hence it can be deduced that the Germans are in the category of less represented nationalities in the party and administration. Of the nationalities with territorial units the Lithuanians have 40 party members for every 1,000 people while the Moldavians have only 25. Of the non-territorial nationalities, the Tatars (including the Crimean Tatars) also have 25 members per 1,000 people, while the Poles in Belorussia have far fewer – five only. We assume that the German figures are somewhere between 5 and 25 per 1,000.[28] It emerges from the published 1978 figures that there were 1,510 German party members in Kirgizia,[29] where the German population numbered about 100,000. In 1984 statistics on ethnic German membership in the Soviet Communist Party and the Komsomol were published for the first time since the 1930s: there were 73,500 Germans in the party and 251,000 in the Komsomol. Comparing this with the 294,774 Jewish party members in 1976 (the Jewish and Germans populations are of roughly similar size), the Germans are clearly much less well represented in the party.[30]

Up till 1970 the Germans had no representation in the central party institutions. In the Russian Republic, in the northern regions of which there is a considerable German population, we find no Germans at all in the higher ranks of the party. On the lower level of party secretaries are two names: J. Enns and Martin Renner. In Kazakhstan, which is full of Germans, we find a number of German regional secretaries: N. Eberhardt, W. Dukkert, A. Wiese, W. Miller, A. Hilgenberg and A. Braun.

The Germans in the soviets.   The Germans are also under-represented in that most representative institution in the USSR – the soviets. Up to the end of the 1960s there was still no representation of Germans in the Supreme Soviet of the USSR. As can be seen in Table 1, since 1970 German representation in this institution has remained fixed at two members, one-third of the Jewish representation (due to the existence of a Jewish Autonomous District) and less than that of the Poles with a very much smaller

Table 5.1.   GERMANS AND OTHER NATIONAL MINORITIES ON THE SUPREME SOVIET OF THE USSR, 1970–78[31]

	Total reps.	Germans	Jews	Poles	Greeks	Finns	Koreans
1970–4	1,517	2	6	2	1	1	1
1974–8	1,517	2	6	3	1	2	–

28 See *Partiinaia zhizn'*, 1962, no. 1, p. 44; 1967, no. 19, pp. 14–15; 1976, no. 10, p. 16.
29 *Radio Liberty Research*, RFE-RL 172/79 (June 6, 1979).
30 *Partiinaia zhizn'*, 1976, no. 10, p. 16; *Freundschaft*, Aug. 21, 1984.
31 *Verkhovnyi Sovet SSSR*, Moscow, 1970; 1975.

population. The Germans constitute 0.8 per cent of the entire population of the Soviet Union, and they have only 0.13 per cent of the representatives on the Supreme Soviet, which means that they are under-represented indeed. The German representatives hitherto have been Sophie Eifeld and Friedrich Schneider from Slavgorod and Jakob Höring from Pavlodar, and today are Natalia Gelbert and Svetlana Schuch.[32]

On the middle level of the Supreme Soviets of the republics, out of a total of 5,879 representatives in 1971 there were 8 Germans, 15 Jews, 27 Poles, 2 Finns and 7 Koreans.[33] In this sphere, too, the Germans are at the bottom of the ladder of representation, with 0.15 per cent of all the representatives, whereas the Jews have 0.32 per cent and the Poles 0.45 per cent. On the lowest level, that of the local soviets, German representation is higher: the first German representatives were elected as early as 1959, with 0.1 per cent. By 1969 the ratio had risen to 0.6 per cent.

Table 5.2. GERMANS ON THE LOCAL SOVIETS IN THE RUSSIAN REPUBLIC, 1961–75[34]

	Total	Urban representatives
1961	906	26
1971	6,132	438
1973	6,505	443
1975	6,952	546

Table 5.3. REPRESENTATIVES OF NATIONAL MINORITIES ON LOCAL SOVIETS IN THE USSR, 1967–73[35]

	Germans	Jews	Poles	Bulgarians	Greeks	Koreans
1967	12,536	7,881	7,777	2,972	2,486	1,705
1969	12,760	6,619	7,815	3,175	2,422	1,808
1971	13,168	6,030	8,042	3,493	2, 596	1,601
1973	14,012	5,173	8,127	3,983	2, 558	1,558

32 *Freundschaft*, May 15, June 18, 1970; *Neues Leben*, Jan. 1, 1976; *Kazakhstanskaia pravda*, Feb. 5, 1980; *Pravda*, Feb. 5, 1980; *Partiinaia zhizn' Kazakhstana*, 1974, no. 7.
33 *Itogi vyborov i sostav deputatov verkhovnykh sovetov soiuznykh i avtonomnykh respublik*, Moscow, 1971, pp. 18–20.
34 *Itogi vyborov i sostav deputatov mestnykh sovetov RSFSR*, Moscow, 1961, 1971, 1973.
35 *Ibid.*, 1967, 1969, 1971–3.

Thus from 1967 till 1973 the number of German representatives on the local soviets increased by 11.8 per cent. In 1973–83 the number of German representatives increased by 25 per cent. As against this, we see a significant decrease for the Jews and the Koreans and stability for the Poles. The satisfactory representation of the Germans precisely at this level, and especially in the rural and regional soviets, is explained by the existence of a wide stratum of German managers of *kolkhozy* and *sovkhozy* (state farms), technicians and the like, who are ideal candidates for local soviets in the USSR. Politically, the need to fit the Germans into the Soviet administration found its best solution precisely at this level.

Germans in the administration. At the republic level there appears not to have been a single minisverial post filled by a German. This is striking in Kazakhstan, for example, where the Germans constitute an appreciable segment of the population, and where another minority, the Ukrainians, do hold senior posts. The army has one German general and several officers of lower rank. In the KGB there are apparently no Germans at all so far.

From what is published in the Soviet German press, we learn that most of the German representatives in the party and in government institutions were born in the 1930s (that is to say they arrived in the deportation regions as children) and received secondary or technical schooling. It is remarkable that the German cultural and scientific intelligentsia is hardly represented at all in Soviet government institutions, unlike the Jews for example. This certainly stems from the socio-economic structure of the German population and perhaps also from suspicion of the German intelligentsia, which is far from negligible and has managed to preserve its national culture.

The 'representatives' of the German public in the Soviet Union have been extremely cautious in their public pronouncements and have taken little part in German national life, such as it is. This does not mean that they do not have a certain behind-the-scenes influence especially at the lower levels of the administration. They are certainly consulted when questions arise concerning their national culture, and they are made use of by the authorities for propaganda purposes abroad.

The socio-economic situation of the Soviet Germans

In the socio-economic field, some important distinctions have to be made. First there are two clearly differentiated sub-periods, the first from 1945 till 1955 during which, as we have seen, the Germans still lived under the special deportation régime, and the other since 1956, during which there has been a gradual but steady improvement in the quality of their lives.

1945–1955

From the early 1930s on, about half a million Germans were living in the Urals, Siberia and the Asiatic republics, as a result of having been deported in the course of the anti-kulak campaign. During the war and after it their position was favourable relative to that of their fellow-nationals who had been deported from 1941 on. There was also a third category of Germans, at least in 1942–7 – namely those in the labour army.

The local Germans. The better situation of the local Germans *vis-à-vis* that of the other Germans was determined by a number of factors. First, they continued to live in their own fixed homes and kept their property. Secondly, they were settled in jobs and were able to keep them even after the declaration of the wartime deportation, although they now had to possess a special identity certificate and come and register as required. Thirdly they knew the local conditions and were used to the harsh climate. And fourthly, various relations had been established between them and the local officials, which greatly helped them to get through the worst period. They were, moreover, mostly a population of peasants in the *kolkhozy* and *sovkhozy*, which also made their position easier. Certainly in the terrible famine years of 1942 and 1943 and again in 1947 and 1948, deaths among them were fewer than among the rest of the Germans. Nevertheless their economic situation worsened not only during the war but after it as well, simply as a result of their being Germans living under the deportation régime.[36]

The deported Germans. The economic situation of the 600,000–700,000 deported Germans was extremely difficult, especially in the places they were sent to. Here one must differentiate between two categories among the deported Germans, regarding not their legal status, which was uniform, but their physical conditions – between those moved to existing places of residence and those sent to new areas, in other words, into the wilderness. Those in the first of these categories were in the better

---

36 Letters reaching the West from the Urals in this period contain detailed descriptions of the life of the Soviet Germans. See P.A. Dyck, *Orenburg am Ural*, Canada, Clearbook, 1951.

situation; because of the urgent need for manpower in wartime they were immediately given work and a place to live.[37] There were, of course, places where the situation was extremely difficult and families of ten or more people lived in one room.[38] The fate of the second category was especially harsh; they arrived in waste lands with no dwellings, sanitation or other basic necessities. Without any real assistance, they had to build their homes with their own hands.

The war period was hard for the whole population of the Soviet Union. For the Germans and the other deported nationalities the bad times continued till 1948, and even up to as late as 1953 there was only slight improvement. Only between 1953 and 1955 did the economic situation of the Soviet Germans begin to improve. What exactly was their situation during and after the war? First, the working day was very long – up to 14 hours – and the high production norms imposed were difficult to fulfill. Especially hard was the lot of mothers with small children, whose husbands had been taken off to the labour army. The bread ration was very low – 200–300 grams for an adult and only 200 grams for a child. There were no proper medical facilities, and there was a constant shortage of medicines, leading to the spread of disease and a high mortality rate. Finally, like the other deported nationalities, the Germans were compulsorily restricted to hard physical labour, which was also the worst paid. If the Soviet Germans were perhaps able to withstand these hardships better than others, it was because of their bitter experience during the great hunger years of the 1920s and the anti-kulak campaign, because of their skills and their capacity for work, and above all because of their strong sense of community and family solidarity throughout all these years.

The Germans in the labour army.   It is difficult to say how many Germans served in this army, but a realistic estimate would have to be in the region of 100,000. In organisation and functioning, the labour army combined the features of a military unit and a concentration camp. The soldiers formed labour brigades, without ranks and under constant close surveillance by the NKVD apparatus. Up to 1944 they did not even have

37 See R. Berler, *Avec elles au-delà de l'Oural*, Paris, 1967, p. 169; W. Leonhard, *Die Revolution enlässt ihre Kinder*, Frankfurt/Main, 1961, p. 145; K. Stirner, *7,000 dana u Sibiru*, Zagreb, 1973, pp. 164–5.

38 See the testimony of Susan Leonhard, who was deported to a different place from her son W. Leonhard; both were German anti-fascists who had escaped to the Soviet Union from Germany. S. Leonhard, *Gestohlenes Leben*, Herford, 1962, p. 421.

the right to send letters to their families. They were dispersed in different regions far from the war zones, in places like Kuibyshev, Sverdlovsk, Cheliabinsk, Novosibirsk, Irkutsk, Vorkuta, Arkhangelsk and Karaganda.[39] The work was mainly building railways, roads and bridges, working in the mines and on canals, and cutting timber. Besides the long working day and high production norms already mentioned there was a constant shortage of working tools and of warm clothing. The food provided, which was restricted enough anyway, was still further reduced through ceaseless thieving by the camp management. The attitude to the Germans in the labour army was never less than humiliating but often crossed the boundary into serious maltreatment – worse indeed than that meted out to prisoners of war.

Since 1956

Whereas a slight improvement in the condition of the Soviet Germans was already perceptible in 1953–5, a real change only took place after the publication of the rehabilitation decree of December 1955. The transition to normal life was very gradual and took until the later 1960s.

The socio-economic life of any people is naturally varied and complex, but in the case of a national minority with no federative unit of its own the data at our disposal are especially limited. Within these limitations we shall outline a number of aspects of the life of the Soviet Germans in the more recent period.

Educational level.   The war and deportations did immeasurable harm to a whole generation of Germans born between 1930 and 1945. If Table 4 is taken to be generally representative of the rural German population (55 per cent of all Soviet Germans in 1970), then we see that close to 12 per cent of this population was illiterate. In contrast to the Ukrainians, the percentage of illiterates among the Germans in the pre-war period had been among the lowest in the Soviet Union. Today this is a high ratio in comparison with the general Soviet population and it was caused by the deportation; the rate of illiteracy in the rural Soviet population in general is only 2.5 per cent.[40] About 68 per cent of all Germans have had up to six classes of elementary education and only 0.4 per cent have

39 P. Reimer, 'Wir waren mit dabei', *Freundschaft*, Feb. 23, 1973; El Campesino, *La vie et la mort en URSS (1939–1949)*, Paris, 1950; S. Nora and P. Zwierniak, *La justice soviétique*, Rome, 1945.
40 B. Karblay, *La société soviétique contemporaine*, Paris, 1977, p. 146.

Table 5.4.   EDUCATIONAL LEVEL OF GERMANS AND UKRAINIANS IN THE NOVOSIBIRSK REGION, 1967[41]

				Classes				Vocational	Incomplete higher	Higher education
	None	1-3	4-6	7-8	9	10-11				
Germans	11.6	25.1	42.6	16.5	0.9	2.2	0.7	0.4	-	-
Ukrainians	19.9	23.2	28.9	19.5	0.8	4.9	2.0	-	0.8	0.8

41 Data taken from research by the Soviet Academy of Sciences in the Novosibirsk region and published by Malinovskii in *Neues Leben*, July 2-16, 1969.

managed to get a partial higher education. The situation is of course better among the urban German population, but they too were badly hurt by the effects on their education caused by the war and the deportation.

Table 5.5.   GERMANS AND OTHER NATIONAL MINORITIES IN HIGHER EDUCATION IN KIRGIZIA, 1960–71[42]

	1960–1	*1965–6*	*1970–1*		
Total	17,379	32,227	48,437		
Germans	132	433	857		*Students in institutions*
Russians	6,345	12,586	16,879		*of higher education*
Jews	263	295	388		
Total	17,202	31,756	41,747		*Students*
Germans	141	837	1,601		*in special*
Russians	7,809	15,496	17,868		*education*
Jews	146	212	130		
	1955–66		*1970–1*		
Total	3,702		6,277		
Germans	–		91		*Scientific researchers*
Russians	1,827		2,880		*(with doctoral or*
Jews	169		228		*candidate degrees)*

Since Kirgizia is the only republic that issues data on the number of German students, and the 70,000 or more Germans there during these years were much like the Germans in the Kazakh Republic, the Kirgizia data can provide an important indicator for the development of higher education in the latter republic as well. Table 5 shows a significant increase in the number of German students throughout the 1960s, and this trend undoubtedly continued and even speeded up in the 1970s. All the same, 3.1 per cent of the whole population of Kirgizia and only 0.8 per cent of students there in the 1960s were Germans. No Germans were to be found among researchers, and they have only begun to enter this sphere in the last decade. Our estimate shows that in Kazakhstan, where about half of all the Soviet Germans are concentrated today, the number of German students increased from about 3,530 in 1960 to 7,900 in 1967 and 11,730 in 1971; that is to say, the percentage

42 *Narodnoe khoziaistvo Kirgizskoi SSR*, Frunze, 1979, p. 285.

of German students in the Kazakh Republic had begun by the beginning
of the 1970s, to approach a 'normal' level. Thus we can conclude that
there was a considerable improvement in higher education for the
Germans in the 1960s and 1970s, but they are still under-represented in
this important field which affects the whole standard of life.

Social and occupational structure. The process of urbanisation was particularly slow among the Soviet Germans in the 1920s and only
accelerated with increased industrialisation in the Soviet Union and as
a consequence of the anti-kulak campaign. In 1939, only 18 per cent of
the Soviet Germans were city dwellers, but in 1959 there were 39.3
per cent and in 1970 45.5 per cent in the towns. Today the ratio is
apparently 50 per cent, that is to say, lower than that of many European nationalities in the Soviet Union and lower than that among the
population in general.

Table 5.6.   OCCUPATIONAL DISTRIBUTION OF GERMAN
POPULATION IN NOVOSIBIRSK REGION, 1967[43]

	Among whole Siberian population	Among Germans in Novosibirsk region
	%	%
Executive posts	4.1	0.9
Specialised workers in agriculture	0.8	0.9
Engineers and technicians	7.0	1.6
Officials	4.5	2.1
Mechanics	14.7	22.4
Cattle and pig breeders etc.	14.2	21.0
Field labourers	26.3	34.0
Industrial workers	1.8	1.6
Building workers	3.5	4.5
Others	23.1	11.0

The data given in Table 6 together with that obtained from among 3,600
Soviet German emigrants who reached West Germany in 1978[44] give us
some idea of occupational distribution. The most numerous group –

43 Malinowski in *Neues Leben*, July 2–16, 1969.
44 *Volk auf dem Weg*, 1979, no. 5, p. 3.

about 28 per cent – were artisans or practised workshop trades such as carpenters, locksmiths, and electricians. Workers in heavy industry, mines and factories accounted for 18 per cent; drivers of all sorts of vehicles from trucks to bulldozers 16 per cent; and office workers – bookkeepers, cashiers, store-keepers and so on – 13.7 per cent. Only about 4.6 per cent were in the liberal professions (engineers, doctors, teachers, journalists, economists). It appears, however, that in the last decade there has been a change in this sphere, and the number of Germans completing university studies is large and rising rapidly to a notable place among German families.[45]

Family incomes, private property and living standards

It is difficult to survey incomes among the German population because of a paucity of statistical data and the complicated nature of categories of payments in the rural population (wages, various wage supplements and income from private property). The Soviet German press occasionally publishes reports on the incomes of German families, with the clear propaganda purpose of showing what high living standards the Germans enjoy.[46] These accounts indicate an average wage for a *kolkhoz* or *sovkhoz* worker of 130 rubles a month and an average family wage income of about 400 rubles, but this is a very exaggerated description. In the Novosibirsk survey already cited, about 50 per cent of the Germans interviewed earned between 60 and 100 rubles a month and only one per cent earned more than 150 rubles. Among the urban population of the western Soviet republics, a worker's income in the 1960s was 124.1 rubles a month, and an average family income 293 rubles, while the income of Jewish families emigrating to Israel was 384.9 rubles.[47] The income of a German family depends on the occupations of the members of the family, the number of workers in the family, their place of residence and additional incomes on the side,

45 The Novosibirsk research shows that 38 per cent of those interviewed would have wished their children to be teachers. However, it did not state whether they would prefer their children to teach German in schools for a German population.

46 *Freundschaft*, Feb. 29, 1972; *Neues Leben*; Nov. 2, 1976, *Dell et ses enfants*, p. 35.

47 G. Ofer and A. Vinokur, *Family Budget Survey of Soviet Emigrants in the Soviet Union*, Jerusalem (Soviet and East European Research Centre, Research Paper no. 32), 1979, p. 35. In 1965 the average wage of a Soviet worker was 101.7 rubles. See *Les Recherches sociologiques en URSS*, Moscow, 1978, p. 107.

these last being of special importance in rural life and among artisans.

If we apply the social stratification and hierarchy used in Soviet sociology to the German population in regard to incomes, the Germans are found to be clustered preponderantly in the two last categories – specialized workers and non-specialised manual workers, who constituted 76.4 per cent of the general Soviet population in 1970 and 93.1 per cent in the *kolkhozy* – while in the first two categories, intelligentsia and officials, the Germans still account for a very small proportion at 8 per cent. The situation of the Germans in the *kolkhozy* and *sovkhozy* is apparently better than that of non-Germans in the same regions: thus the Novosibirsk study shows that 81.5 per cent of the Germans own one cow and 3.3 per cent two cows or more, while only 60 per cent of the general rural population in the Soviet Union own one cow.[48] The proportions are similar for sheep, pigs, poultry and other livestock. In the matter of housing, the remarkable total of 67 per cent of the Germans live in new houses that they have built themselves since 1955.[49]

Table 5.7.   GERMAN OWNERSHIP OF DURABLE CONSUMER GOODS, NOVOSIBIRSK DISTRICT, 1967, COMPARED WITH JEWISH EMIGRANTS AND TOTAL SOVIET POPULATION[50]

	Germans in Novosibirsk, 1967	Soviet Jewish emigrants to Israel, 1978	Soviet population, 1973
	%	%	%
Washing machine	42.2	68.6	60
Television	22.3	90.2	67
Radio	66.5	73.1	74
Record player	8.9	40.5	–
Bicycle	39.3	24.7	–
Motor cycle	23.3	4.5	8
Musical instrument	14.5	16.3	–
Motor-car	–	10.6	3

48 Karblay, p. 88.
49 This emerged from the Novosibirsk survey and from the research in West Germany among recent emigrants from the Soviet Union. See J. Schnurr, 'Die Aussiedler aus dem Sowjetischen Bereich', unpubl. ms., Stuttgart, 1978, p. 22.
50 J. Schnurr; Malinovskii; and G. Ofer and A. Vinokur, p. 69.

As regards that other indicator of living standards, namely ownership of durable consumer goods, we see from Table 7 that the Germans own fewer washing machines, TV sets, radios and telephones not only than the Jewish population, which is mainly urban and in the best-paid occupations, but fewer even than the Soviet average. Figures on means of transport indicate that the Germans are in the lead with bicycles and motorcycles, but not with cars, even though the Soviet press frequently stresses that many German families have private cars of their own.

In sum the Soviet Germans have enjoyed steadily rising living standards since the late 1950s, due to their energy, hard work and increased qualifications. These standards are certainly higher than those of the local population, Kazakh or Russian, in the same occupational classes, but when they are compared with the European population of the Soviet Union the Germans are still a long way behind.

Education and culture

One cannot over-emphasise the importance of national education and culture for minorities living in multi-national countries, all the more so if the minority is an extra-territorial one fighting for its very existence as a nation, as the Soviet Germans have had to do since the early 1940s.

Education. In the last years of Stalin's rule, nearly all the schools of the extra-territorial national minorities were shut down. This was part of the overall policy on nationalities, which was aimed at stifling the cultures of the smaller nationalities and intensifying the process of the russification.

After Stalin's death in 1953 certain national minorities, such as the Hungarians in the Carpathian region of the Ukraine and the Poles in Lithuania and the Ukraine, were given the right to open schools for mother tongue teaching.[51] This privilege was not extended to other national minorities including all the deported nationalities.

In 1956, German was introduced as a foreign language in Soviet

---

51 Thus in 1953–4 there were 98 Hungarian schools in the Ukraine and 263 Polish schools in Lithuania and the Ukraine. *Prosveshchenie i kul'tura litovskoi SSR*, Vilnius, 1964, p. 44; J. Kolasky, *Education in the Soviet Ukraine*, Toronto, 1968, pp. 49–59.

schools in Siberia and Kazakhstan, as a way of enabling thousands of German children to be taught their mother tongue. On April 9, 1957, the Education Ministry of the Russian Republic adopted a regulation on 'The Introduction of the Study of German as the Mother Tongue for Children and Adults of the German Nationality'.[52] Parents in agglomerations with a German majority would be allowed to choose between establishing schools with all the subjects taught in the mother tongue or forming German-language classes in the ordinary schools. It has not proved possible in practice to adopt the first of these options up till now for both objective and subjective reasons. First, the definitions in the regulation itself of such notions as 'considerable majority' and 'according to the parents' choice' were vague enough to admit of differing interpretations. Secondly, the relatively dispersed settlement of the Germans would have made it difficult to apply the first option even if the local authorities had been inclined to adopt it. Thirdly, no German representative institutions such as there had been in the 1920s and 1930s existed in the period in question; these could have influenced and guided the German population and emboldened it to demand the implementation of this option more vigorously. The final and most important reason was unquestionably the trauma resulting from Stalin's reign of terror during and after the war, and the fear it instilled, so that an act expressive of national feeling – sending children to learn their mother tongue, even with official authorisation – called for real courage. The majority of the Germans in the Soviet Union still could not find such courage in themselves.

For the same reasons it was also not easy to implement the second option. The main difficulty was the lack of teachers and textbooks. This was only partly made good in the 1960s by the opening of teaching seminars in different faculties in the Russian Republic and Kazakhstan and by the publication of a number of textbooks and the importation of German books from East Germany. In 1957–8, the first year after the regulation was issued, only a few hundred German pupils learned German as their mother tongue. In the next year there was some improvement as a direct result of efforts by the Ministry of Education and local education inspectors, and by German writers. In 1959–60 some 6,000 pupils were already learning German in the Russian Republic;[53]

52 *Sbornik prikazov i instruktsii ministerstva prosveshcheniia RSFSR*, 1957, no. 26, p. 9, as quoted in *Heimatbuch*, 1965, pp. 5–6.
53 H. Römich in *Heimatbuch*, 1964, p. 113.

the number reached 12,000 in 1960–1 and 16,000 in 1961–2.[54] We lack data from Kazakhstan for 1958–64, but we know that in 1965–7 the number of pupils learning German as their mother tongue dropped from 3,318 to 1,175 in the Tselinograd district and from 1,593 to 790 in Aktiubinsk. In Kirgizia there were 5,000 pupils in 1964–5.[55] In Kazakhstan between 1968 and 1972, the number of pupils learning German rose from 25,000 to 40,884.[56] From 1974 on, the publication of statistical data on everything connected with the numbers of German pupils learning German as their mother tongue ceased – possibly a pointer to negative changes in official policy, and to stagnation or even decline. If we take the high-point in the development of a German educational network among the Soviet Germans – the years 1968–72, – the percentage of German pupils learning German as their mother tongue can be stated as 35 per cent in Kirgizia,[57] 25 per cent in Kazakhstan, 10 per cent in the Russian Federal Republic and less than 10 per cent in Tajikistan. Little is known of the situation in the other republics except for the Ukraine where German is taught as the mother tongue in the Carpathian area. What is important, of course, is not only the numbers being taught but also the quantity and quality of the teaching. From 1957 on there were many changes in the number of hours taught, and in the ages at which the children received instruction. In the Russian Republic in 1965, German as mother tongue was taught in classes 2–5 for 29 hours a week, in Kazakhstan in classes 2–6 for 22 hours, in Kirgizia in classes 2–8 for 26 hours, and in Tajikistan in classes 5–10 for 13–14 hours a week.

The lessons generally include German grammar and language. The standard of teaching remains low, and criticism of teaching methods appears from time to time in the Soviet German press because German students leaving high school are unable to write a composition in German in spite of its being their mother tongue. As for the teaching of German literature, the problems are still worse, and every so often disputes erupt into the open over the question of which German literature

54 *Ibid.*
55 *Freundschaft*, Apr. 11, 1967; *Neues Leben*, Sept. 21, 1966; and *Neues Leben*, Jan. 27, 1965.
56 *Freundschaft*, June 27, 1968; *Neues Leben*, Aug. 7, 1968, Feb. 9, 1972.
57 E.g. the number of pupils in Kirgizia went down from 5,000 in 1964–5 to 2,500 in 1978–9, despite the fact that the German population increased in this period by 50 per cent. *Radio Liberty Research*, 1979.

Table 5.8. HOURS PER WEEK OF LEARNING GERMAN AS
MOTHER TONGUE, 1965[58]

Class	Russian Federal Republic	Kazakhstan	Kirgizia	Tajikistan
1	Grammar & literature	Grammar & literature	Grammar & literature	Literature
2	3	2	2	–
3	3	2	2	–
4	3	2	2	–
5	6	4	5	3
6	5	3	5	3
7	5	3	3	3
8	4	2	5	2
9	–	2	–	1
10	–	2	–	1–2
Total	29	22	24	13–14

should be taught – classical, modern West German, modern East German or Soviet German. A special committee of professors, teachers and education inspectors, headed by Professor A.A. Miroliubov was set up in 1975 by the Soviet Ministry of Education to seek solutions for all the problems which had arisen in German language and literature teaching.[59] It seems, however, that no complete solution has yet been found.

To sum up, despite all the problems and difficulties and the drop in the number of pupils learning German as their mother tongue, the situation of the Germans in this regard is much better than that of other national minorities such as the Jews, Bulgarians and Crimean Tatars, who have not been given the right to have their children taught their mother tongue.

Soviet German literature. Within the compass of this chapter there is no room for an analysis in depth of the development of Soviet German literature over the last quarter of a century. We can do no more than

58 *Neues Leben*, Sept. 8, 1965; D. Jahn in *Zeitschrift für Kulturaustausch*, 1969, no. 1, p. 17; Römich, p. 103.
59 *Neues Leben*, May 11, 1975.

give brief indications of its main problems and show how it has contributed towards strengthening German national sentiment.

Important Soviet German writers of the 1920s and 1930s like G. Luft, F. Bach, G. Sawatzky and D. Schellenberg were swept away in the terrible whirlwind of the purges and deportations. Others were forced to cease all literary activity until 1955. Then after fifteen years of silence Soviet German writers made their first reappearance in December 1955 with the publication in Siberia of the newspaper *Arbeit*. Writers like Österreicher, Kontschak, Frank, Kunz and Hollmann began to write for this paper and then, from May 1957, in the main German newspaper, *Neues Leben*. More will be said below of the German press.

The first organisation of German writers in the Soviet Union was established in the Krasnoiarsk *qblast* in July 1958 as part of the preparations for the Congress of Soviet Writers of the Russian Republic, and by 1960 it already numbered 30 writers, poets and dramatists as its members.[60] In Kazakhstan the German Writers' Section was founded only in 1965, and it too had 30 members. Besides these two groups of 30 each, some 40 more authors and journalists published literary work from time to time. Biographical information has been published on 60 German writers, and of these 9 per cent were born before 1900, 28 per cent in 1900–11, 26 per cent in 1917–29 and only 13 per cent after 1930. Thus very few writers were born in the deportation, and the future of German literature in the Soviet Union will be seriously jeopardised if a new generation of German writers does not emerge soon. About half these writers were born in the German Republic of the Volga and of the others many taught or worked there, which again proves the importance of the existence of a federative national unit for the survival of a national culture in the Soviet Union. Five of these writers were born abroad and went to the Soviet Union in the 1920s and 1930s. Nearly all were educated in the humanities (mainly literature) and had chosen teaching as their occupation. As regards taking part in political life, only some 15 per cent of them were members of the Communist Party, a low percentage indeed compared with other nationalities, especially since this is a German élite. The rate of participation by Germans in the general Soviet Union of Writers was also low – only 16 out of 100 writers are members. However, their non-participation stemmed from reasons independent of their own

60 *Ibid.*, July 26, 1958, and Oct. 24, 1960.

personal wishes, and in recent years there have been requests to take more German writers into the Union because of the many benefits that accrue from membership.

The main event in Soviet German literary life is the Moscow seminar inaugurated in 1968, in which writers from all parts of the Soviet Union take part and the tasks of fostering German literature and art and creating ties with the German public are discussed. At the first seminar it was resolved to establish a Commission for Soviet German Literature as part of the general Soviet Union of Writers, and until 1975 this Commission was headed by the Professor of German Literature at Leningrad University, a former political officer in East Germany, A. Dymshits.[61] When Dymshits, who was of Jewish origin, died, the German writer Robert Wagner was elected to succeed him. In recent years the Commission has been inactive. Another public activity of the German writers is participation by their representatives in writers' conferences and meetings in the different republics.

An anthology of new German writing by 45 authors in the Soviet Union, called *Hand in Hand*, and edited by Gubkina and Richter, appeared in 1960 in an edition of 50,000 copies, the first time such a collection had been published since the 1930s. Between 1960 and 1964, very few books by Soviet Germans and for the Soviet German population were published. Then regulation no. 228, 'Regarding increasing German Publications', issued by the Soviet Government's Committee for the Press on June 23, 1965, led to a certain improvement. In February 1967 a special department for German literature was created within the Kazakhstan Publishing House in Alma Ata, headed first by the poet I. Kurz and after him by K. Ehrlich.

Since the 1960s, German books intended for Soviet Germans have been published by Progress publishers in Moscow, Kazakhstan Publishing House in Alma Ata and the Siberian Publishing House in Kamerovo, and from time to time single works are brought out by other local publishers. In terms of quantity, Kazakhstan is the most important publisher, having brought out some 200 works between 1967 and 1980.[62] We have no data for books from other publishers, but it is possible to assume that since the beginning of the 1970s there has been an annual average of 15–20 books. There are very few translations of Soviet German literature into Russian and other languages, compared,

61 *Ibid.*, June 12, 1968.
62 These data were provided by the head of the German section of the Kazakhstan Publishing House, K. Ehrlich, *Neues Leben*, Feb. 25, 1981.

for example, with translations into Russian from Yiddish.[63] On the
other hand, translations of works by German writers have appeared in
recent years in local (mainly Siberian) periodicals such as *Altai, Enesei,
Leninskii Put', Ogni Sibirii* and *Prostor*. Soviet Germans can of course
enjoy German works that were neither written by nor for them to mention only the works of Goethe, Schiller, Lessing, Heine, Chamisso and
Thomas Mann. In 1962–73, 4,309 German works – an average of 400 a
year – were published in the Soviet Union.[64]

As regards the content of Soviet German literature, one can distinguish two different periods since the war. From 1955 to 1964 there
was much 'timidity', and writers shied away from touching on the
taboo subjects of war and deportation. From 1965 onwards an increasing number of works have dealt with these themes in different ways
and with differing degrees of boldness. The theme of the October
Revolution and the part played in it by Germans was always a favourite
of German writers in the Soviet Union and it is still acceptable today,
especially as regards anything connected with Lenin. Another historical theme that is important for the younger generation of Germans,
who know nothing of their people's history, is the period of the 1920s
and 1930s; today it is widely treated in novels, stories and plays
by veteran German writers such as V. Klein, A. A. Reimgen and D.
Hollmann. In this context, a welcome subject in new Soviet German
literature (and, incidentally, in general Soviet literature as well) is the
heroism of the Cheka and of intelligence people of German origin.
The impact of war and deportation is softened by tales of the heroism
of the Germans in the struggle against the Nazis both at the front and
in the rear – 'on the labour front' is the accepted Soviet terminology –
and the fact that there were only a few traitors among them. The use of
these themes has spread steadily in recent years. Deportation is generally
described as the rescue of Germans from the clutches of fascism, but these
descriptions are frequently interrupted by pages full of bitterness and
anger at the terrible wrong inflicted on hundreds of thousands of innocent people. This post-war softening of the impact of those years covers
every area of experience and is common to the whole of Soviet literature.

A 'changing of the guard' as the veteran writers disappear and die off

---

63 E.g. in 1955–66 198 books appeared, which were translated from Yiddish into
Russian. See B. Pinkus, A. Greenbaum, M. Altschuler (eds), *Russian Publications on
Jews and Judaism in the Soviet Union, 1917–1967*, Jerusalem, 1970, p. 81.
64 *Pechat' v SSSR*, Moscow, 1962–73.

has changed Soviet German literature considerably in recent years. The future of this literature will depend very much on the arrival of a new generation of writers.

Press and radio. The German press began to decline in the mid-1930s and disappeared completely in 1941 with the liquidation of the Autonomous Republic of the Volga. The first German paper in the post-Stalin period, *Arbeit*, appeared shortly after the December 1955 decree abolished restrictions on the Germans. Its editorial board was headed by a Russian appointee, Viktor Pestov, not a Soviet German, although his two principal assistants were the German writers Waldemar Spär and Johann Schellenberg. The paper appeared in Barnaul for two years, and its circulation was 6,400 copies. The main German paper in the Soviet Union, *Neues Leben*, first appeared in Moscow in May 1957, and two others came out the same year: *Arbeitsbanner* in Znamenka and *Rote Fahne* in Slavgorod. In 1960–5 only two papers were appearing – *Neues Leben* and *Rote Fahne* – and then in 1966 a new paper, *Freundschaft*, appeared in Tselinograd, to become the only German-language daily in the Soviet Union. In 1981 a literary periodical, *Heimatliche Weiten*, appeared in the form of an almanac of some 250 pages, with most Soviet German writers participating. It has to be noted that distrust of the Germans is so deep that to this day the main paper, *Neues Leben*, is run by Russians: up to 1975 by Georgii Pshenitsin (whose mother was German, it is true) and thereafter by Vladimir Zapanov. 'nly recently has the name of the editor of *Freundschaft* been published: he is the writer A. Debolskii, and it is even rumoured that he too is not German.

The circulation figures of the papers seem to be low: *Freundschaft* and *Neues Leben* bring out 25,000 to 30,000 copies each, and *Rote Fahne* only 8,000. None of them is sold abroad. From time to time a campaign of sorts is carried out in the papers and in the areas where Germans live to encourage or persuade people to become subscribers. The lack of response that the papers complain of has two main causes. First, there is ignorance of the language (mainly on the part of the younger generation), which is the result of the stifling of German culture; and secondly the Russian press is preferred. This is partly because of its greater importance, but mainly for political reasons: Germans who underwent the trauma of the Stalinist terror are still afraid of being accused of disloyalty. Yet the situation of the Germans with regard to newspaper publishing is much better than that of other extra-territorial nationalities, except

perhaps for the Hungarians. For example, the Jews have only two
periodical publications, the Koreans two and the Greeks and Crimean
Tatars one each.

In their content, the German papers are the same as all the other
Soviet papers. From the German-national viewpoint, the especially
important sections are literature, language, art – and the search for
missing relatives. Some emphasis is given to news concerning individual Germans (most notably workers who have exceeded their quotas,
and such like). The propagandist trend appears in articles attacking
religion and in increasingly frequent and virulent attacks on West
Germany.

The radio plays a role largely similar to that of the press, but broadcasts have an additional function which is of great national importance:
the diffusion of music, poetry and other forms of artistic expression. The
first German broadcasts intended for and arranged by Soviet Germans
began on Moscow Radio in 1956, when W. Rath was appointed head of
the German section.[65] In 1967, after the reorganisation of the Soviet
broadcasting service, a new allotment of two hours a day was given to
the different national broadcasts, and the German section was put under
'Radio Peace and Progress'. The programmes include news, press
reviews, talks on economic and scientific subjects, cultural presentations,
and the anti-religious campaign. Radio Alma Ata began broadcasts
in German in 1957 with a staff of only two; today nine people are
employed.[66] The director of the German radio since its foundation has
been Dietrich Friesen.[67] In the 1970s there was considerable expansion
both of broadcasting hours, which reached 290 minutes a week, and of
the number of programmes. Radio Frunze began German broadcasts
only in 1962, directed by J. Kunz and more recently by Paul Garber.
Since March 19, 1974, there have also been German broadcasts over
Slavgorod radio, directed by Andreas Krammer – 50 minutes a month;
and since September 30, 1974, Omsk Radio has put out 120 minutes
a month directed by K. Ehrlich. Other stations in Kazakhstan and the
Russian Republic occasionally broadcast German programmes.

Culture and the Arts. German cultural activity in the Soviet Union
developed in the 1920s, and there were some successes, mainly theatrical,

65 *Neues Leben*, Mar. 19, 1960.
66 *Ibid.*, July 17, 1974.
67 *Freundschaft*, May 7, 1970.

in the 1930s. The struggle to revive German culture in the Soviet Union after the rehabilitation decree was especially difficult simply because there were practically no high-level artistic organising personnel who could measure up to the difficulties and contend with the administrative and budgetary obstacles. In the first stage, therefore, in 1959, all that was done was to organise choirs in work places and German population centres. In Kazakhstan, after intervention by the administrative institutions, the first choir was established in 1960 alongside the Philharmonic Orchestra of Kustanai,[68] with Nikolai Baumann as its head and Elvira Muth and Peter Zoog among the singers, but it went out of existence soon after it was founded. In 1963 a German cultural circle was founded in Aktiubinsk called 'Edelweiss,' headed by H. Leicht. The first large German professional ensemble, called 'Freundschaft', and including actors, dancers and singers, was formed in Karaganda on December 5, 1968.[69] H. Leicht was its first director, followed in 1975 by Waldemar König. In different regions with large German agglomerations the group presented programmes of sketches, German folksongs, and songs by Soviet German composers and writers, as well as Kazakh songs and dances, but after early successes it ran into difficulties. There were budgetary problems, since proceeds from the sale of tickets did not cover expenses. The group's administrative dependence on the Philharmonic of Karaganda did not make matters easier and quarrels broke out from time to time. There were also serious disputes within the group between the performers and the management over what should be its character – for example, whether it should enlarge its Russian repertoire to attract non-Germans to the shows. And they were short of artists of a high professional standard. It is interesting that in some places they were presented as an East German group and not a Soviet one in order to draw a crowd. In 1975 the Kazakh authorities promised the group financial aid,[70] but this did not solve all the problems and the group's activity has slowed down in recent years. Other groups that have worked in Kazakhstan recently have been 'Lorelei', established in June 1975 in the Dzhambul region, and directed by Alfred Matt;[71] the group of the

68 Neues Leben, Nov. 19, 1960.
69 The most important were Elvira Muth, Heinrich Voth, Erwin Penner, Maria Penner, Semfira Abdratikova, Erich Schulz, and Martha Saks. Freundschaft, July 5, 1963; July 30, 1969; Jan. 1, 1970.
70 Neues Leben, May 17, 1975.
71 Ibid., June 7, 1978.

kolkhoz, 'Thirty Years of Kazakhstan', in the Pavlodar *oblast* directed by Jakob Walter;[72] and 'Jugend' in the Chemkent *oblast*.[73]

Since the late 1950s the possibility of creating a professional German theatre like the one which existed in the German Republic of the Volga and the Ukraine in the 1930s has been discussed from time to time in the Soviet German press, but without practical results. Then the establishment of a national German Studio in the Shchepkin Drama School in Moscow was announced in September 1975.[74] Students taking a five-year course in this Studio performed in public for the first time in 1978 in short plays, and the following year put on Lessing's drama *Emilia Galotti* in Krasnodar and Kustanai. In 1981, when the first class graduated in Moscow, a permanent theatre was established at Termitau in Kazakhstan.

In the field of music, the composer and researcher Oscar Geifuss was especially active, writing the music for the oratorio *Buchenwald* to the words of the Soviet German poet Jaquemien, and the opera *Richard Sorge*.[75]

Apparently there is little painting and sculpture being done. One can only mention the painters Vladimir Eifert and Viktor Busch.[76]

Academic research.   Serious academic research in the fields of history, literature, religion, demography, philology and national folklore calls for established research institutions and numerous experienced researchers as well as considerable funds. All this was of course lacking for Soviet Germans from the 1940s on, and even in the preceding decade German research in the Soviet Union was only just beginning to develop. Does the possibility exist of building it up in the Soviet Union today? The prospects seem slight, but high aspirations and energetic work can produce results even under the most difficult objective conditions – the non-existence of a republic, unhelpful administrative policy and the disappearance of German researchers during and after the war. We must therefore look at what has been achieved by isolated researchers scattered among many different universities.

The historian L. Malinovskii has already been mentioned, especially his doctoral thesis based on archival material, 'The History of the Soviet

72 *Ibid.*, Apr. 29, 1975; May 18, 1976.
73 *Ibid.*, Jan. 25, 1977.
74 *Freundschaft*, Sept. 26, 1975.
75 *Ibid.*, Aug. 17, 1968.
76 *Ibid.*, Nov. 11, 1975.

Germans from the Beginning up to 1917'.[77] The publication of this work will be of great importance to Germans who know nothing of their past because of the prolonged silence imposed by the regime. Other historical contributions, of a more propagandist nature, were V. Danilov, 'The German Internationalists in Siberia in the Years 1917 to 1921';[78] J. Gosnitz and P. Hermann, 'The First Communists in Marienthal';[79] and A. Eirich, 'The First Soviets in the Volga Region'.[80]

In the field of philology and literature, the leading researchers of the previous period (G. Dinges, V. Schirmunsky and F. Schiller) either disappeared or ceased working on the Soviet Germans. An important philologist today is Professor Andreas Dulson of Tomsk University, who trained a whole generation of Germanists in the Soviet Union.[81] Other researchers in this field are O. Zacher of Irkutsk, H. Pankrat of Minsk, A. Herdt of Rostov-on-the-Don, W. Propp of Leningrad and A. Hermann of Alma Ata.[82] V. Klein (also important as a Soviet German author) and Hugo Jedig of Omsk are researching German dialects in the Soviet Union, an important and interesting field both linguistically and historically.[83] Some years ago, Johann Windholz wrote a doctoral thesis on German folksongs.[84]

German national identity in the Soviet Union

In the light of our survey of the legal-political status of the Soviet Germans and their economic and cultural situation, we can now examine German national identity as influenced, on the one hand, by the administration's policies and, on the other, by complex and multi-faceted internal factors.

We have to consider first what are the characteristics of national identity, and how they should be examined, and then the factors that

---

77 In 1976 parts of this thesis were published in *Neues Leben*, Sep. 14 and 19, 1976.
78 *Ibid.*, July 31, 1974; Aug. 7, 1978.
79 *Ibid.*, June 1–July 13, 1976.
80 *Ibid.*, Mar. 22, 1977.
81 *Freundschaft*, Feb. 7, 1970; Mar. 28, 1972.
82 *Ibid.*, Jan. 16, 1973: H. Bolger, *Zweig eines grossen Baumes – Werdegang Sowjetdeutschen Literatur*, Alma-Ata, 1974.
83 *Freundschaft*, Feb. 25, 1972; W. Klein published his book on German folksongs in 1974; *Unversiegbaren Born*.
84 *Freundschaft*, Aug. 14, 1975; Oct. 10, 1975.

help to strengthen national identity and those that hasten its decline. Finally we shall see what solutions to the German problem in the Soviet Union are feasible.

In the Soviet Union there are four quantitative indicators which serve to identify a person's national category:
– the declaration on nationality at the time of a population census;
– the declaration on mother tongue at the time of the census;
– item 5 on the identity card since the decree of December 1932; and
– subjective expressions of national identity, which can surface in various ways (in the Soviet Union this cannot be presented quantitatively because of the non-existence of objective public opinion surveys).

We shall look at these categories with reference to the Soviet Germans only; lack of space rules out comparative study of other nationalities whose legal-political situation is similar.

Nationality according to population censuses, 1959–79. The first population census after the Second World War was in 1959, when 1,619,655 persons declared themselves of German nationality. In the second census, in 1970, there were 1,846,317 Germans, and in the most recent one, in 1979, 1,936,000.[85] An important and difficult question, however, concerns the number of Germans who have 'disappeared' and are now 'hidden', that is those who for various reasons have preferred to hide their real nationality, which they would have registered if they had been free of internal and external compulsion. In other words, what is the answer if one subtracts the number in the first and third categories above from that in the fourth category? We are helped to answer it by surveys made in recent years in Germany and Israel. In a survey entitled 'Patterns of Adjustment of Immigrants from the Soviet Union' carried out by the Israeli Ministry for Absorption of Immigrants.[86] 207 people were asked: 'How did the census-taker put the question regarding nationality: (1) "Are you Russian, Lithuanian, Ukrainian etc.?" or (2) "What is your nationality?" or (3) in some other way?' Over 90 per cent of those questioned said that they had been asked in a neutral way, that is 'What

85 The data cited here are taken from *Itogi vsesoiuznoi perepisi naseleniia* 1970 goda, IV: *Natsional'nyi sostav naseleniia SSSR*, Moscow, 1973, pp. 9–11; *Naselenie SSSR* Moscow, 1980, pp. 23–7.
86 The data cited here are those given by Altshuler, *Soviet Jewry Today: A Socio-Demographic Analysis*, Jerusalem, 1979, p. 29 (Hebrew). On this subject see too the interesting analysis in H. Carrère d'Encausse, *L'empire éclaté*, pp. 63–6.

is your nationality?' The survey also reported that over 90 per cent of those asked said there had been no sense of constraint during the census. Only a very few said they had felt pressure to declare themselves as belonging to another nationality. In a survey by R. Karklins of 200 German emigrants from the Soviet Union in West Germany, questions were also asked *inter alia* about the population censuses of 1970 and 1979[87] regarding declarations on nationality. Part of those questioned said that at the time of the census they found it difficult to answer the question because they belonged to mixed families, or because they had been cut off from the Germans for so long, and in this way the census-takers were given the widest opportunity to 'advise' in the way they wished, which was generally to declare Russian nationality or the predominant nationality in the given republic. Our personal experience gained in talks with recent German, Jewish and Russian emigrants from the Soviet Union, added to the above, leads to the conclusion that there was in fact pressure with the deliberate intention of registering fewer persons as Germans at the time of the census.

A more important question is the possibility of deliberately hiding one's real nationality from the census-taker so as to escape discrimination and hostility on the part of the administration and the local population. As is well known, the census-takers are forbidden to ask for people's identity cards to verify the declaration made, but this rule was not always strictly followed. In the survey in Israel referred to above, 41% of the sample stated that they did present their identity cards to the census-taker (29.5 per cent at his request and 11.5% on their own initiative),[88] whereas in the Karklins survey 90 per cent stated that they were not asked for their identity cards and were registered according to their declaration alone.[89] Where there are many nationalities it could certainly happen that for a given population the census-takers might register a different nationality from that given them without fear that the respondent would check, but it must be assumed that there were not many such instances. Hence one can conclude that among the Germans, unlike the Jews, it was not at all common practice to present identity cards, and town-dwellers especially could register whatever nationality they wished. Did they want to change their nationality, and if so of what percentage is

87 R. Karklins, 'A Note on "Nationality" and "Native Tongue" as Census Categories in 1979', *Soviet Studies*, 1980, no. 3, pp. 415–22.
88 Altshuler, p. 29.
89 Karklins, p. 419.

this true? These questions are hard to answer, but because the Germans constitute one of the 'problem' nationalities facing material and other difficulties, we can conclude that a certain proportion – varying from 10 to 15 per cent in the 1959 and 1970 censuses down to 5 to 10 per cent in the 1979 census – did in fact conceal their German nationality and were registered as Russians, Ukrainians, Lithuanians and the like.[90]

Nationality according to mother tongue. It is in the nature of things that not all the members of a national minority should be able to speak their mother tongue and know it properly in a multi-national state where another language is dominant, like the Soviet Union. However, assimilation by language through acculturation, when it happens by free choice, is something wholly different from language assimilation that is based on coercion through official russification and carried out by stifling the culture of the national minority. Here too there were pressures at the time of the census, and Germans were frequently obliged to register a language (generally Russian) other than German as their mother tongue. (Ethnic Germans were often inclined to register as German speakers although, because of inadequate education and the effects of the deportation, they did not know the language properly.) The number of German speakers decreased significantly between 1939 and 1959, but it was still high – 75 per cent in 1959. In the 1970 census, 66.8 per cent declared German as their mother tongue but in 1979 only 57 per cent did so – a decrease of 18 per cent in twenty years, despite the (limited) facilities granted to Germans to learn German as their mother tongue or as a foreign language.[91]

Partial or even complete language assimilation without the loss of other national elements does not of course necessarily signify national

90 According to a survey carried out by Jewish activists in the Soviet Union in 1976, more than half of those questioned said they had not had any trouble because of their external Jewish characteristics such as accent or facial traits, but they nevertheless said they would be glad to conceal their national identity. B. Fein, Dan Caspi and M. Verbit, 'The Jewish Identity of Jews in the Soviet Union' in D. Prital (ed.), *The Jewish Intelligentsia in the Soviet Union*, 1981, no. 5, p. 88.

91 Another interesting question that we cannot discuss here is the extent of real knowledge of the mother tongue by those claiming it. Not a few Germans, Jews and Poles do this now on national grounds because of the national awakening, although they actually do not know their mother tongue at all. From surveys and conversations with both German and Jewish emigrants it emerges that 23 per cent among the Germans hardly know their mother-tongue and 50 per cent know it only moderately well. See Schnurr, p. 44.

assimilation in the sense of loss of national identity. In periods of linguistic and cultural assimilation, moreover, there were people in the front ranks of the movement for national re-birth in a number of national minorities who were culturally and linguistically assimilated. Whether the process of language assimilation will be accelerated or slowed down will depend on many complex factors, such as securing or not securing a real autonomous unit in the Soviet federal framework, the degree of urbanisation, the possibility of learning the language in national minority schools, and the advance of the national awakening.

Nationality according to identity card. If we could refer to statistical data on all the notations for item 5 of the internal Soviet identity card, we could calculate the number of Germans who for one reason or another prefer to hide their German identity. A survey carried out by Zionist activists in the Soviet Union revealed that 60 per cent of the Jews questioned stated that they would like to see the statement of nationality on the identity card abolished. This is what serves for ethnic identification in the Soviet Union.[92] Surprisingly, this wish is voiced by people with strong Jewish national affiliation, though fulfilment of their wish would certainly lead to a rise in national assimilation. It is well known that item 5 was not abolished despite numerous rumours in the early 1960s, in the Soviet Union itself and in the West, that it would be; this was due to political-administrative considerations that carried decisive weight with the Soviet leadership. Thus the Soviet authorities contributed – and this is only one of the many paradoxes of Soviet nationality policy – to putting a brake on the process of assimilation among many of the nationalities. The abolition of item 5 would, moreover, have slowed down the process of emigration that gained momentum in the 1970s.

At all events, there is no doubt whatever that the number of Germans registered as such on their identity cards is higher than the number who declared themselves as such in the population censuses.

Nationality according to subjective national identification. Besides the objective, material indications signalising national identity, such as language, territory, federal unit or nationality as registered under item 5, there are subjective signs of an intellectual or emotional nature. Such signs are interest in the historical past and in learning about it, a desire to maintain

92 B. Fein, in Prital, p. 88.

national customs and preserve folklore, a sense of special identification with members of one's nationality both inside the Soviet Union itself and outside it, and an affective tie of some kind with the national State, the heartland, of one's people. Since no surveys have been published in the Soviet Union on these matters, we must resort once more to surveys made among emigrants – which, given the nature, size and other characteristics of the sample, do no more than serve as an indicator. A survey at the Hebrew University in the early 1970s among nearly 500 former Soviet Zionist activists indicated that the vast majority of those questioned had had some knowledge of Israel and Jewish history and culture. In the survey inside the Soviet Union already mentioned, half of those answering claimed to have close cultural ties with other Jews. Some two-thirds of those answering felt a sense of belonging with Jews in other countries.[93] From the surveys of Karklins and Schnurr, it appears that a similar state of affairs exists among Soviet Germans, who prefer the company of fellow-Germans, keep up their own national and religious customs and give other signs of a high degree of solidarity. This means that despite the clear advance of especially strong assimilatory processes among extra-territorial national minorities in the Soviet Union, the factors working for national identification are also important.

Mixed marriages and national identity. A factor of great importance that affects the national identity of all the Soviet nationalities – especially the extra-territorial ones, who are more dispersed among a 'foreign' population than those with a recognised territory – is the rate of mixed marriages. It is no accident that Soviet researchers see mixed marriages as one of the principal levers for starting off the process of melting the nationalities together. Already in the 1920s, the rate among Jewish men in the Russian Republic reached 21 per cent (in 1926), among Germans 11 per cent and among Poles as much as 80 per cent.[94] From the incomplete data published in the Soviet Union since the 1960s we can obtain only a very general picture of this important subject. We shall make use here of two quantitative indicators: data on mixed marriages in the Soviet Union and data on mixed families among Soviet German emigrants in West Germany.

Of the three national minorities we are concerned with here – the

93 *Ibid.*, p. 87.
94 *Natsional'naia politika VKP (b) v tsifrakh*, Moscow, 1930, p. 41.

Germans, the Jews and the Poles – the process of mixed marriage continues to be fastest among the Poles. Thus in the Latvian Republic in the 1960s it reached 71.6 per cent for men and 67.6 per cent for women. The Jews come next, with 35 per cent in Latvia.[95] In the city of Kharkov, the mixed marriage rate among Jews was 29.6 per cent,[96] but among Jews in the Ukraine generally it did not rise above 10.3 per cent for the urban population and 9.8 per cent for the rural population.[97] No data on mixed marriages among the Germans have been published in the Soviet Union at all since the 1920s. An analyst of data gathered by German researchers in the Nazi period (1941–4) concluded that the the increase of mixed marriages observed in those years continued at a still faster rate into the 1960s. In the Kokchetav *oblast*, where there was a large German agglomeration (75,485 out of a population of 589,204 in 1970), the rate of mixed marriages was 32 per cent in 1960 and 35.5 per cent in 1967.[98] Among the German emigrants from the Soviet Union who returned to Germany in 1980, only 5 per cent of the families were mixed.[99] The proportion of mixed marriages involving Soviet Germans would seem to be between 10 and 20 per cent.

The crucial question here is what choice the children of mixed marriages will make when they reach the age of 16 and get their identity cards for the first time. Soviet researchers – who may have a tendency to exaggerate in the desired direction – assert that in the majority of the republics 80 per cent of the children of mixed marriages tend to choose the nationality of the majority population of their republic.[100] This means that among national minorities mixed marriages constitute the gravest danger of loss of national identity. However, it is clear that this trend can also change and has apparently already changed partially today under the influence of various factors that we shall discuss later.

Religion and national identity. The Christian churches with which the Soviet Germans are associated – Lutheran, Catholic, Mennonite and

95 A. Kholmogorov, *Internatsional'nye cherty sovetskikh natsii*, Moscow, 1970, p. 84.
96 M. Kurman and I. Lebedinskii, *Naselenie bol'shogo sotsialistich-eskogo goroda*, Moscow, 1968, p. 126.
97 V. Naulko, *Etnichnyi sklad naseleniia ukrainskoi SSR*, Kiev, 1965, p. 109.
98 M. Fazylov, *Religiia i natsional'nye otnosheniia*, Alma Ata, 1969, p. 101.
99 Der Bundesminister des Innern, VEK T-4-933 600/2.
100 V. Kozlov, *National'nòsti SSSR*, Moscow, 1975, pp. 239–48.

Baptist – have to wage a very unequal battle with the forces ranged against them.

Even today religion plays an important role in the Soviet Union in preserving national identity among all national minorities with religions other than Russian Orthodoxy. As far the Germans are concerned, this is first because the language of prayer, German, strengthens the tie with the mother tongue. Secondly, the place where they come to worship is practically the only meeting place the people have. Thirdly, the observance of feast-days and other customs and traditions connected with religion is directly connected with their own history and it deepens national feeling. Finally, there is an important link, even if it can only find limited expression, between believers inside the Soviet Union and abroad.

In 1937 the question of religious affiliation was put for the first and last time in a Soviet census, and no related statistical data have been published. Partial data have been appearing since the 1960s, but of a tendentious character as regards both the choice of regions covered and the way the survey questions were put. From these it emerges that in northern Kazakhstan, with its considerable German population, only 6.7 per cent of the population were practising believers.[101] But according to a different source, the percentage in the whole of Kazakhstan, where there are about a million Germans, was 16 per cent,[102] and in Estonia about 33 per cent.[103] From a survey carried out in the Slavgorod *oblast* (where half of those questioned were Germans of Catholic, Lutheran and Mennonite origin) it appeared that between 21 and 28.6 per cent of the general population were believers.[104]

These partial data together confirm our view that between 25 and 30 per cent of the Soviet Germans are religious believers. To these should certainly be added people of non-religious views who nevertheless value religion as an important factor for strengthening national identity and weakening the strong assimilatory influences.

Factors that help to strengthen national identity

We have now seen that both the objective factors (the very existence of a

101 M. Fazylov, p. 81.
102 I. Rau, 'Wer glaubt heute schon an Gott?', *Freundschaft*, Feb. 9, 1972.
103 Carrère d'Encausse, p. 229.
104 R. Erhardt, 'Aktiver Atheist sein', *Neues Leben*, Apr. 12, 1972.

multi-national country with different nationalities living in close social, economic, and cultural proximity; processes of modernisation and integration, and so on) and the subjective factors (the russification policy; coercion by many and varied methods) all work in the direction of loss, or at least weakening, of national identity. What contrary forces are at work which strengthen German national identity in the Soviet Union? These factors, which are numerous and very complex, can be divided into two main classes, 'negative' or repellent and 'positive' or attractive.

Negative factors are those that discourage Soviet Germans from accepting the idea of integration into Soviet – mainly Russian – society. Their importance lies in their function as catalysts that set off the complex process of awakening or strengthening the sense of national identity. The trauma of the past is one of the prime negative factors promoting national identity. While subjected to much of the same persecution that other national groups received, the Germans had cause to feel that their nationality was at the root of some of the injustice meted out to them. This is particularly true of their wartime and post-war treatment. Their fifteen years of suffering, with over 300,000 dead, all property lost, constant humiliation and innumerable personal tragedies, could not have failed to leave a mark on a whole generation of Germans, even when the sufferings had receded into the past. It is difficult to judge the extent to which this factor now influences young people born in the deportation, but it is certain that they are aware of the wrong done to their parents. This must have its effect in awakening national feelings.

But although the trauma of the past may have varying effects, present-day discrimination has a decisive influence, whether it exists in fact or is subjectively felt to exist. The policy of discrimination against the extra-territorial national minorities in the post-Stalin period differs in application to various minorities. Thus, for example, the Hungarians, Poles and Greeks have been given the possibility of having their children taught in their national schools in some regions, while others – Jews and Crimean Tatars – are not so privileged. Some minorities have newspapers in their mother tongue and others do not, and so on. How is discrimination against the Soviet Germans manifested in the post-Stalinist period, even after the years of rehabilitation from 1955 to 1972?

First, there is no practical possibility of living wherever they choose in the Soviet Union, notably in the region that was once the Autonomous Republic of the Volga. Secondly, the Germans are not admitted into a number of government institutions and services including the KGB, the Foreign Ministry, the Ministry of Foreign Trade and certain army institutions. Thirdly, there is a bar to advance and promotion in various undertakings and institutions. It is hard to verify how far this is true, but it is a contention commonly voiced by Soviet German emigrants in West Germany. Further, we see under-representation in administrative institutions and the Communist Party. And, finally, there is discrimination in education and culture.

Up to the present time, the Soviet media present an unfavourable image of the Germans. It is hard to explain the political grounds (if there are any) for this hostile attitude, apart from the bitterness and the hatred felt towards Germans in general since the war. For many years up till the 1970s the very existence of the Germans in the Soviet Union was consistently ignored, but since then references to them in various contexts and writings about them – books, newspaper articles, radio and TV reports – have begun to appear, all hostile in tone. We shall give only a few examples. A book by P. Vershigora, *People with a Clear Conscience*,[105] was published after the war and continues to appear in many editions. There has been no revision of passages about the Soviet Germans full of falsifications and blind hatred, despite the well-known, normal and accepted Soviet practice of altering such tendentious passages when there has been a change in the official political line. Nor has there been any revision of the history textbooks used in Soviet schools which falsify the Germans' role in Russian history and contain a marked anti-(Soviet) German trend. Thus in the book by Pankratova, one of the most blatantly Stalinist historians, we find: 'The Volga Germans . . . quickly transformed themselves into the most prosperous and reactionary part of the rural population, behaving in a disdainful and hostile way to the Russian inhabitants.'[106] In the textbook for second grade in Kazakhstan schools there still appears to this day the well-known wartime patriotic poem by Sergei Mikhalkov with the lines: 'Did we not tell the fascists/Our people will not suffer/Russian bread – bread of the spirit-/to be called by the name of "*Brot*". . .' The poem ends: 'We hit the Germans hard – there and here![107] This gives great joy

105 P. Vershigora, *Liudi chistoi sovesti*, Moscow, 1956.
106 *Istoria SSSR Uchebnik 9go klassa*, Moscow, 1963, 23rd edn, quoted from A.S. no. 1776.
107 According to the unpublished memoirs of Herta Vogel, who emigrated to West Germany from Pavlodar in 1979.

to the Russian pupils in mixed classes with German children.

The hostile attitude of the press continues in spite of protests from the Germans; K. Wukert has reported on it extensively in *samizdat*.[108] The local population is naturally influenced by the hostility of the media, which they see as giving 'official ratification' to popular dislike for the German national minority. This dislike shows itself in many ways in personal encounters: for example, Germans are frequently called 'fascist', 'Nazi' and 'traitor' as well as the more innocuous 'Fritz'. In the city of Pavlodar, the Russian teacher tells the pupils in second grade the 'historical' story of how the German traitress Fania Kaplan[109] assassinated good grandfather Lenin.[110] Numerous other insults, either personal or collective, have been documented in recent years. They are predominantly connected with the Nazis and the war against fascism.[111]

In the Baltic Republics, in contrast to the Russian Republic and Kazakhstan, the Germans are regarded sympathetically by the local Baltic people and have a favourable image. This is due to their long shared history, and similarities in their respective national characters and patterns of behaviour.[112]

Soviet German literature cannot ignore this burning issue but attempts to treat it cautiously. In a play by the Soviet German writer Friedrich Bolger, the Russian Sergei loves the German girl Erna in spite of the fact that his first wife and children were murdered by the Nazis. It is he who tries to calm Erna's pangs of conscience, saying, '*Nu* – there now, what do you have in common with those Germans? How can you be responsible for the criminal acts of the fascists, just because you are German? You were born in the Soviet Union, you went to school here, you were brought up here.' To this Erna answers, 'Ah, if only they all thought like you!'[113] Bolger is giving a broad hint that such thoughts are very exceptional and that hatred for

---

108 A.S. no. 2811–6, p. 16.

109 The absurdity of this story can be seen in the fact that Fania Kaplan, a Jewess, shot Lenin in 1918 but did not kill him.

110 Herta Vogel.

111 See, for example, A. Pierrard and M. Wartin, *Vivre en Sibérie*, Paris, 1966, p. 77 and A.S. no. 2811–b, pp. 14–15.

112 I. Kazlas, 'Social Distance among Ethnic Groups' in E. Allworth (ed.), *Nationality Survival*, New York, 1975, pp. 258–99.

113 *Freundschaft*, Aug. 26, 1973. We should stress here that such things are published only in German.

the Germans – including the Soviet Germans, and perhaps them in particular since they are close at hand – has not yet died down.

The breakdown of Communist ideology was perhaps more immediate and more general among Soviet Germans, most (if not all) of whom had not been supporters of communism before the war either. The Twentieth Party Congress in 1956 – news of which only reached them much later – and the great political events of the 1950s and 1960s such as the Berlin uprising in 1953, the Hungarian revolt in 1956 and the Soviet invasion of Czechoslovakia in 1968 still further undermined any faith they might have had in the Soviet regime. Most of the Germans, however, were apolitical and what apparently affected them most decisively was their not being granted full rehabilitation, as well as the virulent propaganda against them and against West Germany in all the Soviet communications media. This factor, as we shall see, spurred on the search for a more radical solution than anything envisaged before, leading to the desire to leave the Soviet Union and build their personal and national life elsewhere.

The rising tide of nationalism in the Soviet Union, which began during the war, not only did not stop in the post-Stalin era but rose even higher. The extra-territorial national minorities had perhaps been more inclined than others to believe in the myth of 'the socialist fraternity of peoples' and to combine in a cultural 'melting together'. They were soon disenchanted, however, on finding that all it meant was russification. They were not prepared to be alone in renouncing their national identity while all the other peoples were reinforcing theirs. This important factor is hard to pin down, and unfortunately no question about it was put in the surveys carried out among Soviet German emigrants in West Germany. However, its effect cannot be doubted and this will certainly continue in the future if nationalistic trends continue to gain strength in the Soviet Union in the future.

Although these negative factors stimulate the complex process of national awakening and the search for solutions to the specific national problems of each nationality, positive factors can undoubtedly determine the nature of a given solution at a given time.

Chronologically, priority has to be given to the historic encounter of the 350,000 Germans with the German *Reich*, both in the German-occupied areas of the Soviet Union and in Germany itself. Even though this unforeseen encounter was short, and took place amid the tragedy of war and deportation, it made a deep emotional impression on the Soviet Germans, who had been cut off from the rest of the German nation for so long. Family relations were renewed, there was once again the possibility of learning about the past and imbibing elements of German culture, even if these came in the chauvinistic guise of Nazi imperialism, religious life was revived with observance of customs and feast-days – all this influenced not only the generation that lived through it but the next generation as well. From the 1950s on, this encounter also fed the aspiration to leave the Soviet Union, which began with the many Gemans who had obtained German citizenship and could thus get exit visas more easily.

It is necessary to stress how very strong was the Catholic and other religious solidarity among the Soviet Germans, which had held firm all through the ordeals of war and deportation. Keeping up the prescribed religious observances and customs enshrined in German community life for generations reinforced the will to preserve them in the future, and immeasurably strengthened national sentiment. This solidarity and cooperation within the German community was strongest in the countryside, but in the cities too it survived and increased under the influence of the other factors we have discussed. Official education policy and cultural activity also had a considerable influence. The German language was taught in class in the context of German literature, theatre, the press and so on. But even if this cultural activity took place within a framework of official censorship and restrictions, it still strengthened national identity.

The existence of two German states is an important factor, since these states can – if they choose – influence the Soviet Union and intervene on behalf of the Soviet Germans. They influence the Soviet Germans directly too by making them feel that they are not isolated and abandoned but can receive assistance in their hour of need. However limited the cultural and religious ties with these states may be, they are important in that they strengthen the Soviet German national identity. From 1955 on, as we have seen, West Germany, became not only a symbol and a pole of attraction but also an active, dynamic factor.

The German population in the Soviet Union divides into four very heterogeneous groups, hard to evaluate quantitatively, which manifest various degrees of vacillating national identity. These are: the group that is entirely assimilated or in an advanced stage of assimilation; the national communist group; the religious group; and the national group.

— The *assimilated group* is mainly urban and is to be found among the intelligentsia, whose numbers have risen in recent years. Up till now this group has not possessed the means to express itself and therefore has not publicised its assimilationist attitude. These are Germans who are already linguistically and culturally assimilated, or are well on the way to being so, and have decided to abandon the rest of their German national identity as well. Although some of them are still Germans, this is not due to any wish of theirs, but because of compulsory registration of nationality in the identity card and the absence of any legal possibility of changing it.

The wish to assimilate is directed mainly towards Russian culture. The reasons are many and varied, but all are connected in one way or another to two main axes. On the one hand are economic interests, opportunity to advance in one's professional career and the desire to shed the burden of belonging to a 'problem' nationality with an unfavorable public image, and on the other is the attraction of Russian culture.

— The *national-communist group* is the only one that has the opportunity and the means to express itself legally in the Soviet Union within the bounds and according to the patterns which have been acceptable in the country at different times since the revolution. The group began to grow in the late 1920s, but after suffering severe blows already in the 1930s, it was almost wiped out in the deportation. In the 1950s, as a result of the rehabilitation processes, it took shape again and even began to expand, aided by the means put at its disposal by the Soviet régime. Making use of the four German periodicals, the special departments in the publishing houses, radio broadcasts, theatre groups and so on, it can reach every part of the German public, although the extent and power of this influence is hard to judge because of the absence of data from statistical surveys. However, the German writers themselves – novelists, poets, playwrights and journalists – provide the clearest expression of this group's outlook. Within the bounds of what is permitted, they are able to express their Soviet-German national identity. R. Leiss, A. Reimgen, K. Welz, D. Hollmann, A. Saks and F. Bolger are among those who have shown their desire to expand the bounds of German culture in the Soviet Union and strengthen the German national awakening with all the means at their disposal.

— The *religious* group. These Germans belong mainly to the Mennonite and Baptist Churches, which emphasise the central and absolute value of religion in the life of the individual, over and above all other elements, including national ones. This group works to spread the faith in the community, defend the believers and fight Soviet anti-religious coercion. Insofar as the national factor does not run counter to their religious aspirations, they are prepared to support the preservation of German national identity, but when there is any conflict between the two, it is the struggle to save the faith which has priority.

— It is hard to judge the scope of the *nationalist* group, but there can be no doubt that it has increased steadily in recent years, as the size of the German emigration from the Soviet Union bears witness. Unlike the national-communist group, which seeks partial solutions within the official Soviet political framework, this group seeks solutions that are both radical and immediate. It is also the group that, most of all, apprehends the serious dangers threatening the Soviet Germans as they are in the process of being worn down and crushed nationally by accelerated assimilation.

Possible solutions to the German national problem in the Soviet Union

By 'possible' solutions we mean proposals that have been put before the Soviet authorities or have been brought up in some other fashion by Soviet Germans, mainly representatives of the German nationalist movement that began to take form in the 1960s. The solutions are not merely theoretical, but are based on Soviet legal-political realities and are capable of being implemented if the authorities judge them desirable. If we ignore the assimilationist solution, which is of course the opposite of national survival, there are three solutions proposed to solve the German national problem in the Soviet Union. These are the exterritorial solution, the territorial solution, and emigration.

— The *exterritorial solution*, based on the principle of national-cultural autonomy, was rejected in theory by Soviet leaders but was in fact applied after the October Revolution with some amendments. It would mean leaving the Germans where they are now and not concentrating them in one area or giving them a federative unit. The solution adopted for them with the publication of the rehabilitation decrees was in fact along these lines and is being carried out in a limited way. It had the official backing of the Chairman of the Supreme Soviet, Mikoyan, who received the second German delegation in 1965[114] and declared, 'As for the reconstruction of the German Republic, that is certainly the best solution, but it is not feasible, since for this purpose it would be necessary to put half a million people there. Can't the Germans really live without a republic? When it existed, two-thirds of them lived outside it.'[115] Mikoyan promised the delegation that he would take steps to extend the rights of the Soviet Germans in education and culture.

National-communist circles, some of whose representatives were also in this German delegation to Moscow, have had no choice but to accept this solution. All they can do is to try and widen the bounds of the national-cultural autonomy accorded them as best they can. They call for extensions and improvements in the German educational network by the creation of German national schools like those that existed in the 1920s and 1930s. They also concern themselves with securing large budget allocations for cultural purposes, expanding art institutions, increasing the number of German publications, and so on.

This minimalist solution is generally acceptable to the Soviet authorities, but even this can only be kept going by means of unremitting struggle. On its success depends the very survival of the German nationality in the Soviet Union. It can also, incidentally, help advance the claims of other national minorities which for various reasons were accorded fewer rights than the Germans in the fields of education and culture.

— The *territorial solution* – the reconstruction of the German Republic of the Volga and permission to concentrate there for those Germans wishing to do so – was the insistent German demand immediately after the publication of the rehabilitation decrees in August 1964, but as we have seen, it was rejected by the Soviet régime. In 1972–4, with the growing strength of the illegal German nationalist movement (the

114 For the visits of the German delegations to Moscow (two in 1965 and one in 1967) see E. Schwabenland-Haynes. 'The Restoration of the German Volga Republic', *American Historical Society of Germans from Russia*, 1973, Working Paper no. 12, p. 12; A. Sheehy in AMHSGR 1973, no. 13, p. 5, and 1976, no. 22, p. 1.

115 Cited from B. Lewytzkyj, *Politische Opposition in der Soujetunion, 1960–1972*, Munich, 1972, pp. 231–235.

second phase after the failure of the legally permitted efforts) a proposal was raised to enable the Germans who wished to come together to do so in the Kaliningrad *oblast* (formerly East Prussia). The latter could, in the future, become a German national unit within the Soviet Federation, or it might conceivably join up with East Germany.[116] After a long interval, the question of establishing an autonomous German republic in the Siberian *krai* of the Russian Socialist Republic or in Kazakhstan ` has been brought up repeatedly in recent years: more than two-thirds of all Soviet Germans now live in these two areas. According to news reaching the West via journalists and from Soviet German emigrants, there was even a secret discussion in June 1979 in the Presidium of the Supreme Soviet of Kazakhstan on the possibility of establishing an autonomous German republic there, with its centre in the Ermentau *raion*. Kazakh students reacted with an angry protest demonstration and carried the slogan 'Kazakhstan one and indivisible'.[117] Rumours spread that the Soviet German representative on the Supreme Soviet, Lydia Kritz, even launched an attack on 'imperialist circles' that were spreading rumours to the effect that the Germans wanted to set up a republic of their own, when in fact they were perfectly happy where they currently lived.[118]

— Finally, there is the solution of *emigration*. But here it is important to distinguish emigration by isolated individuals, however many these may be (and there are indeed many), who see leaving the Soviet Union and settling in some other country as their personal solution, from emigration as an overall national solution for the Germans in the Soviet Union. In the first phase, from 1955 right until 1969, the Germans who wanted to emigrate were mainly German citizens by virtue of the agreements between the Soviet Union and Nazi Germany in 1939–41 or by Germany unilaterally granting citizenship in the years 1941–45. Even if others wanted to emigrate, they could not envisage that it might be possible for them to do so. The situation changed from the beginning of the 1970s because of both the general changes in Soviet emigration policy and the Germans' bitter disappointment over not receiving full rehabilitation. The struggle for emigration by any

---

116 G. Rar, 'Nemtsy khotiat uekhat', *Posev*, 1974, no. 6, p. 30; H. Mickoleit 'Das Schicksal der Russland Deutschen', *Akademische Blätter*, 1977, no. 6, p. 193.
117 See memoirs of Herta Vogel and *Der Spiegel*, Oct. 15, 1979.
118 See *Kulturpolitische Korrespondenz*, 1979, no. 382, pp. 15–16; *Sowjetunion heute*, 1979, no. 8.

means, whether legal or not, was intensified in the second half of the 1970s.[119]

Between 1955 and 1981, 89,544 persons emigrated from the Soviet Union to West Germany, and over 2,000 to East Germany and a few hundred more to the United States, Canada and South America. This total of 92,000 is less than 5 per cent of the total German population in the Soviet Union. From the drastic drop since 1980 in the number of Soviet German emigrants (for example, from 7,226 in 1979 to 3,773 in 1981 and only 910 in 1984) it is clear that if no change takes place in the opposite direction soon, the solution of emigration will cover only a tiny minority of the Soviet Germans. For the majority of the German population, the first two solutions will hold good, but the prospect is that only the first of them can be carried out in actual practice. The Soviet administration is afraid that other national minorities (such as Tatars, Koreans, Armenians, Greeks, Bulgarians, Poles and Hungarians) will start demanding a similar solution.

119 On the many and complex problems connected with emigration from the Soviet Union to Germany by Germans and other national minorities, see B. Pinkus, 'Emigration of National Minorities from the USSR in the Post-Stalinist Period', *Soviet Jewish Affairs*, 1983, no. 1, pp. 3–36.

EPILOGUE

Edith Rogovin Frankel

The restlessness and dissatisfaction of at least a portion of the Soviet Germans has become abundantly clear over the past twenty-five years. Their loss of a territorial base within the borders of the Soviet Union; their wartime treatment by Stalin and the long wait for rehabilitation after his death; the distrust and discrimination many still experience in their new places of residence – all these things have created unhappiness and national discontent. Realising that there is little hope of return to the *status quo ante* and that there is at least a chance of leaving the country in which their people have lived for some 200 years, many Germans have come to see emigration as their best option. Although this strategy cannot provide a solution to the national problem of the Germans inside the Soviet Union, it does offer personal hope for many who see no other viable alternative.

Emigration as a national policy existed in various forms before the 1970s, when it became a phenomenon attracting world attention; throughout the post-war years, the Soviets permitted emigration of specific groups for various reasons. People who had been Polish citizens and found themselves within the Soviet borders as a result of the Second World War were given permission to return to Poland in the years immediately after the end of the fighting. Another agreement to allow those in this category still in the Soviet Union to leave was implemented in the 1957–9. The ex-citizens of other countries long resident in the Soviet Union, for example Greeks and Spaniards, were likewise given the opportunity to return to their native lands. It was in the mid-1950s that the West German Chancellor Konrad Adenauer received a similar concession from Khrushchev to allow German ex-prisoners of war to return to (West) Germany. At that time Adenauer also expressed concerned interest in the ethnic Germans.

It has not been unusual for foreign policy considerations of various kinds to play a role in Soviet internal policy moves. Thus, the early establishment of the Autonomous Soviet Socialist Republic of the Volga Germans – the first such republic to be formed in the Soviet Union – was motivated in part by the hope of influencing public opinion in Germany and thus strengthening the Communist Party in that country. Again, the 1955 decree has been called the 'Adenauer amnesty' and was clearly a result of his visit to Moscow. Emigration policy in the 1970s, though not solely a function of foreign policy considerations, almost certainly hinged on East-West relations, and in this respect the striking similarity in pattern between the emigration of the Germans and of the Jews from the Soviet Union is instructive. True, German emigration reached its high point in 1976–7, whereas that of the Jews came in 1979, and the outflow of the Germans was generally less subject to violent oscillations. It is true also that German emigration in the 1970s did not reach the size of the Jewish exodus – at its height over 51,000 Jews left in one year, while the number of Germans leaving in one year never passed 10,000. All in all, German emigration since the early 1970s now totals slightly less than 75,000 as against the 260,000 Jews who have left the Soviet Union since 1971. (A result of this is that almost the same number of Jews and Germans now remain inside the Soviet Union.) Despite these variations in the pattern of emigration, the experiences of the two groups are analogous: relatively high emigration figures throughout the 1970s, and then both dropping to inconsequential levels in the 1980s. In 1984 fewer than 900 Jews and 1,000 Germans were given permission to leave. Statements made by Soviet spokesmen at various meetings implied that improvements in East-West relations or, alternatively, in trade with the West would bring about an increase in emigration.

The emigration of Armenians, the third of the major groups given permission to leave the Soviet Union during this period, has followed a roughly similar curve, although their peak year was 1980, with just over 6,000. Late in that year the first signs of the cutback appeared, and the numbers dropped to about 2,500 in 1981 and less than 400 in 1982.

Each of these groups differs from the others in major respects. The Germans are 'returning' to a country where neither they nor their grandparents were either born or bred; even their more remote ancestors did not necessarily originate in what is today West Germany, the country to which the majority head once they leave the Soviet Union. On the other hand, they have to a considerable extent maintained the language and even the religion of their forebears, and a sense of community: adversity and alienation have heightened their sense of attachment to each other and to the German state which has fostered their exodus. A few thousand of them, however, have opted for

EMIGRATION FROM THE USSR, 1954–84

	Germans	Jews	Armenians*
1954	18	53	
1955	608	105	
1956	800	454	
1957	1,221	149	
1958	4,681	12	
1959	5,960	3	6,000
1960	3,460	60	
1961	451	202	
1962	927	184	
1963	242	305	
1964	262	537	
1965	365†	891	
1966	1,245	2,047	
1967	1,092	1,406	5,000
1968	598	229	
1969	316	2,979	
1970	340	1,027	
1971	1,145	13,022	?
1972	3,426	31,071	?
1973	4,493	34,733	1,494
1974	6,541	20,628	1,074
1975	5,985	13,221	1,162
1976	9,704	14,261	2,574
1977	9,274	16,736	?
1978	8,455	28,865	?
1979	7,226	51,320	3,600
1980	6,954	21,471	6,000
1981	3,773	9,447	2,500
1982	1,958	2,692	400
1983	1,447	1,315	193
1984	910	897	88

Source: Benjamin Pinkus, 'The Emigration of National Minorities from the USSR in the Post-Stalin Era', *Soviet Jewish Affairs*, vol. 13, no. 1, 1983, and unofficial sources.

*Armenian figures are approximate.
†Between 1965 and 1970, an additional 600 Germans emigrated to East Germany; and approximately 1,000 in addition did so between 1971 and 1979.

Canada or the United States, where earlier groups of Russian Germans had settled.

The Jews are in at least as anomalous a situation. Their 'return' is to a homeland whose language few of them speak and from which they and their forebears have been separated for almost 2,000 years. However, in spite of the degree to which they have become absorbed into the main fabric of Soviet life, achieving a high level of individual success, there still remains a strong tie binding the Jews as well. This is partly to be attributed to the identification by nationality required in the internal passport; partly to the anti-Jewish discrimination prevalent in certain occupations and in entry to institutions of higher learning; and in part to the virulently anti-semitic propaganda frequently published under a thin guise of anti-Zionism. The percentage of Jews who have chosen not to go to Israel, for which their emigrant visas are issued, is far higher than that of the Germans going on to countries other than West Germany.

The case of the Armenians is different again. They alone among these three groups actually have a national republic established for their people within the borders of the Soviet Union, complete with the various assets provided by such status: a vast number of schools, many churches and native language publications, and a majority status in their territory. In leaving the Soviet Union, the Armenians are, in effect, leaving their 'native' area (keeping in mind, however, that their traditional area extends to Turkey, which is of course not their destination) and dispersing to join a great range of Armenian communities in a far-flung diaspora. Their emigration was relatively negligible until 1976, when 1,800 exit visas were issued; however, in their case a sizeable proportion of those seeking to emigrate were not natives of the Soviet Union, but had come in the post-war years from elsewhere – North America, France, Lebanon, Syria, Iran and Greece – to settle in the Armenian republic.

It is improbable that emigration can provide a total solution to the national problems of the Germans and the Jews of the Soviet Union. It is unlikely to serve as more than a palliative – a personal solution for those who succeed in leaving and a way for the régime to relieve pressure by ridding itself of those who are most troublesome and cause dissatisfaction among their co-nationals. Thus what happens to those who remain is still the central problem. The dilemma of what is to be done about the extraordinary number of nationalities in the Soviet Union has never been satisfactorily resolved. If the aim is to allow each nationality to flourish and retain its separate identity while participating as equal members in a multi-national society, it is still far from attainment. And if the true aim is to erase those characteristics which differentiate peoples from each other and to produce a new, universal, Soviet man, then, according to the voices ringing out in dissent, the régime also has a very long way to go. The German issue is by no means one of the most difficult or dangerous. It is just one of many such problems, each one unique but each also part of the complex pattern of inter-acting forces in Soviet society.

BIBLIOGRAPHY

Ackermann, J. *Heinrich Himmler als Ideologe*. Göttingen, 1970.

Adenauer, K. *Erinnerungen, 1953–1955*. Stuttgart, 1966.

Allard, H. *Politik vor und hinter den Kulissen*. Düsseldorf-Vienna, 1979.

Allworth, E. *Nationality Group Survival in Multi-Ethnic States*. New York, 1977.

Altshuler, M. *Soviet Jewry Today: A Socio-Demographic Analysis* (Hebrew). Jerusalem, 1979.

Amburger, E. *Die Anwerbung ausländischer Fachkräfte für die Wirtschaft Russlands vom 15. bis 19. Jahrhundert*. Wiesbaden, 1968.

——. *Die van Brienen und ihre Sippe in Archangel*. Berlin, 1936.

——. *Geschichte des Protestantismus in Russland*. Stuttgart, 1961.

Ammende, E. *Muss Russland hungern? Menschen- und Völkerschicksale in der Sowjetunion*. Vienna, 1935.

Anger, H. *Das Deutschtum in Sibirien. Reise durch die deutschen Dörfer Westsibiriens*. Berlin, 1930.

Anthologie der sowjetdeutschen Literatur. 2 vols, Alma Ata, 1981.

The Anti-Stalin Campaign and International Communism. New York, 1956.

Arkhiv Samizdata. Radio Svoboda. Vols 1–30, Munich, 1968–79.

ASSR Nemtsev Povolzhiia. Verkhovnyi Sovet. Stenograficheskii Otchet. Pervyi sozyv. Engels, 1938; *Vtoroi sozyv*. Engels, 1939; *Tretii sozyv*, Engels, 1940; *Chetvertyi sozyv*. Engels, 1941.

ASSR der Wolgadeutschen. Politisch-ökonomischer Abriss. Engels, 1938.

Aubin, H. *et al.* (eds). *Deutsche Ostforschung. Ergebnisse und Aufgaben des ersten Weltkrieges*. Leipzig, 1942–3.

Auerbach, H. *Die Besiedlung der Südukraine in den Jahren 1774–1787*. Wiesbaden, 1965.

Auhagen, O. *Bei den deutschen Bauern an der Wolga*. Berlin, 1927.

——. *Die Schicksalswende des russlanddeutschen Bauerntums in den Jahren 1927–1930*. Leipzig, 1942.

Auslanddeutschtum in Osteuropa einst und jetzt. Troisdorf, 1963.

Bachmann, H. *Durch die deutschen Kolonien des Beresaner Gebietes der UdSSR*. 2nd edn, Stuttgart, 1974.

Bährens, K. *Deutsche in Straflagern und Gefängnissen der Sowjetunion*. Munich, 1965.

Bailes, K.E. *Technology and Society under Lenin and Stalin: Origins of the Soviet Technological Intelligentsia, 1917–1941*. Princeton, 1978.

Baltenbriefe zur Rückkehr ins Reich. Berlin-Leipzig, 1945.

Bartels, B. *Die deutschen Bauern in Russland. Einst und jetzt*. Moscow, 1928.

Barton, B. *The Problem of 12 Million German Refugees in Today's Germany*. Philadelphia, 1949.

Baumhauer, F. *Der Unterricht im Deutschen an dem deutschen Realgymnasium in Tiflis.* Stuttgart, 1926.

Becker, J. *Bessarabien und sein Deutschtum, Bietigheim und Fabelle.* Pokrovsk, 1923.

Beiträge zur Heimatkunde des deutschen Wolgagebiets. Pokrovsk, 1923.

Belimov, A. *Kto takie mennonity?* Moscow, 1972.

Bellendir, L. *Deutsches Liederbuch.* Pokrovsk, 1927.

Belov, A., and A. Shilkin. *Diversiia bez dinamita.* Moscow, 1972.

Bender, P. *Die Ostpolitik Willy Brandts oder die Kunst des Selbstverständlichen.* Hamburg, 1972.

Beratz, G. *Die deutschen Kolonien an der unteren Wolga in ihrer Entstehung. Gedenkblätter zur 150-jährigen Ankunft, 1764-1914.* Saratov, 1915.

Bereday, G., W. Brickman and G. Read (eds). *The Changing Soviet School.* Cambridge, Mass., 1960.

Berger, R. *Das deutsche Dorf auf dem Wege zum Sozialismus.* Moscow, 1930.

Bericht des Kommissariats für deutsche Angelegenheiten im Wolgagebiete über seine Tätigkeit vom 30. April bis 1. September 1918. Saratov, 1918.

Berkova, P., and R. Kuzmenko. *Viktor Maksimovich Zhirmunskii.* Moscow, 1965.

Berler, R. *Avec elles au-delà de l'Oural.* Paris, 1967.

Beschlüsse des Zweiten Rätekongresses der Autonomen Sozialistischen Räte-Republik der Wolgadeutschen. Zolotoe, 1925.

Beschlüsse des Dritten Rätekongresses der Autonomen Sozialistischen Räte-republik der Wolgadeutschen. Pokrovsk, 1926.

Bethell, N. *The Last Secret: Forcible Repatriation to Russia, 1944-1947.* London, 1974.

Bibliographisches Handbuch des Auslandsdeutschtums. Stuttgart, 1935.

Bier, F., and A. Schick. *Aus den Leidenstagen der deutschen Wolgakolonien.* Darmstadt, 1921.

Billig, J. *Rosenberg dans l'action idéologique, politique et administrative du Reich hitlérien. Inventaire commenté de la collection de documents conservés au C.D.J.C. provenant des archives du reichsleiter et ministre A. Rosenberg.* Paris, 1963.

Birenbaum, W. *Christenheit in Sowjetrussland.* Tübingen, 1961.

Bis zum letzten Atemzug. 3 vols, Alma Ata, 1968–75.

Bociurkiw, B., J. Strong and J. Laux (eds). *Religion and Atheism in the USSR and Eastern Europe.* London, 1975.

Bohmann, A. *Menschen und Grenzen. Strukturwandlung der deutschen Bevölkerung im sowjetischen Staats- und Verwaltungsgebiet.* Cologne, 1970.

Böhme, K. *Die deutschen Kriegsgefangenen in sowjetischer Hand. Eine Bilanz.* Munich, 1966.

——. *Gesucht wird. Die dramatische Geschichte des Suchdienstes.* Munich, 1965.

Bollmuss, R. *Das Amt Rosenberg und seine Gegner.* Stuttgart, 1970.

Bongs, R. *Harte herrliche Strasse nach Westen.* Berlin, 1942.

Bonwetsch, G. *Geschichte der deutschen Kolonien an der Wolga*. Stuttgart, 1919.

Böss, O. *Materialen zur Geschichte der Volksdeutschen in der UdSSR*. Munich, 1960.

Bosse, H. *Der Führer ruft. Erlebnisberichte aus den Tagen der grossen Umsiedlung im Osten*. Berlin, 1941.

Bourdeaux, M., and M. Rowe (eds). *May One Believe in Russia? Violations of Religious Liberty in the Soviet Union*. London, 1980.

Brahm, H. (ed.) *Opposition in der Sowjetunion*. Düsseldorf, 1972.

Brandt, W. *Begegnungen, Einsichten. Die Jahre 1960–1975*. Hamburg, 1976.

—— and R. Löwenthal. *Ernst Reuter. Ein Leben für die Freiheit*. Munich, 1957.

Bräutigam, O. *So hat es sich zugetragen. Ein Leben als Soldat und Diplomat*. Würzburg, 1968.

——. *Überblick über die besetzten Ostgebiete während des Zweiten Weltkrieges*. Tübingen, 1954.

Brettmann, A. *Bin Russlands Sohn*. Alma Ata, 1981.

Broederich-Kurmahlen, S. *et al. Deutsche Bauern in Russland*. Berlin, 1916.

Broszat, M. *Nationalsozialistische Polenpolitik 1939–1945*. Stuttgart, 1961.

Brown, M. (ed.) *Ferment in the Ukraine*. London, 1971.

Brüder in Not. Dokumente der Hungersnot unter den deutschen Volksgenossen in Russland. Berlin-Steglitz, 1933.

Brüder in Not! Dokumente des Massentodes und der Verfolgung deutscher Glaubens- und Volksgenossen im Reich des Bolschewismus. Berlin, 1933.

Brügel, J.W. *Stalin und Hitler. Pakt gegen Europa*. Vienna, 1973.

Buber-Neumann, M. *Als Gefangene bei Stalin und Hitler*. Stuttgart, 1968.

Buca, E. *Vorkuta*. London, 1976.

Buchholz, E. *Erlebte Geschichte zwischen Weichsel und Wolga. Erinnerungen an das Deutschtum im slawischen Raum*. Bonn, 1979.

Buchsweiler, M. *German Raiony and their Newspapers 1927–1941*. Research Paper no. 58, Soviet and East European Research Centre, Hebrew University, Jerusalem, 1984.

——. *Volksdeutsche in der Ukraine am Vorabend und Beginn des Zweiten Weltkriegs – ein Fall doppelter Loyalität?* Gerlingen, 1984.

Captured Germans and Related Records. Washington, DC (no date).

Carrère-d'Encausse, H. *L'empire éclaté. La révolte des nations en URSS*. Paris, 1978.

Carroll, W. *We're in this with Russia*. Cambridge, Mass., 1942.

Cartellieri, D. *Die deutschen Kriegsgefangenen in der Sowjetunion*. Munich, 1967.

Ciszek, W.J. *L'espion du Vatican*. Paris, 1966.

Conquest, R. *The Great Terror: Stalin's Purge of the Thirties*. London, 1968.

——. *The Nation Killers: The Soviet Deportation of Nationalities*. London, 1970.

——. *Power and Policy in the USSR*. New York, 1961.

—— (ed.). *Religion in the USSR*. London, 1968.

——. *The Soviet Deportation of Nationalities*. London, 1960.

Craig, G., and F. Gilbert (eds). *The Diplomats, 1919–1939*. Princeton, 1953.

Crankshaw, E. *Russia and the Russians*. London, 1947.

Dallin, A. *The German Occupation of the USSR in World War II*. New York, 1955.

——. *German Rule in Russia, 1941–1945: A Study in Occupation Policies*. London, 1957.

——. *Odessa, 1941–1944: A Case Study of a Soviet Territory under Foreign Rule*. Santa Monica, Calif., 1957.

Dallin, D., and B. Ničolaevsky, *Forced Labor in Soviet Russia*. London, 1948.

Das Deutsche Auslandsinstitut im neuen Reich. Stuttgart, 1935.

Däs, N. *Wölfe und Sonnenblumen. Eine Russlanddeutsche erzählt von ihrer Kindheit*. Baden-Baden, 1969.

De-Fehr, S.P., *Im Wandel der Jahre*. Winnipeg, 1975.

Deiatel'nost' Soveta Natsional'nostei i ego Prezidiuma. Moscow, 1929.

Dell und seine Kinder. Aus dem Leben der Sowjetdeutschen. Moscow, 1975.

Demelt, W. *Der grosse Treck der Volksdeutschen, 1939–1941*. Breslau, 1941.

Der Bote. Index. 1924–1947. Winnipeg, 1976.

Der Treck der Volksdeutschen aus Wolhynien, Galizien und dem Narew-Gebiet. Berlin, 1943.

Der Zug der Volksdeutschen aus Bessarabien und dem Nordbuchenland. Prague, 1942.

Deriabine, P., and F. Gibney. *Policier de Staline*. Paris, 1966.

Deutschbaltisches biographisches Lexikon, 1710–1960. Im Auftrag der Baltischen Historischen Kommission. Cologne, 1970.

Deutsche Brüder schreiben aus russischer Hungersnot. Geilenkirchen, 1935.

Deutsche Bücher, 1933. Moscow, 1933.

Deutsch-sowjetische Beziehungen von den Verhandlungen in Brest-Litowsk bis zum Abschluss des Rapallovertrages. Berlin (East), 1971.

Deutsche Volkslieder. Alma Ata, 1971.

Die deutschen Ostseeprovinzen Russlands. Geschichtlich, kulturell und wirtschaftlich dargestellt von Kennern der Baltischen Provinzen. Berlin, 1918.

Die 1. Parteikonferenz der RKP(b) des Gebiets der Wolgadeutschen. Marxstadt, 1921.

Diezel, P. *Exiltheater in der Sowjetunion, 1932–1937*. Berlin (East), 1978.

Dimanshtein, S. (ed.) *Itogi razresheniia natsional'nogo voprosa v SSSR*. Moscow, 1936.

Dinges, G. *Beiträge zur Heimatkunde des deutschen Wolgagebiets*. Pokrovsk, 1923.

——. *Wolgadeutsche Volkslieder mit Bildern und Weisen*. Berlin, 1932.

Dirksen, H. von. *Moskau, Tokio, London. Erinnerungen und Betrachtungen zu 20 Jahren deutscher Aussenpolitik, 1919–1939*. Stuttgart, 1949.

Dukmeyer, Fr. *Die Deutschen in Russland*. Munich, 1916.

Dunn, D. *The Catholic Church and the Soviet Government, 1939–1949*. New York, 1977.

Durdanevskii, V. *Ravnopravie iazykov v sovetskom stroe*. Moscow, 1929.

Durksen, M. *Die Krim war unsere Heimat*. Winnipeg, 1977.

Dyck, H.L. *Weimar Germany and Soviet Russia, 1926–1933: A Study in Diplomatic Instability*. London, 1966.

Dyck, P. *Orenburg am Ural*. Clearbook, 1951.

Ehrt, A. *Das Mennonitentum in Russland von seiner Einwanderung bis zur Gegenwart*. Berlin-Leipzig, 1932.

El Campesino. *La vie et la mort en URSS (1939–1949)*. Paris, 1950.

Emma, N. *Die Auswanderung ist eine konterrevolutionäre Aktion*. Moscow, 1930.

Engelhardt-Kyffhäuser, O. *Das Buch vom grossen Treck*. Berlin, 1940.

Epp, F. *Mennonite Exodus*. Altona, Manitoba, 1966.

Epstein, F. T. *Germany and the East*. Bloomington-London, 1973.

Epstein, J. *Operation Keelhaul: The Story of Forced Repatriation from 1944 to the Present*. Old Greenwich, Conn., 1973.

Er lebt in jedem Volk. Sowjetdeutsche Presse und Prosa dem grossen Lenin gewidmet. Moscow, 1970.

Fabry, P. *Die Sowjetunion und das Dritte Reich. Eine dokumentierte Geschichte der deutsch-sowjetischen Beziehungen von 1933 bis 1941*. Stuttgart, 1971.

Fast, G. *Das Ende von Chortitza*. Winnipeg, 1973.

——. *Schatten des Todes. Erlebnisbericht aus Sowjetrussland*. Winnipeg, 1956.

Fazylov, M. *Religiia i natsional'nye otnosheniia*. Alma Ata, 1969.

Feldbrugge, F. *Samizdat and Political Dissent in the Soviet Union*. Leiden, 1975.

Fiechtner, F. (ed.) *Heimat in der Steppe: Aus dem Schrifttum der Bessarabiendeutschen*. Stuttgart, 1964.

Fisher, A. *The Crimean Tatars*. Stanford, Calif., 1978.

Fisher, H.H. *The Famine in Soviet Russia, 1919–1923*. New York, 1927.

Fittbogen, G. *Wie lerne ich die Grenz- und Auslandsdeutschen kennen? Einführung in die Literatur über die Grenz- und Auslandsdeutschen*. Munich-Berlin, 1927.

Fleischhauer, I. *Das Dritte Reich und die Deutschen in der Sowjetunion*. Stuttgart, 1983.

Fletcher, W. *The Russian Orthodox Church Underground, 1917–1970*. London, 1970.

Fondis, Fr. *Kanada, Deutschland oder die Sowjetunion*. Kharkov, 1930.

Forndran, E., F. Golczewski and D. Riesenberger (eds). *Innen- und Aussenpolitik unter nationalsozialistischer Bedrohung*. Opladen, 1977.

Frederiksen, O. *The American Military Occupation of Germany, 1945–1953*. Darmstadt, 1953.

Freund, G. *Unholy Alliance: Russian-German Relations from the Treaty of Brest-Litovsk to the Treaty of Berlin*. London, 1957.

Frick, K. *Umdenken hinter Stacheldraht. Österreicher in der UdSSR*. Vienna, 1967.

Garadza, V. *Protestantizm*. Moscow, 1971.

Gazety v SSSR 1917–1980. Bibliograficheskii spravochnik. 4 vols, Moscow, 1970–80.

Gebhardt, E. *'Deutsche Hungernot' Wo?* Moscow-Leningrad, 1933.

Geilfus, O. *Deutsche Volkslieder.* Alma Ata, 1971.

Geilke, G. *Das Staatsgehörigkeitsrecht der Sowjetunion.* Frankfurt-Berlin, 1964.

Geissler, B. *Vom Deutschtum in Russland.* Leipzig, 1934.

Genocide in the USSR: Studies in Group Destruction. Munich, 1958.

Gerlach, F. *Auf neuer Scholle.* Berlin-Leipzig, 1941.

German Workers in the Soviet Union: German Foundry Workers tell their own Story. Moscow, 1932.

Geyer, D. (ed.) *Sowjetunion, Aussenpolitik, 1917-1955.* Cologne-Vienna, 1976.

Gidulianov, P. *Otdelenie tserkvi ot gosudarstva v SSSR.* Moscow, 1926.

Giesinger, A. *A Key to Microfilm of the German Captured Documents.* Lincoln, Neb., 1977.

——. *From Catherine to Khrushchev: The Story of Russia's Germans.* Winnipeg, 1974.

Giesinger, A., F. Haynes and M. Olsen. *Bibliography of the AHSGR Archives and Historical Library, Greeley, Colorado.* Lincoln, Neb., 1976.

Ginsburgs, G. *Soviet Citizenship Law.* Leiden, 1968.

Ginzberg, L., and S. Drabkin. *Nemetskie antifashisty v bor'be protiv gitlerovskoi diktatury (1933-1945).* Moscow, 1961.

Girchak, E. *Na dva fronta v bor'be s natsionalizmom.* Moscow, 1933.

Gitelman, Z. *Jewish Nationality and Soviet Politics: The Jewish Section of the CPSU, 1917-1930.* Princeton, 1972.

Glinsky, A. *Der greikhengen un felern in der arbet tsvishn di natsionale minderhaiten.* Kharkov, 1931.

Gollwitzer, H. *Und führen wohin du nicht willst. Bericht einer Gefangenschaft.* Munich, 1952.

Goncharskaia, S. *Rabota sredi natsional'nykh men'shinstv. Opyt moskovskoi partiinoi organizatsii.* Moscow, 1929.

Gosudarstvennaia planovaia kommissiia. Itogi khoziaistvennogo stroitel'stva ASSR za 15 let (1918-1933). Engels, 1933.

Götz, K. *Das Schwarzmeerdeutschtum.* Folge 1: *Die Mennoniten.* Posen, 1944.

Greife, H. *Zwangsarbeit in der Sowjetunion.* Berlin-Leipzig, 1936.

Grieser, H. *Die Sowjetpresse über Deutschland in Europa, 1922-1932.* Stuttgart, 1970.

Grimm, W. and S. Österreicher (eds). *Durch der Heimat weite Fluren. Sowjetdeutsche Poesie und Prosa.* Moscow, 1967.

Gross, E. *Avtonomnaia Sotsialisticheskaia Respublika Nemtsev Povolzh'ia.* Pokrovsk, 1926.

Grosse (Die) Sozialistische Oktoberrevolution und Deutschland. Berlin (East), 1967.

Grube, F., and G. Richter. *Flucht und Vertreibung. Deutschland zwischen 1944 und 1947.* Hamburg, 1980.

Gulkina, I. (ed.) *Wir selbst. Sammelband sowjetdeutscher Prosa.* Moscow, 1968.

Haarmann, H., L. Schirmer and D. Walsch. *Das 'Engels' Projekt: Ein anti-*

faschistisches Theater deutscher Emigranten in der UdSSR (1936–1941). Worms, 1975.

Hahn, G. *Die deutschen Bauernsiedlungen am Schwarzen Meer.* Stuttgart, 1965.

Haller, J. *Die Deutschen in Russland in Reden und Aufsätzen zu Geschichte und Politik.* Stuttgart-Berlin, 1934.

Hammond, E. *Soviet Foreign Relations and World Communism.* Princeton, 1965.

Hans, N., and S. Hessen. *Educational Policy in Soviet Russia.* London, 1930.

Hayward, M., and W. Fletcher (eds). *Religion and the Soviet State: A Dilemma of Power.* New York, 1969.

Height, J. *Homesteaders on the Steppe: A Cultural History of the Evangelical-Lutheran Colonies in the Region of Odessa, 1800–1945.* Bismarck, N.D., 1972.

——. *Paradise on the Steppe: A Cultural History of the Katschurgan, Beresan and Liebental Colonists, 1804–1944.* Bismarck, N.D., 1972.

Heitman, S. (ed.) *Germans from Russia in Colorado.* Fort Collins, Colo., 1978.

——. *The Soviet Germans in the USSR Today.* Cologne, 1980.

Helby, J.A. *Protestants in Russia.* Belfast, 1976.

Herling, G. *Welt ohne Erbarmen.* Cologne, 1953.

Herzog, R. *Die Volksdeutschen in der Waffen-SS.* Tübingen, 1955.

Hesse, E. 'Der sowjetrussische Partisanenkrieg 1941 bis 1944 im Spiegel deutscher Kampfansweisungen und Befehle.' Unpubl. dissertation, University of Göttingen, 1969.

Hodnett, G. *Leadership in the Soviet National Republics: A Quantitative Study of Recruitment Policy.* Oakville, 1978.

Hoffmann, E. *Neues Heimat Polen.* Berlin-Leipzig, 1940.

——and A. Thoss. *Der vierte Treck.* Berlin-Leipzig, 1941.

Hollmann, D. *Kern des Lebens.* Moscow, 1973.

——. *Menschenschicksale.* Alma Ata, 1974.

Hummel, I. *Die Deutschen in Transkaukasien.* Langensalza (no date).

Hummel, Th. *100 Jahre Erbhofrecht der deutschen Kolonisten in Russland.* Berlin, 1936.

Huppert, H. *Wanduhr mit Vordergrund.* Halle (Saale), 1977.

Ipatov, A. *Wer sind die Mennoniten?* Alma Ata, 1977.

Ischchanian, B. *Die ausländischen Elemente in der russischen Volkswirtschaft.* Berlin, 1913.

Jacobsen, H.A. (ed.) *Misstrauische Nachbarn. Deutsche Ostpolitik, 1919–1970.* Düsseldorf, 1970.

Janecke, A. *Wolgadeutsches Schicksal. Erlebnisse Auslandsdeutscher.* Leipzig, 1937.

Janowsky, O. *Nationalities and National Minorities.* New York, 1945.

Jenny, E. *Die Deutschen im Wirtschaftsleben Russlands.* Berlin, 1920.

Jeschonnek, E. *Wo der Landser denken lernte. Die sowjetische Kriegsgefangenschaft im Spiegel der Zeitung 'Nachrichten'.* Berlin (East), 1959.

Joachim, S. *Towards an Understanding of the Russian Germans.* Morhead, 1969.

Jong (de), L. *Die deutsche fünfte Kolonne im Zweiten Weltkrieg*. Stuttgart, 1959.

Joost, W. *Botschafter bei den roten Zaren. Die deutschen Missionschefs in Moskau, 1918 bis 1941*. Vienna, 1967.

Kahle, W. *Geschichte der evangelisch-lutherischen Gemeinden in der Sowjetunion, 1917–1938*. Leiden, 1974.

Kamenetsky, I. *Secret Nazi Plans for Eastern Europe*. New Haven, 1961.

Kantor, Ia. *Natsional'noe stroitel'stvo sredi evreev v SSSR*. Moscow, 1934.

Karblay, B. *La société soviétique contemporaine*. Paris, 1977.

Karklins, R. 'The Interrelationship of Soviet Foreign and Nationalities Policies: the Case of Foreign Minorities in the USSR'. Unpubl. dissertation, University of Chicago, 1975.

Karklins, R. *Interviews mit Deutschen Spätaussiedlern aus der Sowjetunion*. Cologne, 1978.

Katz, Z. (ed.) *Handbook of Major Soviet Nationalities*. New York, 1975.

Keller, C. *The German Colonies in South Russia, 1804–1904*. 2 vols, Saskatoon, 1968–73.

Kent, G. *A Catalog of Files and Microfilms of the German Foreign Ministry Archives, 1920–1945*. 4 vols, Stanford, Calif., 1962–72.

Keussler, J. *Zur Geschichte und Kritik des bäuerlichen Gemeindebesitzes in Russland*. 3 vols, St Petersburg, 1887.

Khanzarov, K. *Reshenie natsional'no-iazykovoi problemy v SSSR*. Moscow, 1977.

Kholmogorov, A. *Internatsional'nye cherty sovetskikh natsii*. Moscow, 1970.

Khrushchev Remembers. The Last Testament. Boston, Mass., 1974.

Klauss, A.A. *Unsere Kolonien. Studien und Materialien zur Geschichte und Statistik der ausländischen Kolonisation in Russland*. Odessa, 1887.

Klein, F. *Die diplomatischen Beziehungen Deutschlands zur Sowjetunion, 1917–1932*. Berlin (East), 1953.

Kleindienst, A. *Ein Leben im Dienst an Kirche und Volk*. Hannover, 1968.

Kleist, P. *Die Europäische Tragödie*. Göttingen, 1961.

——. *Zwischen Hitler und Stalin, 1939–1945*. Bonn, 1950.

Klibanov, A. *Iz mira religioznogo sektantstva*. Moscow, 1974.

——. *Mennonity*. Moscow, 1931.

Klinger, G.K. *Sovetskaia politika za 10 let po natsional'nomu voprosu v RSFSR*. Moscow, 1928.

Koch, F. *The Volga Germans in Russia and the Americas: From 1763 to the Present*. State University of Pennsylvania Press, 1977.

Kochan, L. *Russia and the Weimar Republic*. London, 1954.

Koehl, R. *RKFDV: German Resettlement and Population Policy, 1939–1945*. Cambridge, Mass., 1957.

Kolarz, W. *Die Nationalitätenpolitik der Sowjetunion*. Frankfurt/Main, 1956.

——. *Religion in the Soviet Union*. London, 1961.

——. *Russia and her Colonies*. London, 1952.

Kolasky, J. *Education in the Soviet Ukraine*. Toronto, 1968.

König, L. *Die Deutschtumsinsel an der Wolga*. Dülmen, 1938.

Koslow, I. *Über Aufbau in der Krim. Bericht auf dem IV. Vereinigten Plenum des Krimer Gebietskomitees und der Kontrollkommission der KP(b)*. Simferopol, 1931.

Kozlov, V. *Natsional'nosti SSSR*. Moscow, 1975.

Krachker, D., and H.G. Schneege. *Die Deutschen in Osteuropa heute*. Bielefeld, 1970.

Kräenbring, A. *Bibliographie über das Bessarabiendeutschtum*. Hannover, 1970.

Kraft, S. *Die russlanddeutschen Flüchtlinge des Jahres 1929–1930 und ihre Aufnahme im Deutschen Reich*. Halle, 1939.

Krahn, C. *The Mennonites: A Bibliography of Mennonite Literature*. Newton, Kansas, 1966.

Krausnick, H., and H. Wilhelm. *Die Truppe des Weltanschauungskrieges. Die Einsatzgruppen der Sicherheitspolizei und des SD, 1938–1942*. Stuttgart, 1981.

Kreindler, I. *The Soviet Deported Nationalities: A Summary and an Update*. Research Paper no. 59, Soviet and East European Research Centre, Hebrew University, Jerusalem, 1985.

Krest'ianinov, V.F. *Mennonity*. Moscow, 1967.

Kroeker, A. *Unsere Brüder in Not! Bilder vom Leidensweg der deutschen Kolonien in Russland*. Striegau, 1930.

Kroll, H. *Lebenserinnerungen eines Botschafters*. Cologne-Berlin, 1967.

Lange, F. *Ostland kehrt Heim*. Berlin-Leipzig, 1940.

Langhans-Ratzeburg, M. *Die Wolgadeutschen. Ihr Staats- und Verwaltungsrecht in Vergangenheit und Gegenwart*. Berlin, 1929.

Laqueur, W. *Russia and Germany: A Century of Conflict*. London, 1965.

Lasst sie selber sprechen. Berichte russlanddeutscher Aussiedler. Hannover, 1978.

Leibbrandt, G. *Die deutschen Kolonien in Cherson und Bessarabien*. Stuttgart, 1926.

——. *Die deutschen Siedlungen in der Sowjetunion*. Berlin, 1941.

Leitelt, H. *Menschen in Menschenhand*. Munich, 1958.

Leonhard, S. *Gestohlenes Leben*. Frankfurt/Main, 1956.

Leonhard, W. *Die Revolution entlässt ihre Kinder*. Frankfurt/Main, 1961.

Lewis, R.A., R.H. Rowland and R.S. Clem. *Nationality and Population Change in Russia and the USSR: An Evaluation of Census Data, 1897–1970*. New York, 1976.

Lewytzkyj, B. *Die linke Opposition in der Sowjetunion*. Hamburg, 1974.

——. *Die politische Opposition in der Sowjetunion, 1960–1972*. Munich, 1972.

Librach, J. *The Rise of the Soviet Empire: A Study of Soviet Foreign Policy*. New York, 1964.

Lindemann, K.E. *Prekrashchenie zemlevladeniia i zemlepol'zovaniia poselian sobstvennikov*. Moscow, 1917.

——. *Von den deutschen Kolonisten in Russland. Ergebnisse einer Studienreise, 1919–1921*. Stuttgart, 1924.

Lipper, E. *Onze ans dans les bagnes soviétiques*. Geneva (no date).

Lisann, M. *Broadcasting to the Soviet Union: International Politics and Radio*. New York, 1975.

Lobsack, G. *Einsam kämpft das Wolgaland. Ein Bericht aus sieben Jahren Krieg und Revolution*. Leipzig, 1936.

Loesch, K. *Deutsche Züge im Antlitz der Erde: Deutsches Siedeln, deutsche Leistung*. Munich, 1935.

Loew, R. *Deutsche Bauernstaaten auf russischer Steppe*. Charlottenburg, 1916.

Long, J.W. *The German Russians: A Bibliography of Russian Materials*. Santa Barbara-Oxford, 1979.

——. *Russian Language Sources relating to the Germans from Russia*. Fort Collins, Colo., 1976.

Lorimer, F. *The Population of the Soviet Union: History and Prospects*. Geneva, 1946.

Löwenthal, P., and H. Vogel (eds). *Sowjetpolitik der 70er Jahre*. Stuttgart, 1972.

Maas, L.L. *Handbuch der deutschen Exilpresse, 1933-1945*. Munich-Vienna, 1976.

Malinovskii, L.V. *Nemetskoe selo v Sibiri v periode sotsialisticheskogo stroitel'stva*. Novosibirsk, 1971.

Malinovsky, J.A. *Die Planerkolonien am Asowschen Meere*. Stuttgart, 1928.

Marguliers, S.R. *The Pilgrimage to Russia: The Soviet Union and the Treatment of Foreigners, 1924-1937*. Madison, Wis., 1968.

Marshall, R. (ed.) *Aspects of Religion in the Soviet Union 1917-1967*. Chicago, 1971.

Martel, R. *Le mouvement antiréligieux en URSS (1917-1932)*. Paris, 1933.

Matthaei, Fr. *Die deutschen Ansiedlungen in Russland. Ihre Geshichte und ihre volkswirtschaftliche Bedeutung für die Vergangenheit und Zukunft. Studien über das russische Kolonisationswesen und über die Herbeiziehung fremder Kulturkräfte nach Russland*. Gera, 1865.

Maurer, H. *Leistung und Schicksal des bäuerlichen Deutschtums im Ostraum*. Berlin, 1943.

Mayenburg, R. von. *Blaues Blut und rote Fahnen. Ein Leben unter vielen Namen*. Vienna-Munich-Zürich, 1969.

McSherry, J. *Stalin, Hitler and Europe: The Origins of World War II*. Cleveland, Ohio, 1968.

Medvedev, R. *Politicheskii dnevnik, 1964-1970*. Amsterdam, 1972.

Meisner-Lindsay, M. *A Window into the Iron Curtain: A Series of Interviews with Russian-German Displaced Persons who Fled Russia during World War II*. 1941.

Mende, G. von. *Die Völker der Sowjetunion*. Reichenau, 1939.

Meyer, Th. *Nach Sibirien*. Dresden-Leipzig, 1927.

Morton, A., and R. Tőkés. *Soviet Politics and Society*. London, 1974.

Müller, A. *15 Jahre Oktoberrevolution im deutschen Dorfe*. Kharkov, 1932.

Müller-Henning, E. *Wolgakinder: Geschichte einer Flucht*. Berlin, 1941.

Münzenberg, W. *Solidarität. Zehn Jahre internationale Arbeiterhilfe, 1921–1931*. Berlin, 1931.

Myllyniemi, S. *Die Neuordnung der baltischen Länder, 1941–1944. Zum national-sozialistischen Inhalt der deutschen Besatzungspolitik*. Helsinki, 1973.

Nabatov, G. *Respublika Nemtsev Povolzhiia*. Leningrad, 1930.

Nadolny, R. *Mein Beitrag*. Wiesbaden, 1955.

Nekrich, A. *The Punished Peoples: The Deportation and Fate of Soviet Minorities at the End of the Second World War*. New York, 1978.

Neusats, H., and D. Erka. *Ein deutscher Todesweg*. Berlin, 1930.

Niclaus, K. *Die Sowjetunion und Hitlers Machtergreifung*. Bonn, 1966.

Nolde, B.E. *Russia in the Economic War*. New Haven, 1928.

Nora, S., and P. Zwierniak. *La justice soviétique*. Rome, 1945.

Ofer, G., and A. Vinokur. *Family Budget Survey of Soviet Emigrants in the Soviet Union*. Research Paper no. 32, Soviet and East European Research Centre, Hebrew University, Jerusalem, 1979.

Oktiabrskaia revoliutsiia i proletarskii internatsionalizm. Moscow, 1970.

Olsen, M.M. *Bibliography of Materials in the Collection of the American Historical Society of Germans from Russia*. Greeley, Colorado, 1973.

——. *A Bibliography on the Germans from Russia. Material found in the New York Public Library*. Lincoln, Nebraska, 1976.

Ostrovskii, Z. *Problemy ukrainizatsii i belorussizatsii v RSFSR*. Moscow, 1931.

Pampuch, A. *Heimkehr der Bessarabiendeutschen*. Breslau, 1942.

Parigi, I. *Die Sowjetdeutschen zwischen Moskau und Workuta*. Gütersloh, 1965.

Pashukanis, E. (ed.). *15 let sovetskogo stroitel'stva*. Moscow, 1930.

Petrus, E. *Euer Heim ist meine Burg*. Alma Ata, 1969.

Phillips, I. *The Tragedy of the Soviet Germans*. 1983.

Pierrard, A., and M. Warten. *Vivre en Sibérie*. Paris, 1966.

Pinkus, B., A. Greenbaum and M. Altshuler (eds). *Russian Publications on Jews and Judaism in the Soviet Union, 1917–1967*. Jerusalem, 1970.

Pipes, R. *The Formation of the Soviet Union*. Cambridge, Mass., 1954.

Poletika, E.W. *Annulierte Volkszählung von 1937 und Bevölkerungsstand in der Sowjetunion*. Jena, 1937.

Pollock, J.C. *The Christians from Siberia*. London, 1964.

Priess, A. *Verbannung nach Sibirien*. Steinbach, 1972.

Proudfoot, M.I. *European Refugees, 1939–1952: A Study in Forced Population Movement*. London, 1957.

Quiring, I. *Die Mundart von Chortitza in Süd-Russland*. Munich, 1978.

Quiring, W. *Russlanddeutsche suchen eine Heimat*. Karlsruhe, 1938.

Radio Liberty Register of Documents. Munich, 1975.

Radio Liberty Register of Samizdat. Munich, 1971.

Radkey, O.H. *The Election to the Russian Constituent Assembly of 1917*. Cambridge, Mass., 1950.

Rampel, J. *Der Sowjethölle entronnen*. Kassel, 1931.

Rau, G. *Kasachstaner Kaleidoskop*. Alma Ata, 1973.

Rauch, G. von. *The Baltic States: Years of Independence, 1917–1940*. London/ Berkeley, Calif., 1974.

Reddaway, P. (ed.) *Uncensored Russia: Protest and Dissent in the Soviet Union*. New York, 1972.

Redlich, C. *Deutschbaltische Arbeit, 1945–1955*. Bonn, 1957.

Reimgen, A. *Menschen aus unserer Mitte*. Moscow, 1971.

Reinmarus, A., and O. Langner. *Güldendorf. Ein deutsches Stürmer-Kollektiv zur 15ten Oktoberfeier*. Kharkov, 1932.

Reitlinger, G. *The Final Solution: The Attempt to Exterminate the Jews of Europe, 1939–1945*. London, 1953.

——. *The House Built on Sand: The Conflicts of German Policy in Russia, 1939–1945*. London, 1960.

——. *The SS: Alibi of a Nation, 1922–1945*. Melbourne, 1956.

Remer, C. *Deutsche Arbeiterdelegation in der Sowjetunion*. Berlin (East), 1963.

Reuter, E. *Briefe, Aufsätze, Referate 1904 bis 1922*. Berlin, 1972.

Revesz, L. *Volk aus 100 Nationalitaten. Die sowjetische Minderheitenfrage*. Bern, 1979.

Richter, W. *Aus der wolgadeutschen Sowjetrepublik*. Berlin, 1926.

Rigby, T. *Communist Party Membership in the USSR, 1917–1967*. Princeton, 1968.

Rimland, J. *The Wanderers*. St Louis, Missouri, 1979.

Rimscha, H. *Die Umsiedlung der Deutschbalten aus Lettland im Jahre 1939*. Hannover-Döhren, 1958.

Ritter, A. (ed.) *Nachrichten aus Kasachstan. Deutsche Dichtung in der Sowjetunion*. Hildesheim, 1974.

Ritter, E. *Das Deutsche Auslandsinstitut in Stuttgart, 1917–1945. Ein Beispiel deutscher Volkstumsarbeit zwischen den Weltkriegen*. Wiesbaden, 1976.

Robinson, J. *Das Minoritätenproblem und seine Literatur*. Berlin-Leipzig, 1928.

Rohrbach, P. *Deutschtum in Not*. Berlin, 1926.

Russland, O Russland! Stuttgart, 1934.

Saks, G. *Rabota sredi natsional'nykh men'shinstv. Opyt leningradskoi oblasti*. Leningrad, 1931.

Schaufler, J. *Gedichte*. Engels, 1935.

——. *Die wolgadeutschen Schulen – einst und jetzt*. Moscow, 1933.

Scheffer, P. *Sieben Jahre Sowjetunion*. Leipzig, 1930.

Scheibert, P. (ed.) *Die Russischen Politischen Parteien von 1905 bis 1917*. Darmstadt, 1972.

Schellenberg, D. (ed.) *Sammlung sowjetdeutscher Dichtung vom Jahre 1931*. Kharkov-Kiev, 1931.

Schiller, F. *Literatur zur Geschichte und Volkskunde der deutschen Kolonien in der Sowjetunion für die Jahre 1764–1926*. Pokrovsk, 1927.

Schirmunski, V. *Die deutschen Kolonien in der Ukraine*. Kharkov, 1928.

Schleuning, J. *In Kampf und Todesnot*. Berlin, 1930.

——. *Die Stummen reden. 400 Jahre evangelisch-lutherische Kirche in Russland*. Erlangen-Rothenburg, 1954.

——. *Die deutschen Siedlungsgebiete in Russland*. Würzburg, 1955.

Schmid, E. *Die deutschen Kolonien im Schwarzmeergebiet Südrusslands*. Berlin, 1919.

Schmidt, D. *Studien über die Geschichte der Wolgadeutschen*. Pokrovsk, 1930.

Schmitt, W. *Krieg in Deutschland. Strategie und Praxis der sowjetrussischen Deutschlandpolitik seit 1945*. Düsseldorf, 1961.

Schnurr, J. 'Die Aussiedler aus dem sowjetischen Bereich'. Unpubl. ms., Stuttgart, 1979.

——. (ed.) *Die Kirchen und das religiöse Leben der Russlanddeutschen. Evangelischer Teil*. Stuttgart, 1978.

Schoenberg, H.W. *Germans from the East: A Study of their Migration, Resettlement and Subsequent Group History since 1945*. The Hague, 1970.

Schrenk, Fr. *Geschichte der deutschen Kolonien in Transkaukasien*. Tiflis, 1869.

Schröder, H. *Die systematische Vernichtung der Russlanddeutschen*. Berlin-Leipzig, 1934.

Schultze-Gävernitz, G. von. *Volkswirtschaftliche Studien aus Russland*. Leipzig, 1899.

Schwabenland, E. *A History of the Volga German Relief Society*. Portland, Oregon, 1941.

Schwager, G. *Erlebnisbericht. Im Herzen die Heimat*. Osnabrück, 1978.

Schwarz, B. *Wolhyniendeutsches Schicksal*. Munich, 1942.

Schwarz, L. *Refugees in Germany Today*. New York, 1957.

Schwarz, M. *Die Umsiedlung und die Sowjets. Erlebnisse einer deutschen Frau*. Berlin-Leipzig, 1942.

Seaton, A. *The Russo-German War, 1941–1945*. London, 1971.

Seidel, G. *Das Wort. Moskau 1936–1939. Bibliographie einer Zeitschrift*. Berlin (East), 1975.

Seraphim, E. *Grundriss der Baltischen Geschichte*. Reval, 1908.

Seraphim, H.G. *Die deutsch-russichen Beziehungen 1939–1941*. Hamburg, 1949.

Serebriakov, F. *Nemetskaia kommuna na Volge i vozrozhdenie iugovostoka Rossii*. Moscow, 1922.

Sharapov, Ia. *Natsional'nye sektsii RKP(b)*. Kazan, 1967.

Shechtman, J.B. *European Population Transfers, 1939–1945*. New York, 1946.

Shindler, C. *Exit Visa*. London, 1978.

Simon, G. *Die Kirchen in Russland. Berichte-Dokumente*. Munich, 1970. English edn: *Church, State and Opposition in the U.S.S.R.*, London/Berkeley, Calif., 1974.

——. *Der Kampf für die Glaubenstoleranz. Die innerkirchliche Opposition*. Cologne, 1972.

——. *Die nichtrussischen Völker in Gesellschaft und Innenpolitik der UdSSR*. Cologne, 1979.

Simonov, K. *Soldatami ne rozhdaiutsia*. Moscow, 1964.

Smith, A.L. *The Deutschtum of Nazi Germany and the United States*. The Hague, 1965.

Solzhenitsyn, A. *The Gulag Archipelago 1918–1956*. New York, 1978.

Sommer, E.F. *Die Einigungsbestrebungen der Deutschen im Vorkriegs-Russland (1905–1904)*. Leipzig, 1940.

Sommer, H. *135,000 gewannen das Vaterland*. Berlin-Leipzig, 1940.

Sontag, R.J., and J. Beddie. *Nazi-Soviet Relations, 1939–1941*. New York, 1948.

Sotsial'nyi i natsional'nyi sostav VKP(b). Itogi vsesoiuznoi partiinoi perepisi. Moscow-Leningrad, 1928.

Sowjet-Russland und seine Kinder. Berlin, 1921.

Stach, J. *Das Deutschtum in Sibirien, Mittelasien und dem Fernen Osten*. Stuttgart, 1938.

———. *Grunau und die Mariupoler Kolonien. Materialien zur Geschichte deutscher Siedlungen im Schwarzmeergebiet*. Leipzig, 1942.

———. *Ocherki iz istorii i sovremennoi zhizni iuzhnerusskikh kolonistov*. Moscow, 1916.

Starodubsky, L. *Das Volkszählungswesen in der Union der Sozialistischen Sowjetrepubliken*. Vienna, 1938.

Statisticheskoe upravlenie ASSR Nemtsev Povolzh'ia. Pokrovsk, 1924.

Stern-Rubarth, E. *Graf Brockdorff-Rantzau. Wanderer zwischen zwei Welten*. Berlin, 1929.

Stirner, K. *7,000 dana u Sibiru*. Zagreb, 1973.

Stricker, W.D.M. *Deutsch-russische Wechselwirkungen oder die Deutschen in Russland und die Russen in Deutschland*. Leipzig, 1849.

Stumpp, K. *Bericht über das Gebiet Chortitza*. Berlin, 1943.

———. *Bericht über das Gebiet Kronau-Orloff*. Berlin, 1943.

———. *Die deutschen Kolonien im Schwarzmeergebiet, dem früheren Neu-(Süd-) Russland*. Stuttgart, 1926.

———. *Die Russlanddeutschen. Zweihundert Jahre unterwegs*. Freilassing, 1964.

Stupperich, R. *Kirchenordnungen der evangelisch-lutherischen Kirchen in Russland*. Ulm/Donau 1959.

Sulkevich, S. *Administrativno-politicheskoe stroenie SSSR*. Leningrad, 1926.

Teich, G., and H. Rübel (eds). *Völker, Volksgruppen und Volkstämme auf dem ehemaligen Gebiet der UdSSR*. Leipzig, 1942.

Thorwald, J. *Wen sie verderben wollten*. Stuttgart, 1952.

Thoss, A. *Heimkehr der Volksdeutschen*. Berlin, 1942.

Toews, G. *Die Heimat in Trümmern. Deutsche Schicksale im Russland der Anarchie*. Manitoba, 1936.

Toews, J. *Lost Fatherland: The Story of Mennonite Emigration from Soviet Russia, 1921–1927*. Scottdale, 1967.

———. *The Mennonites in Russia from 1917 to 1930*. Winnipeg, 1975.

Toews, S. *Trek to Freedom: The Escape of Two Sisters from South Russia during World War II*. Manitoba, 1976.

Tőkés, R. (ed.) *Dissent in the USSR*. Baltimore, Md., 1975.

Tolstoy, N. *The Victims of Yalta*. London, 1978.

Trainin, I.P. *Der Verband der Sozialistischen Sowjetrepubliken.* Hamburg, 1923.

Trainin, I.T. *SSSR i natsional'naia problema. Po natsional'nym respublikam i oblastiam Sovetskogo Soiuza.* Moscow, 1924.

Transferts (Les) internationaux de la population. Paris, 1946.

Trials of War Criminals before the Nuremberg Military Tribunals. Washington, DC, 1950.

Unger, A. *Der Auszug der Deutschen aus Litauen.* Oldenburg, 1971.

Unruh, B. *Fügung und Führung im Mennonitischen Welthilfswerk, 1920–1933.* Karlsruhe, 1966.

Vaatz, A. *Deutsche Bauernarbeit im Schwarzmeer-Gebiet.* Berlin, 1942.

Vardys, V.S. *The Catholic Church, Dissent and Nationality in Soviet Lithuania.* New York, 1978.

Velitsyn, A.A. (pseud.) *Nemtsy v Rossii.* St Petersburg, 1893.

Vershigora, P. *Liudi chistoi sovesti.* Moscow, 1956.

Vins, G. *Three Generations of Suffering.* London, 1976.

Vladimirov, V. *Chto zhe skazat' komissaram.* Alma Ata, 1975.

Völker in Ketten. Bern, 1978.

Vor den Toren Moskaus oder Gottes Gnädige Durchhilfe in einer schweren Zeit. Canada, 1958.

Wagner, D. *Ritter ohne Furcht.* Alma Ata, 1973.

Wagner, G. *Die Deutschen in Litauen. Ihre kulturellen und wirtschaftlichen Gemeinschaften zwischen den beiden Weltkriegen.* Marburg, 1959.

(Der) Wanderweg der Russlanddeutschen. Stuttgart, 1930.

Weber, R. (ed.) *Sage über meine Freude. Sowjetdeutscher Almanach.* Moscow, 1974.

Weinberg, G. *Guide to Captured German Documents.* Maxwell, 1952.

Weinberg, G.L. *Germany and the Soviet Union, 1939–1941.* Leiden, 1959.

Weinert, E. *Das Nationalkomitee 'Freies Deutschland', 1943–1945.* Berlin (East), 1957.

Weingartner, Th. *Stalin und der Aufstieg Hitlers. Die Deutschlandpolitik der Sowjetunion und der Kommunistischen Internationale, 1929–1934.* Berlin, 1970.

Weissberg, A. *Conspiracy of Silence.* London, 1952.

Weissbuch über die menschenrechtliche Lage in Deutschland und der Deutschen in Osteuropa. Bonn, 1977.

Werner, P. *Ein schweizer Journalist sieht Russland.* Olten, 1942.

Wettig, G. *Broadcasting and Detente: Eastern European Policies and their Implication for East-West Relations.* London, New York, 1977.

Williams, R.C. *Culture in Exile: Russian Emigrés in Germany, 1881–1941.* Ithaca, NY, 1972.

Winter, E. *Die Sowjetunion und der Vatikan.* Berlin (East), 1972.

Wittram, R. *Baltische Geschichte. Die Ostseeländer Livland, Estland, Kurland, 1180–1918.* Munich, 1954.

——. *Drei Generationen. Deutschland-Livland-Russland, 1830–1914*. Göttingen, 1949.

——. *Geschichte der baltischen Staaten*. Stuttgart, 1939.

Wogau, W. *Die Bauernschaft und die Religion*. Kharkov, 1928.

Wolfrum, G. *Das Russlanddeutschtum. Die Deutschen aus Wolhynien*. Posen, 1944.

——. *Das Schwarzmeerdeutschtum. Geschichte und Charakter*. Posen, 1944.

——. *Das Schwarzmeerdeutschtum. Die Deutschen aus Transnistrien*. Posen, 1944.

Wolin, S., and R. Slusser. *The Soviet Police*. New York, 1957.

Yarmolinsky, A. *The Jews and other Minor Nationalities under the Soviets*. New York, 1928.

Zakovskii, L. *Podryvnye raboty tserkovnikov i sektantov*. Leningrad, 1937.

Zakharov, M. *Natsional'noe stroitel'stvo v Krasnoi Armii*. Moscow, 1927.

Zayas, A. de. *Die Anglo-Amerikaner und die Vertreibung der Deutschen*. Munich, 1978.

Zehn Jahre Wolgadeutsche Autonomie, 1918–1928. Pokrovsk, 1928.

Zinger, L. *Natsional'nyi sostav proletariata v SSSR*. Moscow, 1934.

Zinner, P. *Nemtsy Nizhnego Povolzh'ia. Vydaiushchiesia deiateli iz kolonii Povolzh'ia*. Saratov, 1925.

Ziuriukin, V. *Mennonity koppental'skogo raiona oblasti Nemtsev Povolzh'ia v bytovom i khoziaistvennom otnoshenii*. Pokrovsk, 1922.

INDEX

Adenauer, Konrad, 107–8, 154
administrative units, 38–40
Advensbote, Der, 55
Adzhubei, A.I., 110
agriculture: 46; *kolkhozy* and *sovkhozy*, 10, 38, 76, 78, 117, 123–4; livestock, 46, 124; during Second World War, 70; tsarist period, 2–3, 4, 14, 20–2, 26; *see also* collectivisation, *Kombedy*, kulaks, Virgin Lands
Aktiubinsk, 127, 134
Alexander I, 5
Alexander II, 4, 23
Alexander III, 5
Alexanderheim (Aleksandrovka), 74
Aleksandrovsk–on–the–Dnieper, 25
Allrussischer Verband der russischen Bürger deutscher Nationalität und Mennoniten, 28
Alma Ata, 130, 133,136
Altai, mountains, 81, 103
Altai, 131
amnesty: 107; decrees: *Sept. 17, 1955*, 108; *Sept. 20, 1955*, 108; *Dec. 13, 1955*, 109, 112, 119; *Dec. 22, 1956*, 112; *Aug. 29, 1964*, 110-11; *Nov. 3, 1972*, 111; Crimean Tatars, 9; Germans, 9, 109; Meskhetians, 9
Andersberg, 74
Anticomintern, 95
anti-fascist, 131, 146; propaganda, 65; theatre, 58, 65
Arbeit, 129, 132
Arbeitsbanner, 132
Arbeitsdienst, 101
Arkhangel'sk, 16, 119
Armenians: 41, 153; in Communist Party, 113; emigration of, 155, 157
army, tsarist/Soviet: Germans in, 27, 63–4, 106, 112, 145; *see also* officers
art, German, 133, 135
Artemovsk, 85
assimilation, 44; *see also* ethnic Germans

Autonomous Soviet Socialist Republic of the Volga Germans: 7, 11, 33–4, 46, 53, 58, 64, 67n, 111, 129, 144; abolished, *Sept. 7, 1941*, 8, 9, 84, 132, 154; collectivisation, 47; Communist Party members in, 40, 43; deportation, 78–84; establishment, 35, 37, 41–2, 154; German schools, 54–5; higher education, 54; importance, 7, 42; possible re–establishment of, 151; publications in, 56, 132; purges, 63; size, 42, theatre in, 58, 135; urban population, 48
Azerbaijan, German *raion* in, 39
Azov, Sea of, 67n, 75

Bach, F., 58, 129
Balkars, 8, 110
Baltic Germans (*ostzeiskie nemtsy*): 13, 14–16, 24, 25, 26, 29, 48, 67n, 94; origins, 2; significance under tsars, 17–18
Baltic provinces/states/republics: 2, 25, 26, 27, 49, 112; attitude toward ethnic Germans, 146; German–owned land in, 22; independence between wars, 29; Second World War, 94; *see also* Courland, Estonia, Livonia
banks, German–owned, 23
Baptists, 49, 50, 143, 150
Barnaul, 132
Bartels, B., 59
batrak (hired agricultural labourer), 46
Baumann, Nikolai, 134
Baumtrog, Bishop August, 50
Belorussian Republic: 54; Germans in, 69; German soviets in, 39; national courts in, 40; Poles in, 114
Belorussians, 2
Berdiansk, 85
Berlin crisis, 110
Bessarabia, 3, 30, 67n; refugees from, 80
Black Sea, 2, 50, 67n

175